The Words and Music of Brian Wilson

Recent Titles in
The Praeger Singer-Songwriter Collection

The Words and Music of Van Morrison
Erik Hage

The Words and Music of Joni Mitchell
James Bennighof

The Words and Music of George Harrison
Ian Inglis

The Words and Music of Paul McCartney: The Solo Years
Vincent P. Benitez

The Words and Music of Jimi Hendrix
David Moskowitz

The Words and Music of Billy Joel
Ken Bielen

The Words and Music of Dolly Parton: Getting to Know Country's "Iron Butterfly"
Nancy Cardwell

The Album: A Guide to Pop Music's Most Provocative, Influential, and Important Creations, 4 volumes
James E. Perone, Editor

The Words and Music of Melissa Etheridge
James E. Perone

The Words and Music of Alanis Morissette
Karen Fournier

The Words and Music of Elvis Costello
James E. Perone

The Words and Music of Sheryl Crow
Christopher Gable

THE PRAEGER SINGER-SONGWRITER COLLECTION

The Words and Music of Brian Wilson

Christian Matijas-Mecca

James E. Perone, Series Editor

PRAEGER™

An Imprint of ABC-CLIO, LLC
Santa Barbara, California • Denver, Colorado

Library of Congress Cataloging-in-Publication Data

Names: Matijas-Mecca, Christian, author.
Title: The words and music of Brian Wilson / Christian Matijas-Mecca.
Description: Santa Barbara, California : Praeger, 2017. | Series: The Praeger singer-songwriter collection | Includes bibliographical references and index.
Identifiers: LCCN 2016053004 (print) | LCCN 2016054669 (ebook) | ISBN 9781440838989 (hardcopy : alk. paper) | ISBN 9781440838996 (ebook)
Subjects: LCSH: Wilson, Brian, 1942——Criticism and interpretation. | Popular music—United States—History and criticism.
Classification: LCC ML420.W5525 M36 2017 (print) | LCC ML420.W5525 (ebook) | DDC 782.42166092—dc23
LC record available at https://lccn.loc.gov/2016053004

ISBN: 978–1–4408–3898–9
EISBN: 978–1–4408–3899–6

21 20 19 18 17 1 2 3 4 5

This book is also available as an eBook.

Praeger
An Imprint of ABC-CLIO, LLC

ABC-CLIO, LLC
130 Cremona Drive, P.O. Box 1911
Santa Barbara, California 93116-1911
www.abc-clio.com

This book is printed on acid-free paper ∞

Manufactured in the United States of America

Contents

Series Foreword

Although the term "singer-songwriter" might most frequently be associated with a cadre of musicians of the early 1970s such as Paul Simon, James Taylor, Carly Simon, Joni Mitchell, Cat Stevens, and Carole King, the Praeger Singer-Songwriter Collection defines singer-songwriters more broadly, both in terms of style and time period. The series includes volumes on musicians who have been active from approximately the early 1960s through the present. Musicians who write and record in folk, rock, soul, hip-hop, country, and various hybrids of these styles are represented.

What do the individuals included in this series have in common? Some have never collaborated as writers, whereas others have, but all have written and recorded commercially successful and/or historically important music and lyrics at some point in their careers.

The authors who contribute to the series also exhibit diversity. Some are scholars who are trained primarily as musicians, whereas others have such areas of specializations as American studies, history, sociology, popular culture studies, literature, and rhetoric. The authors share a high level of scholarship, accessibility in their writing, and a true insight into the work of the artists they study. The authors are also focused on the output of their subjects and how it relates to their subjects' biographies and the society around them; however, biography in and of itself is not a major focus of the books in this series.

Given the diversity of the musicians who are the subject of the books in this series, and given the diversity of viewpoint of the authors, volumes in the series differ from book to book. All, however, are organized chronologically around the compositions and recordings of their subjects. All of the books in the series also serve as listeners' guides to the music of their subjects, making them companions to the artists' recorded output.

James E. Perone
Series Editor

Acknowledgments

This study of Brian Wilson's music will focus on work that, as of 2016, has been commercially released and where Brian has served as the composer, primary performer, producer, collaborator, or secondary (backing) performer. He has produced a significant body of work that has never been released and for which much is unfinished, so I will limit this study to those works that have been available on vinyl, tape, compact disc, or as digital downloads. I have made two exceptions and included *Adult/Child* (1978) and *Sweet Insanity* (1991). Both have circulated as complete, albeit bootleg, albums that inform the larger study of his work.

I am indebted to a number of authors whose prior and exhaustive work has allowed me to present a thorough, narrative arc of Wilson's creative work. The Beach Boys have been written about perhaps more than any other American group, and conflicting accounts across multiple sources in regard to what happened when, where, and with whom, present challenges for any researcher. Many people in this story have passed on, and the memories of those who remain are fluid and subject to extensive revisionism, as is expected over the course of a half-century. Memoirs by both Brian Wilson and Mike Love have been published as this volume enters production, and have supplied two additional layers to their complex story. Many who were present in the early years: Hite and Dorinda Morgan, Herb Newman, Joe Saraceno, Gary Usher, Roger Christian, Nik Venet, Chuck Britz, members of the Wrecking Crew, and of course, Murry, Audree, Dennis, and Carl Wilson, have all passed on.

A significant thanks goes to Brad Elliott, David Leaf, Mark Lewisohn, Stephen Kalinich, and James B. Murphy, for their generous time addressing my questions. I would also like to thank (in alphabetical order) Kingsley Abbott, Keith Badman, Peter Ames Carlin, Mark Dillon, Andrew G. Doe, Steven Gaines, Andrew Hickey, Philip Lambert, Mark Linett, David Marks, Stephen McParland, Dominic Priore, Peter Reum, Ian Rusten, Jeff Sellars, Jules Siegel, Jon Stebbins, John Tobler, Timothy White, and Paul Williams. This book would have been infinitely more difficult without their dedicated and enthusiastic research. In addition, I would like to thank Jean Sievers, Carl Caprioglio at Oglio Entertainment, and University of Michigan's Undergraduate Research Opportunity Program, who sponsored my assistants, Laura Dzubay and Bailey Minney. They compiled the database and comprehensive works list for use as an online resource, and I owe Laura and Bailey sincere thanks for their contributions. The accompanying works list for this book, www.wilsonsingersongwriter.com, will catalog Brian Wilson's creative work as composer, producer, performer, and collaborator over the course of his 50-plus year career. Thank you to ArtSite Design, Daniel Worley and the late O'Bryan Worley, for their Web site design. At the University of Michigan, I would like to thank Dr. Angela Kane for her support in this endeavor and Dr. Marie McCarthy, Director of Research.

Like Brian, I attended El Camino College in Torrance, CA, where I discovered the inspiration to think and believe beyond what I had been told was possible. While there I had four professors whose guidance, encouragement, and influence continues to inform my own teaching at the University of Michigan. For the past 25 years, I have recalled their gestures at the start of every academic year. For Joseph Bloch, who kicked me out of his English class for my intransigent refusal to think, but introduced me to Joyce's "The Dubliners." Melinda Barth, who took me into her English class and introduced me to Kafka's "The Hunger Artist." Two music professors, the late Dr. Robert Haag, who, before a music history class, matter-of-factly handed me two brand-new volumes of Mozart Piano Concerti and said, "I already have copies of these, and thought you might make use of them." As one of the least advanced, but blindly enthusiastic pianists in the school, he encouraged me to be a completest, but more importantly, he taught me to always look (and think) beyond a given moment. To James Mack, who let me join the percussion section of his orchestra when I had no prior orchestral or percussion experience, but kicked me out for an unprofessional lack of dedication, then took me back after I wised up and apologized to him. He taught me that second chances are never to be wasted. At Interlochen Arts Academy I have to thank the late Edward Banghart, with whom I developed my skills of argumentation on composers from Spontini to Berlioz and Honegger. Before meeting him, music was only something I performed.

Special Thanks go to my editor, James Perone, for the opportunity to prepare this volume. Additional thanks to Catherine Lafuente and Elana Palace at ABC-CLIO. I am fortunate to consider five esteemed scholars as friends who have mentored and encouraged me, posed pointed questions, and have engaged in conversations from A to Z: Andrew Mead, Abigail Stewart, Roland John Wiley, David Winter, and Albin Zak. My feline companions, Cassiel, Eliot, Isabel, and Josie, who temper the isolation of writing, and without question, my partner, Karen Fournier, without whom I could never have transformed this wish into reality.

Lastly, I would like to thank Brian Wilson who has given so much of himself through his music . . . Columnated ruins domino . . .

Prelude

October 22, 1966

Brian Wilson stood on the stage of Hill Auditorium at 825 N. University Ave in Ann Arbor, MI, to rehearse the Beach Boys for the world premiere live performance of "Good Vibrations."[1] "Good Vibrations" would be the Beach Boys's biggest hit and their last chart-topping single until 1988's "Kokomo," the first and only Beach Boys number one record to not involve Brian Wilson. But in the fall of 1966, "Good Vibrations," one of the most progressive and richly produced singles in pop music, enabled Brian to demonstrate that popular music could no longer be dismissed as irrelevant or disposable.[2] This was not the only time Brian Wilson would make music history in Ann Arbor. Thirty-two years, five months later, and two blocks west of Hill Auditorium, Brian would make pop music history on one more occasion.

March 9, 1999

Brian Wilson is scheduled to perform a solo concert at the Michigan Theater, 603 E. Liberty St., Ann Arbor, MI, nine months after the release of his second solo album, *Imagination*, a pleasant collection of middle-of-the-road pop. Brian Wilson, the stage-phobic aural auteur who, by 1968, had relinquished artistic control of the Beach Boys and slowly withdrawn into semi-seclusion while he battled psychological and substance abuse issues for over two decades, was back once again. Over the course of his post-1968 career, Brian had become a phantom presence in the world of popular music, and each time it was announced he was back, fans were treated to the image of a man whose vocal prowess and physical well-being had seemingly vanished. As described by Peter Ames Carlin, "(his) public suffering had transformed him from a musical figure into a cultural one."[3] Over the course of his life, myths, rumors, and legends would emerge, and stories of drug abuse, obesity, and mental illness would color his legacy. It would not matter because this concert would be a game changer not only for Brian but also for the 1700 fans that filled the theater. Minutes after the scheduled 7:30 pm show time, a collage of images and video clips from the earliest days of the Beach Boys to the present day signaled the start of the show. A wave of emotions washed over the house when images of Brian, Dennis (who died in 1983), and Carl (who succumbed to cancer in 1998) appeared on the screen. Images of Wilson as a young man performing with the Beach Boys were interspersed with images from the 1976 NBC special that presented the obese and emotionally shattered artist, a sad buffoon in the not-so-funny side show that formally fetishized his "condition," and gave us an indelible image of Brian that would be remembered for the next 12-plus years.[4] Fifteen minutes later, a figure was led downstage and the lights came up to show Brian, front and center, seated behind a keyboard, and over the next two hours he sang and led his band through a lengthy collection of masterfully executed hits.

July 5, 2015

In the splendor of the Art Deco, Fox Theatre in midtown Detroit, Brian Wilson, with his band and special guests, Al Jardine and Blondie Chaplin, performed songs from his extensive catalog and selections from his newest album, *No Pier Pressure*. Sixteen years after Brian's improbable return as a concert artist, the Fox Theatre was filled with more than 4000 fans that were there to hear the then 73-year-old artist. His career over the past 12-plus years was filled with live performances that included complete performances of *Pet Sounds*, but it was his 2004 release, *Brian Wilson Presents SMiLE (BWPS)*, that placed everything else into perspective. *SMiLE*, the mythical, widely bootlegged, and unreleased Beach Boys masterpiece, represented Brian Wilson's musical and emotional undoing in 1967. Brian's 2004 recording presented the songs in what might have been his intended track order before he walked away from the project in mid-1967. To complete the work 35 years later, a few musical links were composed with his original collaborator, Van Dyke Parks.

Other solo albums, *Gettin' in Over My Head* (2004) and *Lucky Old Sun* (2008), showed Brian as an active and creative musical force. He released a collection of works by George Gershwin and a disc of songs from Disney movies. In 2011 Capitol Records released *The SMiLE Sessions*, Brian's "teenage symphony to God" as performed and recorded by the Beach Boys in 1966–1967 proved Brian was at the cutting edge of popular music in the year of *Sgt. Pepper's Lonely Hearts Club Band*, Jimi Hendrix, and the Monterey Pop

Festival. The 50th anniversary of the Beach Boys in 2011–2012 brought Brian, Mike, Al, Bruce, and David Marks together for a golden anniversary tour and a new album composed entirely of original material, *That's Why God Made the Radio* and their first group effort since 1985's eponymous, Steve Levine-produced album. The album reached number 3 on the Billboard charts and was their highest charting album of new material since 1965's *Summer Days (and Summer Nights!!)*. In 2015, Brian's life was dramatized into the critically acclaimed movie *Love and Mercy*, which brought his story to the attention of younger audiences, and he released a new solo album, *No Pier Pressure*.

Location, Location, Location to Mt. Vernon and Fairway

Brian Wilson and the Beach Boys were unlikely candidates for pop music stardom. Though raised in a musical family, Brian displayed no significant aptitude for any particular instrument and had limited skills in reading music notation.[5] He developed a beautiful tenor voice through singing at home with his parents, Murry and Audree, and brothers, Dennis and Carl. Murry taught his sons the pleasures that could be found in making music and the importance of singing from the heart. With these simple tools, Brian created a body of work that has been central to the popular music canon for over five decades.

Who is Brian Wilson? To many, he is the artist who cofounded the iconic American band, the Beach Boys, and for whom he created a body of work that has few rivals in the canon of American popular music. Dennis Wilson, speaking about his older brother in 1976, said, "He is the most vulnerable human being I know . . . I am dumbfounded . . . in awe of him." But "what" made Brian Wilson, and how was he able to create musical tapestries that reflected both place and time and captured the ethos of the California experience in ways that few artists have achieved? Like so many families in mid-century Southern California, Brian descended from Midwesterners who had migrated to California in the first decades of the twentieth century. The Wilsons were from Hutchinson, KS, having moved there from Meigs County, OH, in the late nineteenth century. The ingenuity and dreams that fired Brian's creative spirit had passed through multiple generations of Wilsons, Stohles, and Korthofs, before they settled into Brian's magical and mystical imagination. Brian created a body of work with a DNA that was shaped over four generations across the United States. Through his songs we can witness, observe, and experience an expansive range of emotions and events that encompass feelings of joy, humor, melancholy, beauty, and irrepressible fun. Brian was not only a singer, songwriter, and producer for the Beach Boys, but he also produced and composed songs for numerous other artists, and in the later decades of his career has lent his creative imprint to a variety of projects that include children's songs, songs for animated shows, and tribute albums to artists whom Brian has admired, such as Buddy Holly, Harry Nilsson, Doc Pomus, and Woody Guthrie.

Through his music, Brian Wilson became the primary architect of a mythical and magical Southern California. Tapped directly from his imagination since he could never live in that world, Brian created a reality all of us wanted to believe because we too wanted to escape into that same world. While living almost exclusively in his own mind, the world Brian created disappeared many years ago. The recordings he made with the Beach Boys allow us to hold onto a belief in the perpetual existence of a magical Southern California, and we show no indication of letting that escape our grasp. People will always remember Brian Wilson when they hear "Fun, Fun, Fun," "The Warmth of the Sun," "Surfer Girl," and countless other of his songs. Without him, Los Angeles and the Pacific Coast would still have lured tens of millions of people, but our mystical belief in that magical place would be very different. Why did we place so much importance upon this artist? Why did we not allow him to continue his search for the personal contentment that had eluded him for so long, and why did we insist that he tell us that same wonderful story again and again. The "Magic Transistor Radio" he sang of in "Mount Vernon and Fairway" was confirmation that we continued to live in a dream that no longer existed, but instead we asked why was it that Brian insisted on creating strange music. Why did he do this to all of us, and why did he not write songs that allowed us to sustain a dream that never really existed?

Brian Douglas Wilson was born on June 20, 1942, in Inglewood's Centinela Hospital to Murry Gage Wilson and Audree Korthof Wilson, both of whom were born in the later years of the First World War and whose families had migrated from the Midwest to California between the end of the war and the onset of the Great Depression.[6] Murry and Audree met at George Washington High School in south Los Angeles, and were drawn together through their shared love of music. They married in March 1938, three years after graduation, saved for a home, and four years later, Brian, the first of three boys, was born. He was joined by brothers Dennis Carl (December 4, 1944–December 28, 1983) and Carl Dean (December 21, 1946–February 6, 1988), three brothers in America's first wave of the "Baby Boom" generation.

The Wilsons were a musical family. Audree sang and loved to play boogie-woogie piano. Murry was an aspiring songwriter who composed in his spare time while he supported his family and rose to own his own machining company. He had a handful of songs recorded by professional musicians, but his greatest achievement "Two Step Side Step" was performed in 1953 by the Lawrence Welk Orchestra and broadcast nationally on Welk's "On the Air from the Aragon."[7] It was recorded by Johnnie Lee Wills on RCA Victor and published by Guild Music. Guild was owned by Hite and Dorinda Morgan, and the Morgans, with their son Bruce, would figure into the Beach Boys story less than a decade later. Brian attended Hawthorne High School, received a used 1957 Ford Fairlane from Murry and Audree for his 17th birthday, and was a talented, if not outstanding, athlete who graduated in 1960 with fellow athlete and music enthusiast, Al Jardine. He was well-liked by his peers and is remembered for his sense of humor. He did not have a steady girlfriend, and though plenty of girls liked Brian, none were ever drawn to him as a boyfriend. His first girlfriend was Judy Bowles, a pretty, blonde-haired girl, four years his junior, and the inspiration for "Surfer Girl."[8]

Brian's cousin, Mike Love (b. March 15, 1941), loved to sing doo-wop and rhythm and blues. He was the eldest son of Murry Wilson's sister, Emily (Glee) and Milton Love. They lived at Mt. Vernon and Fairway in the upscale and affluent (when compared to Hawthorne) Baldwin Hills neighborhood of Los Angeles. Like their Hawthorne cousins, Milton and Glee's family loved music, and sing-alongs were as common in the Love household as they were in the Wilson home. As the eldest children in their respective families, Brian and Mike would sing together to escape the flurry of joint family activities and learned to blend Brian's clear, high tenor, with Mike's flexible and resonant bass-baritone. Mike was a year older than Brian and had his own challenges. He attended Los Angeles City College for one year, but dropped out upon learning his girlfriend was pregnant. Before long he was married with a baby on the way while he worked two jobs, one for his father's sheet metal stamping company and an evening job pumping gas at a Standard Oil station.[9] Most narratives about Brian focus on the magical vocal blend created by the three Wilson brothers, but Brian's voice is as inextricably linked to his cousin Mike as it was to Dennis and Carl, because Mike's distinctive baritone was the foundation in so many of Brian's arrangements. Mike did not have the creative DNA with which Brian was gifted, but his voice was as central to Brian's initial efforts as were those of Carl and Dennis.

In *The Nearest Faraway Place*, Timothy White shares a story of Brian and Mike's grandfather Buddy, "the unfulfilled hothead," and his brother Johnny (great-uncle to the Wilson and Love families), the "vulnerable but productive dreamer," in a story that has numerous parallels to Brian and Mike's relationship and their respective personalities.[10] Johnny Wilson was an imaginative inventor and builder who suffered from shell shock after he served in the First World War and was never able to fulfill the exceptional promise he had shown before the war. Johnny and Buddy's brother, Charlie Wilson, described Johnny's challenge as, "Maybe if he'd gone slow ... But no one let him go slow, and he's too sensitive. He was the hero of the family, full of ideas and dreams bigger than all the rest of us ..."[11] Uncle Charlie's words about his adored brother can also frame many of Brian's personal challenges. Brian is averse to conflict, but his complex relationship with Mike has endured simply because they are family. Mike was there in 1961 to encourage Brian to do something with music as he desperately needed an escape from his prematurely settled life as a working family man. Brian attended El Camino College but dropped out one semester short of an Associate of Arts degree. In the year that followed Brian's graduation from high school, he managed to "do" something with music that involved Mike and his brothers Dennis and Carl. He wrote, recorded, and released his first single, "Surfin'."

A Sea of Tunes . . . Surf's Up!

In the introduction to the 1993 boxed set *Good Vibrations: Thirty Years of the Beach Boys*, David Leaf opens with "*An American Family making music just because they loved the way it made 'em feel . . .*". Brian's songs continue to move people of all ages, and it is for this reason that he is as relevant an artist now as he was a half-century ago. Fans go to his concerts because they love his music, and many know of the challenges he has survived over the course of his career, and are there to enjoy an artist who continues to flourish and surprise his fans with every new record. Brian is a survivor who has continued to create wonderful music and can share with his fans the extraordinary masterpieces upon which his legacy was created. David Anderle, the first president of Brother Records, stated in late-1967, "The next big Brian Wilson thing will not happen with the Beach Boys."[12] That "next big thing" ultimately had to wait for two decades, and though Brian's solo career would run with fits and starts until the late 1990s, he has, in the new century, pursued a path that allows him to do what he wants to do, not what a band, the family, or his record company, want him to do.

David Leaf wrote about Brian in performance with the Beach Boys in the late 1970s, "For Brian . . . any concert is an ordeal . . . Stoically, he sat at his grand piano, sometimes playing, sometimes singing . . . and while his voice revealed no emotion, his onstage behavior was a spectacle of nervousness."[13] The Beach Boys were a job to which he felt obligated because the group was a family concern, and when Brian first retired from touring, his father Murry called him a "traitor" for having left the band.[14] From the band's first record in 1961, the Beach Boys have been both a family and a business entity. At first they were led and directed by Murry Wilson, father to Brian, Dennis, and Carl and uncle to Mike Love. As the band quickly developed into an industry with albums, tours, a record label, and later, a recording studio, Brian's creative agenda would often be at odds with the various business and family agendas that reside at the center of Brian's many challenges.

In any study of Brian Wilson's music, it is important to consider his relationship with Murry. Murry demanded that Capitol provide Brian with the autonomy he desired in order to produce records without executive oversight in studios of Brian's choosing, and he managed the band until mid-1964 when tensions escalated to a point where Brian would fire him. Murry often wanted to impose his own creative ideas on the band and though he believed in Brian and pushed him to try harder, he also bullied, criticized, and abused Brian for what he perceived to be laziness or weakness. He was a man of his time who came of age through the depression and worked hard for his family to make a life that was far more comfortable than what he experienced as a young man. Some biographers have been generous in their analysis of Murry, while others describe him as a sadistic bully. The loss of his left eye in an industrial workplace accident drove Murry to always work harder than the next guy, which shaped and hardened his views towards raising his boys and later on, managing their band. The stories of Murry's parenting methods can sound like "a demented mixture of Charles Dickens and David Lynch."[15] Tony Asher remembered him as "a really sick man ... pathetically so." Still, there was a genuine respect between Brian and Murry, however dysfunctional it may have been. In 1969, Murry sold the Sea of Tunes publishing company he founded for Brian for $700,000 because he felt the band was past its prime by the end of the decade and their music would never be as popular or able to generate income equal to what they earned in the 1960s. Murry constantly stressed the importance of family (though he would cheat both family and nonfamily members, especially Mike) and the guilt associated with his father's actions dogged Brian through much of his life and surely influenced career and life choices that were not in his best interests.[16] For every horrific story about Murry and Brian's relationship, there is a story that gives credit to Murry for his persistence and dedication to the group. Instead, I will look at Brian's extraordinary body of music, his extensive collaborative relationships, and the musical narratives that have endured across multiple generations of listeners and defied the continually evolving landscape of popular music.

"Genius musician but an amateur human being," "washed-up," "bloated," "another sad fucking case," and "a loser." Those were some of the kinder opinions of industry insiders who dealt with Brian in the first half of the 1970s. By the middle of that decade, Brian was pushed back into a world he had created 14 years earlier and "encouraged" to compose, produce, and lead the Beach Boys. He delivered work that was considered by many to be uneven in quality, and though he was capable of producing work with enthusiasm and passion, it was with different varieties of passion and precision than he exhibited in earlier records. We always want to look at the Brian Wilson of 1963–1966 and are reluctant to acknowledge that he has grown, changed, and discovered new interests and ideas and are inclined to view him as a commodity rather than as an artist. Marilyn Wilson, Brian's first wife, has said "He doesn't just think of music; his body was just music ... you know, creating music for Brian, sitting down at the piano and writing music is just as easy for Brian as walking. That was the easy part. Life was hard for Brian."[17] Between the unfortunate mid-1970s marketing agenda of "Brian's Back" and the 2004 release of *Brian Wilson Presents SMiLE*, Brian's work was never evaluated on its own merits because it would be compared unfavorably to his work before *SMiLE*. For over 30 years, the culture of "what-if-Brian-had-continued-on-in-1967" used to weigh the value of every musical work he composed. Marilyn, in speaking about one of Brian's most beautiful songs, "Caroline, No," has said that Brian "... constantly remembers his past and still relates to it and everybody in it."[18] While true, the irony is that Brian had moved forward, but we chose to look over our shoulder to a past where Brian used to reside. David Anderle, in a 1997 conversation with *Crawdaddy* founder Paul Williams said "... There's no way Brian can go back and pick up the pieces ... the magic of Brian was his innocence ... to me personally, *Smile's* finished ... it was never meant to have, a shape ... it's just a, a, a large moment of music, of literal musics."[19] In his view, "It was finished when Brian stopped working on it. And that is the way it was supposed to have been."[20] Anderle's argument makes sense when we consider the life Brian endured in the years that followed *SMiLE*, but he surprised everyone with the 2004 release of *Brian Wilson Presents SMiLE*, an album that allowed him to reclaim his own legacy and creative agenda.

The many collaborators with whom Brian chose to work throughout his career helped him to create an extraordinarily rich body of work and include such artists as Gary Usher, Bob Norberg, Mike Love, Roger Christian, Jan Berry, Tony Asher, Stephen Kalinich, Russ Titelman, Van Dyke Parks, Andy Paley, and Darian Sahanaja. As early as 1962, Brian collaborated as coauthor, producer, or performer with a number of artists outside of the Beach Boys, but the dysfunctional dynamics within the Wilson family challenged and ultimately ended many of those relationships. Murry Wilson brought Brian's collaborative partnerships with both Usher and Christian to a premature end, and Mike Love's strong opinions were responsible in limiting Brian's work with Tony Asher, Van Dyke Parks, Danny Hutton, and other artists. Brian created his best work when he was in a healthy and supportive partnership, but his most dynamic collaborations were often thwarted as a result of family pressures. In that same 1997 interview with David Anderle, he states "... 'Cause Brian needs somebody there all the time ... Because Brian functions really well in the company of friendship. It's a good thing for him. So if he can find ... these people, who will encourage him to continue just to make music, and not worry about what the music means."[21] Former publicist Derek Taylor talked about Brian being good company when he was all right, but his need for people would turn against him as he encountered resistance to his work. Taylor quit working for Brian in May 1967 because he found him too demanding and too difficult to handle. Anderle worried that the pressures upon Brian continue(d) (in 1997) to add to the baggage of *SMiLE*, but with the 2004 release of *Brian Wilson Presents SMiLE*, Brian was able to free himself of that legacy and pursue new projects. The past 15 years have been among his most prolific in terms of recordings, new projects, and live performances.

"Don't fuck with the formula," a quote frequently attributed to Mike Love was a reminder that Brian should not forget what brought success, fame, and riches to the band: namely, a winning formula that encompassed themes of fun, sun, surf, cars, and girls.[22] Anderle believes this quote has been taken out of context, as Mike was focused on the bottom line and less concerned with the "artistic" side of the business equation.[23] This quote has also served as the thesis for the perpetual Wilson-Love conflict, so while *Pet Sounds* and *SMiLE* may have been artistic ventures, they did not fit with Mike's world view of the Beach Boys. When Brian announced to the Beach Boys that he would no longer tour, he presented the scenario as, "There's no need to worry ... I foresee a beautiful future for the Beach Boys. But the only way we can achieve it is if we all do our separate jobs. You guys will tour. I will stay in the studio and make music."[24] Mike and the rest of the band assumed that if Brian said he would stay home and make music, that he would make "their" music. This was the first of many volleys in the battle for Brian's creative spirit that would set him against his family, his band, and the record labels who would have him under contract for the next 20 years. Those parties usually won, but always at great cost to Brian.

The Beach Boys's first five studio albums, from *Surfin' Safari* through *All Summer Long*, were filled with upbeat themes and remain among the band's most popular records. The more complex and elaborate work heard on *Beach Boys Today!* and *Summer Days (and Summer Nights!!)* were within acceptable creative boundaries but still produced good sales and chart activity, but with *Pet Sounds* and then with *SMiLE*, the band's opinions and the expectations of Capitol Records were pushed to their limits. Brian's confidence unraveled and he relinquished creative leadership and control over the Beach Boys and passively acquiesced to a democratically led concern. As a result, the Beach Boys would struggle for the rest of their careers to find their way out of a storm of their own creation. When, in June 1974, Capitol Records released the triple platinum "oldies" compilation, *Endless Summer*, the band's niche as a nostalgia act was set. Though the Beach Boys would continue to produce new records in the decade that followed *Endless Summer*, those records never attained the level of popularity, respect, or audience (to the frustration of Warner Brothers Records and later, Columbia Records) of their earlier work because the thousands who came to hear them perform, came to hear Brian's "classic" hits. Many Beach Boys albums from 1969 to 1985 contained wonderful music from Brian, but, with the exception of *Love You* (1977), neither the songs nor their attendant albums should be wholly considered as Brian's work, but work that his band and producers sought to make sound like Brian Wilson.

From 1963 to mid-1967, Brian Wilson created an extraordinary body of work that had few rivals in the field of popular music. He controlled every aspect of the work, from composition and arrangement to performance and production. The resistance he faced both from his band and his record company when making *Pet Sounds* and *SMiLE* resulted in his refusal to complete the latter, his "teenage symphony to God," the work he believed would be his greatest achievement. Once his masterpiece was shelved, his compositional output declined, and after 1968's *Friends*, the number of songs he placed on Beach Boys albums would decline in number to a point where the Beach Boys might take whatever "piece" of a Brian Wilson song they could acquire, and turn it into a complete work. As he removed himself from the band, others believed they could (or should) provide their own input to "help" Brian along. Perhaps he needed different lyrics or some other element because they believed the song lacked the "punch" it needed to become a hit record, or he may have left the song in a partially finished state and it would require someone to take it upon themselves to "complete" Brian's work. The change in the power structure within the Beach Boys allowed for the development of outrageous narratives about Brian so his band and record company could construct and manage the public image of an artist whose creative vision they had chosen to shut down in 1967.

When the Beatles broke up and each of the four members evolved into solo artists, no one expected that any one of them would make records that sounded like those they had made as the Beatles. Fans chose either to like or dislike the very different work created by each of the four, but no one expected the "sound" of the Beatles to have carried on. When Brian shut down *SMiLE*, he only shut down his latest work, not the group who performed his music. As the band continued on, people expected Brian would want to create hits, just as he had done prior to 1967. When he chose to pursue creative avenues that were distinct from the Beach Boys, fans waited impatiently for Brian to return to what both he and the Beach Boys used to be, and he was never allowed to stand outside our need for him to serve the commercial expectations of the Beach Boys. Bob Dylan and Miles Davis are perhaps the only musical artists in the popular arena to choose, throughout the course of their respective careers, to evolve through the adoption of radical and commercially defiant changes. Unlike those artists, Brian Wilson was synonymous with another entity, the Beach Boys, and they continued to perform his music, even when they barely had an audience. The Beach Boys continued to pursue their role as the vehicle for Brian's music, even when his music no longer was "Beach Boys Music."

If we scan the titles of Brian's songs from 1968 to 1971, they provide some indication of where Brian was and can be interpreted as notice that perhaps it was everyone else who had it all wrong. Brian composed a number of works that are best described as "a-day-in-the-life-of" songs, simple litanies of his activities on a given day. Titles such as "Passing By," "Busy Doin' Nothin," "I Went to Sleep," "Games Two Can Play," and "Time to Get Alone," are just a few of his songs from the late 1960s that are thematically distinct from what he had composed just a few years earlier. Ironically, two of his late decade hits, "Do It Again" and "Break Away" could be read as his willingness to, in fact, "do it again," or to literally "break-away" and leave it all for someone else.[25] In the early 1970s, glorious songs such as "All I Wanna Do," "This Whole World," "Add Some Music to Your Day," "At My Window," "H.E.L.P. Is on the Way," and "Til' I Die" bring us to the edge of Brian's inner world that was miles away from the exuberance of "Fun, Fun, Fun." One of Brian's most stunning works, "Til' I Die," with its swirling canvas of aural colors, possesses a depth and richness comparable to (and perhaps beyond) "The Warmth of the Sun," "California Girls," or "Wouldn't It Be Nice."[26] The lyrics expose Brian's most honest and heartfelt emotions and were as intimate and personal as anything Tony Asher composed for *Pet Sounds.* "Til I Die" is 2 minutes and 44 seconds of absolute, crystalline magic, and might be the last song Brian released that was wholly his creation in the way the "classic" records from 1963 to 1967 were, when the Beach Boys were simply the vehicle through which he expressed his purest visions. Six years after "Til' I Die" Brian recorded two songs, "Still I Dream of It" and "It's Over Now," for the never-released *Adult/Child* album, that express feelings similar to "Til' I Die." But where "Til' I Die" may "sound" like the Beach Boys, the *Adult/Child* songs were in a style so removed from anything that could be considered Beach Boys-like, that they were roundly rejected and would not be issued for over 15 years.

Beginning in the mid-1980s, Brian would once again find creative, respectful, and enthusiastic collaborators. He was reunited with Gary Usher in 1986 for sessions that would lead to the recording of *Brian Wilson* and would collaborate with Andy Paley, who would work with Brian throughout much of the 1990s. Joe Thomas, Scott Bennett, Jeffrey Foskett, Darian Sahanaja, and by extension, the Wondermints became Brian's collaborators, and, by all appearances, have been supportive collaborators and creative foils for Brian. These partnerships have enabled Brian to create a significant body of work that includes the reconstruction and recording of *Brian Wilson Presents SMiLE*, the work that represented the end of his "classic" period, and the beginning of an era when fans chose to not listen to what Brian "said" and instead "wished" for him to say something different. Fans and critics have, since the 1988 release of *Brian Wilson*, debated the value, worth, and quality of Brian's output of the past 25 years when, in truth, Brian's return to creating music was an artistic triumph and a gift to his fans. After years of denying its existence with claims that it was incomplete, in fragments, or unable to be salvaged, Brian presented *SMiLE* on record and in concert, and put an end to the legend that surrounded this work.

Beach Boys records are perhaps the most reissued documents in the history of popular music. From *The Best of the Beach Boys* in 1966 and for nearly every year beyond, themed compilations, greatest hits collections, and reconfigured albums on a variety of labels have made it a challenge to evaluate Brian's music in the order or context in which it was originally created and released. When Capitol Records began to reissue the Beach Boys catalog on compact disc in 1990, they paired many of the original albums in "two-fer" configurations with two albums on one CD and included previously unreleased tracks to maximize the usable time afforded by the compact disc. These presented fans with the most comprehensive and chronological collection of Beach Boys albums ever made available at any period in the band's history. The 1993 release of *Good Vibrations: Thirty Years of the Beach Boys* offered a wealth of material that included the familiar hits in addition to previously unreleased tracks known only to serious collectors and excerpts from *SMiLE*. The 2013 boxed set, *Made in California*, offered more previously unreleased songs to an already extensive body of work.

The Wilson, Love, and Jardine, families were not dissimilar to other suburban families in the California of post-World War II United States. This was the American middle-class in a newly created land of opportunity that comprised stay-at-home moms, community activities, church, PTA, with fathers who earned a living wage in one of the state's many burgeoning industries. Brian grew up in Hawthorne, CA, a suburb south of downtown Los Angeles that was like so many other nearly identical suburbs in the Los Angeles basin that rose from the nether fields, first in the depression, then during and after the Second World War, as a home for the thousands of new residents who came to California in search of work and a better life.[27] When Tom Nolan described Hawthorne as a "post-World War II stucco community," he could be describing any number of the small towns dotted with modern, but modest, homes that expanded southward on numbered streets from downtown Los Angeles to the port cities of San Pedro and Long Beach. These modest, bungalow-style homes were fronted by comfortable lawns with new sidewalks and curbs, fitted with two or three bedrooms, one bath, a modern kitchen, and a garage because every family would have an automobile. While these newly designed suburbs might serve a family's immediate needs, it was assumed the family breadwinner would drive to a job located in Los Angeles or one of its nearby towns.[28] These suburbs were the new "Anytown USA" of post-war United States. They were provincial, homogenous, culturally bereft, and suffocating in their conservative and ordinary comforts. This newly created reality is where the Wilson, Love, Jardine, Marks, and countless other post-war families raised their children.[29] As victors in two world wars, the United States developed a military, aeronautic, and space agenda that was second to none in what was then called the free world. Many of the industries needed to support this new chapter in America's history were developed in California and warranted the construction of factories, subsidiary industries, and new suburbs in which semiskilled and skilled workers could build a life that was unlike any world their parents would have known. New schools and a nation-leading, state-funded system of junior, four-year, and graduate colleges educated these new citizens, taught valuable job skills, and made postsecondary education available to all, at little-to-no cost. Television programs beamed into these homes featured the standard fare of the new medium: serials, dramas, comedies, game shows, sports, family entertainment, children's shows, in short, wholesome entertainment for the entire family.[30]

Many biographies about Brian Wilson tell a story that "stands as one of the saddest and strangest in rock history."[31] It is generally acknowledged that Brian responds to questions in, and of, the moment, and regularly contradicts himself. We should not be too focused on the fluidity of memory because the truth exists in all of Brian's songs, and as with many artists, the small details of memory and day-to-day life are not as crucial to the narrative. When we listen to, study, or analyze the music of Brian Wilson, we have to consider the sincerity and honesty that is present in each of his works. Themes may appear, as described by one-time Beach Boy David Marks, as "campy and corny" or "naïve and honest," but we should remember that, even when packaged inside humor, honesty is at the core of every Brian Wilson composition.[32] Anderle explains it as "... to have that much genius on one hand and that much innocence on the other ... there was no preconceived notions about anything ... just whatever came from his heart or his mind."[33] Whether his songs convey his innermost feelings or the ordinary of day-to-day life, he is completely honest, and when he is humorous, it is sincere and seldom ironic. The themes of his earliest compositions reflect the simplicity of teenage life at mid-century in the perpetually sunny, vibrant, wholesome, and endlessly optimistic culture of southern California. It is not at all surprising that the same author who wrote "Surfin' Safari" and "All Summer Long" could also create "God Only Knows" and "Surf's Up." When Brian expressed his heart and his most personal feelings in songs such "She Knows Me Too Well" or "Caroline, No," he helped to lead popular music from the marketplace of temporary and faddish entertainments into a canon that continues to speak across generations and genres. I am interested in the musical, geographic, and emotional landscapes conveyed in Brian Wilson's music and will focus on the work of an artist who used the recording studio as his medium to create records that serve as artifacts of both a time and place. Brian's story is that of an artist's rise, fall, and recovery through personal and professional redemption. He has endured and survived enormous challenges and been allowed to witness how deeply his music has affected his millions of fans and informed the world of popular music. Brian Wilson's first recorded composition, "Surfin'" (b/w "Luau"), was released on the Candix record label in November 1961, and it is at this juncture that our story begins.

Lead Up, Wind Up, and Hits (1961–1964)

1

Lead Up

Surfin' is the only life, the only life for me .... The first Beach Boys single, "Surfin'," was composed by Brian Wilson and Mike Love and was the affirmation of a lifestyle that helped to shape the trajectory of popular music in the 1960s and beyond. "Surfin' " was first demoed in October 1961 at Hite and Dorinda Morgan's home studio at 2511 Mayberry St in Los Angeles, and recorded with Hite Morgan in November 1961 at World Pacific/Third Street Studios at 8715 W. Third St. in Los Angeles and released later that month as Candix 331.[1] "Surfin' " is Brian Wilson's debut as a pop songwriter, and it showed he was a competent tunesmith who could capture fun and sun in a two-minute bottle, though the record's minimal production and campfire sing-along arrangement makes it difficult to envision how this person would become one of the most influential architects of popular music in the last half of the twentieth century. The Beach Boys did not invent surf music, and real surfers did not care for the Beach Boys because they considered both the band and their music as being inauthentic and considered them as poseurs and sellouts.[2] Neither Brian nor the band ever claimed to play an authentic form of surf music, but they did create a new voice in what had been, to that point, a largely instrumental genre.

Surf music originated in Southern California and took its inspiration from rock and roll instrumentals such as those recorded by the Ventures and Link Wray. Surf music's most identifiable color is a guitar drenched in reverberation, the aural signature of a "wet" sound that is intended to give the listener a sense of the waves and ocean. Legendary guitarist, Dick Dale is perhaps the greatest and most influential practitioner of instrumental surf music, and while the Beach Boys's sound had little in common with the adrenaline rush of Dale's music, by singing about the surf culture in "Surfin'," Brian helped to create a subgenre of "vocal surf" music.[3] In Wilson's hands, the glories and joys of sun, water, cars, and girls were transformed into enviable and wholly sincere personal narratives conveyed from an exclusively male perspective and described scenes of an idyllic life on the beaches of Southern California. Brian's unintended expansion of the "surf music" genre inspired musicians in landlocked states to form "surf-inspired" bands. Groups such as the Astronauts (Colorado), the Trashmen (Minnesota), and the Rivieras (Indiana) merged Dick Dale's electric, reverb-washed sound with Brian's coastal fantasy narratives to create hit songs whose popularity has endured for over five decades. Wilson was not a surfer, and neither were three-fourths of the remaining Beach Boys (brother Carl Wilson, cousin Mike Love, or Brian's friend, Al Jardine). It was Dennis, the middle Wilson brother, who was the surfer and teenage rebel who was constantly in trouble both at school and at home and would provide the cache of California "cool" for the entire band.

Of all the songs in the Brian Wilson/Beach Boys canon, "Surfin' " is perhaps the least important song in his catalog, but it is one of the most debated records among scholars and fans of the band. Originally released on Candix Records on November 27, 1961, it ultimately appeared under three different catalog numbers (with five matrix variations) on two different labels: Candix and X Records.[4] For decades it was unclear which of these labels released the first version, which catalog number was first released, and what exactly was the relationship between "X" and Candix. In their individual efforts to determine the correct order of releases, Stephen J. McParland and James B. Murphy posit the following order based on record matrix numbers that indicate first and second pressings of the record:[5]

- Candix 331
- X 301
- Candix 301[6]

The release of the single was concurrent with a change in the band's name from the Pendletones to the Surfers to the Beach Boys. The accepted legend is that Los Angeles record promoter Russ Regan and Candix A&R man Joe Saraceno came up with the name "The Beach Boys" because Regan did not care for the name "The Pendletones" and could not use "The Surfers" when both realized the name was already taken by another band. Murphy identifies additional parties who claim to have renamed the band and whose stories have been embedded into the band's history.

On February 8, 1962, the Beach Boys made their second visit to World Pacific Studios with both Murry and the Morgans to record "Surfin' Safari" and "Surfer Girl." The American Federation of Musician (AFM) contract for this session lists only three musicians: Brian, Dennis Wilson, and Val Poliuto (session musician and engineer at World Pacific). Though Al Jardine's name appears on the contract, it is crossed out.[7] Carl's name was not listed because, at 15, he was too young to apply for union membership, and Mike, as a singer, not an instrumentalist, would not have been listed. This session produced the first iteration of a song that would, in June 1962, become the Beach Boys's debut single for Capitol Records and the title track of their debut album, *Surfin' Safari*. Al Jardine, whose name was crossed out on the AFM sheet, left the group days after this session and was replaced by Carl's friend and neighbor, 13-year-old David Marks, who served as the band's rhythm guitarist into the fall of 1963.

In the months between the session on February 8 and their first sessions at Western Recorders in April 1962, the Beach Boys's activities have been well documented by a range of authors.[8] With "Surfin'" in the charts by early 1962, Murry booked the Beach Boys anywhere he could place them: high-school dances, radio-sponsored teen dance shows, department stores, screenings of surf movies, miscellaneous local venues, and on March 8, for a single recording session done as a favor for the Morgans.[9] Otherwise, the band's recording career had stalled until Brian met his new friend and collaborator, Gary Usher. Gary's uncle Benny lived at 118th Pl. and Yukon in Inglewood, one street over from the Wilson's Hawthorne address at 3701 W. 119th St. (at Kornblum), and encouraged Gary to introduce himself to the band in early 1962. Five years older than Brian and with two singles to his name, Gary was Brian's first serious collaborator outside of the Wilson/Love family, and he provided Brian with the impetus to move forward when "Surfin'" had begun its slide down the charts and no follow-up single waited in the wings. Gary and Brian connected immediately, and the first song written on the night they met was the gentle and haunting ballad, "The Lonely Sea."

Brian never had a permanent, or fixed, collaborator with whom he would work for an extended period of time, and he did not have the equivalent of a George Martin who, as a collaborator/producer with both technical and musical skills, enabled the Beatles to focus solely on creating music. Though Western Recorders engineer Chuck Britz was an invaluable partner behind the console until 1967, he could not provide Brian with the breadth of creative support that Martin had provided to the Beatles, which makes Brian's accomplishments all the more remarkable. Throughout Wilson's career, the quality and tone of his work would be shaped by the people with whom he chose to collaborate. Mike Love was his first collaborator and by default would become, over the next two decades, his most consistent songwriting partner, but Gary Usher was the first partner who informed and shaped Brian's musical vision. Usher was followed by Roger Christian, Tony Asher, and Van Dyke Parks—all of whom provided the narrative canvases upon which Brian could create his most loved and recognized works.

Brian's best songwriting partnerships often were short lived. Murry Wilson distrusted people outside of the family, especially those who disagreed with him, and when Gary crossed that line, he found his access to Brian would be limited. In spite of this, over a dozen Wilson-Usher songs would end up on records by the Beach Boys, the Hondells, Jan & Dean, and the Super Stocks, and it was Gary who inspired Brian to write his first car song "409." In his quest to capture an authentic feel for this song, Brian used David Marks's Roberts reel-to-reel tape recorder to record the sound of Gary's Chevrolet Impala 348 as he sped down Kornblum Ave between 119th and 120th St. at 11:00 pm which, once this sample was mixed into the song, provided the work with a palpable and electric energy.[10] Gary and Brian collaborated again in the 1980s as Brian began to work on material for his 1988 solo debut album, *Brian Wilson*. History would be repeated when Gary was denied access to Brian by Dr. Eugene Landy, Wilson's controversial doctor and surrogate abuser.[11]

Usher arranged two recording sessions in April 1962 at Western Recorders that were paid for by Murry Wilson.[12] At the first session, Usher led Brian and the Beach Boys through four songs: "Beginning of the End," "One Way Road to Love," "My Only Alibi," and "Visions."[13] None of these would ever see an official Beach Boys release, although elements of "Visions" would be recycled and given new lyrics for a single, "Number One," which served as the B-side of Rachel and the Revolvers's "The Revo-lution" (Dot 45-16392). Before the October 1962 release of the *Surfin' Safari* album, Brian received his first official production credit (albeit a coproduction with Usher) with this little-known single, which was a Wilson and Usher manufactured project. Rachel was Betty Willis an African-American singer and sister of Los Angeles-based doo-wop singer, Alonzo Willis, while the Revolvers were Brian Wilson, Carl Wilson, and Gary Usher.[14] Both sides were authored by Wilson and Usher and were recorded on September 4 at Harmony Recorders Studio. "Revo-lution" was Brian's take on Little Eva's then-popular hit single from May 1962, "The Loco-motion." "The Revo-lution" is fresh if only that in no way does it sound like a Beach Boys song, but captures the feel of a Goffin/King, Brill Building work with elements of Phil Spector's early production aesthetic.

The name "Brian Wilson" is synonymous with the Beach Boys, and it is assumed that the band was his primary, if not sole, creative vehicle until the release of his eponymous 1988 solo album. The reality is that Brian collaborated with other artists from the very start of his career and worked to develop a second identity as composer/producer in the model of Phil Spector. This "other" side of Brian would become a source of friction with Murry, the band, and unfortunately, within himself. Before these familial conflicts crippled his creative psyche, Brian juggled collaborations with other artists alongside his commitments to the Beach Boys, their unforgiving tour schedules, and Capitol's requirement for three albums per year. The late Billboard editor and critic, Timothy White described Brian's non-Beach Boys projects as fulfilling a "need to communicate creatively with other artists outside his immediate sphere ... [he] wanted to build a body of production credits at a pace comparable to Spector."[15]

Three tracks recorded at the second April session at Western, "Surfin' Safari," "409," and "The Lonely Sea" were among the dozen songs Murry left with Nik Venet, an Artists & Repertoire (A&R) man for Capitol Records who signed the band, and from which he selected the Beach Boys debut single on Capitol.[16] The move from the Candix label to Capitol is not entirely clear as the period between March 29, when Murry drafted an agreement with Hite Morgan to produce the Beach Boys, to May 10, when Capitol assigned matrix numbers for the single of "Surfin' Safari"/"409," becomes a challenge to date with any authority. Capitol released "409" b/w "Surfin' Safari" on June 4, 1962, but the B-side became the band's first national hit and opened with one of the most recognizable lines in pop music, "Let's go surfin' now, Everybody's learning how, Come on a safari with me." Capitol committed to the band on July 16, and they cut the remaining tracks for their debut album on August 8 and September 5 and 6.

Wind Up

The Beach Boys debut LP, *Surfin Safari*, was released on October 1, 1962, and of the 12 tracks on the album, 9 were written by Brian in collaboration with either Gary Usher or Mike Love. In addition to their debut Capitol single, the album also contained the Hite Morgan master for "Surfin' " and nine songs recorded at Capitol Studios in August and September 1962.

For the first two Beach Boys albums, *Surfin' Safari* and *Surfin' U.S.A.*, Nik Venet is listed as the producer, though David Marks and others have confirmed that Brian really ran the sessions, set all balance levels, handled the arrangements, and was in charge of the session, though he received no production credit.[17] White described Venet's contribution as that of a "corporate liaison," so regardless of the credit accorded to Venet, it should be assumed the first two albums were produced by Brian.[18] The majority of the first album was recorded at Capitol Tower where "County Fair," "Ten Little Indians," "Chug-A-Lug," "Heads You Win, Tails I Lose," "Cuckoo Clock," "The Shift," and "Land Ahoy" were recorded. Music critic Andrew Hickey refers to the Beach Boys of the *Surfin' Safari*-era as a "garage band," which is an accurate, though fleeting, description. Despite a narrow range of themes limited to surfing, cars, and parties, the album featured a buffet of performance styles and abilities that included one song recorded with Al Jardine in September 1961 (Surfin'), two songs recorded at Western with new guitarist David Marks ("Surfin' Safari" and "409"), in April 1962, with the remainder of the album recorded at Capitol Tower over August–September 1962. Over the 12 months in which the album was recorded, we can hear their development as an ensemble unit. They evolved from an energetic but unremarkable group into a taut and tight (if not technically advanced) studio band. We also hear in *Surfin' Safari*, the first stages in Brian's growth as a songwriter and arranger. The songs recorded in August and September 1962 are similar in sound and structure, but the band sounds like an entirely different group when compared to their earlier sessions. Hickey points out that the majority of *Surfin' Safari* was recorded before the Beatles recorded "Love Me Do" on September 4, 1962, to support his opinion that, regardless of its shortcomings, *Surfin' Safari* offers a "fresh, interesting sound."[19]

Fresh and interesting, yes, but there is nothing exceptional about the songs that make up the balance of the album, except for "County Fair," which matches the energy, drive, and novelty of "Surfin' Safari"/"409." "County Fair" was the second song composed by Wilson-Usher and is equal to "409" in terms of its sonic palette and creative wordplay. It possesses one of the album's most inventive arrangements and includes spoken roles for a carnival barker and the narrator's girlfriend (provided, respectively, by Venet and David Marks's aunt).[20] The song owes more than a bit to Freddy Cannon's hit, "Palisades Park" (Swan Records, June 1962), a song the Beach Boys would cover in 1976 on, *15 Big Ones*. "County Fair" ended up as the B-side to their second Capitol single, "Ten Little Indians," released in November 1962. Though the B-side was far more interesting, "Ten Little Indians" is not the sort of material that one might expect for a single. By contemporary standards, this song may be culturally insensitive, but given the Cowboys-and-Indians programming fed to a generation of American kids raised on TV and movies in the 1950s, its selection as a single is not that far-fetched. A wave of western-themed hit songs had scored on the charts over the previous few years, so while "Ten Little Indians" bore a similarity to Johnny Preston's 1960 number one hit, the J.P. "The Big Bopper" Richardson penned "Running Bear," its release made good business sense to Capitol.[21] Still, this was a misfire as the single would only reach number 49 on the national chart and would be the band's lowest charting record for five years.

A week after tracking sessions for *Surfin' Safari*, Brian was at work on another extracurricular project. Bob Norberg was Brian's first roommate at the Crenshaw Park Apartments in Inglewood and would collaborate with Brian on a handful of songs over 1962–1963. On September 13, 1962, Brian produced one of their projects, "The Surfer Moon," for the vocal duo Bob & Sheri, which was simply Norberg and his girlfriend, Cheryl Pomeroy.[22] "The Surfer Moon" was released in October 1962 on a Murry Wilson home-label imprint, Safari Records, and was a departure for Brian as it is a very pretty song in the style of a 1950s pop ballad that could have been sung by any number of artists of the period. Why would Brian write in a style that was more closely aligned to earlier pop styles than to rock and roll? When we consider Brian's appreciation for vocal groups such as the Four Freshmen, the Four Preps, and the Lettermen, his comfort with hybridization makes perfect sense, and he would cross-pollinate styles with relative ease throughout his career.[23] The single made no impact in the charts, but Brian did not let this minor gem slip into obscurity. He returned to it on May 9, 1963, at United Recorders with a few members from the top-notch Los Angeles session players who would become known as "The Wrecking Crew."[24] On that occasion, he paired Norberg with a local singer named Victoria Hale and renamed the song "The Summer Moon." Jan Berry provided an effective string arrangement, but this version would remain unreleased until the 2014 digital-only release *The Big Beat 1963*.[25] The song made a third, final, and perfect appearance, with Brian's vocals and Jan Berry's string arrangement, on the Beach Boys's third album, *Surfer Girl*.

Hits

On January 2, 1963, Brian and the band recorded the instrumental "Punchline" at Western Recorders. This would have been a perfect track on the upcoming *Surfin' U.S.A.* album, but it would remain unreleased until the *Good Vibrations* boxed set. Like his earlier effort on "The Revo-lution," "Punchline" is a rich production and in many ways is a more developed work than any number of songs that appear on *Surfin' U.S.A.* It opens with a classic boogie-woogie riff on piano with drums and gives way to a bass and Hammond Organ riff that is punctuated with obnoxious, howling laughter. While *Surfin' U.S.A.* would be the most "surf-like" album in their canon, "Punchline" is Brian's well-developed contribution to the genre of the "surf instrumental."

Surfin' U.S.A. was recorded over five sessions at three studios in Los Angeles and New York City, and this exuberant album moves beyond the band's modest debut released just five months earlier. With the inclusion of familiar instrumental covers such as "Misirlou," "Honky Tonk," and "Let's Go Tripping," alongside Brian's "Stoked" and Carl's "Surf Jam," this album is the closest the Beach Boys would come to producing an album of authentic surf music. The album also marked a departure for Brian as a producer. Interviewed by Stephen McParland in 1997, Nik Venet claimed that "Brian was fooling around with the Beach Boys' sound at that time . . . trying to alter it . . . I think he was experimenting."[26] The band on *Surfin' U.S.A.* sounds like an entirely different group from the one that recorded *Surfin' Safari*, and it reflects a substantial change in Brian's approach to recording and the band's growing confidence as an ensemble. One technique heard on this album is Brian's adoption of double-tracked vocals, which add a richness and depth to the finished product.

Nik Venet was listed as the producer for this album, but as before, Brian was in charge of the sessions.[27] The band's next album, *Surfer Girl*, would be their first album to read "Produced by Brian Wilson." Murry's persistence pushed Capitol Records executives to release Brian from having to record in their studios (he would use Capitol's studio for selected projects) and allowed him to work in any studio of his choice. Venet's influence has often been portrayed as an obstruction to Brian's development as a producer, but this narrative was likely developed by Murry Wilson to demonstrate his own managerial acumen and his influence upon Brian's evolution as a producer. Venet's memories as to exactly when he met with Brian, Murry, and Gary Usher were never clear as Venet himself has given contradictory accounts about their first meetings. It appears, based on Usher's more objective account, that they met on May 7, 1962, a month prior to their Capitol records debut. Venet respected Brian, and they would collaborate on a variety of projects over the next three years.

Surfin' U.S.A. is one of the most recognizable songs in the Beach Boys canon and is built on the harmonic progression and melodic structure of Chuck Berry's "Sweet Little Sixteen." Jimmy Bowles, the younger brother of Brian's first girlfriend, Judy (who was his inspiration for "Surfer Girl"), provided him with many of the locations mentioned in the song because Brian would not have known where surfers would hangout. The second track on side one, "Farmer's Daughter," is an unusual Wilson-Love collaboration. The song clips along at a moderate pace and features the predictable teenage innuendo often found in Mike Love's lyrics to which is added a bit of material borrowed from Rachel and the Revolvers's "Number One."[28] Brian's falsetto is effortless on the lead vocal, and the call-and-response in the background vocals are tastefully arranged. Recorded the same day as "Lana" (the middle track on side two), one can hear that a similar melody is used in both tunes. Following a cover of Dick Dale's "Misirlou," Brian's "Stoked" is his effective take at writing an "authentic" surf instrumental. It is such a well-crafted piece that one might expect it too is a cover, similar to "Misirlou" or "Let's Go Trippin." Brian's arrangement of "Stoked" places the bass and guitar on the same melodic line, though an octave apart, which provides a thick sound in place of the traditional wet and reverb-heavy melody found on Dale's records. "The Lonely Sea," the first song composed by Brian and Usher in January 1962, was recorded on April 19, 1962, at the same session that produced their debut Capitol single, "Surfin' Safari" and "409." Brian's lead vocal on this ballad does not convey the confidence he would display on their next album, but this does not lessen the song's impact. The harmonic progression for this song was composed by Usher with a melody added by Brian, and in this we hear references to Phil Spector's classic 1958 single, "To Know Him Is to Love Him," especially in the accompaniment's triplet pattern and in Mike's handling of the text "*The-Lonely-Sea.*" Side one of the album closes with "Shut Down," the B-side of the "Surfin' U.S.A." single, which provides a liberal dose of expert automotive vocabulary, and is the first song on a Beach Boys record to come from Brian's collaboration with Roger Christian. Christian was an avid car enthusiast and DJ on KFWB radio and was introduced to Brian by either Gary Usher or Murry Wilson. Murry has been given the credit for their initial meeting, though Murphy and McParland offer strong evidence that Usher (who had worked with Christian) introduced the two. Roger was eight years older than Brian, but the age difference was no impediment to their working relationship. Roger provided Brian's songs with a range of technical automotive vocabulary that was new territory in popular music. The Wilson-Christian collaboration is as important as the Wilson-Usher relationship in Brian's creative development. Though "Shut Down" was the first of their songs to appear on a Beach Boys album, their first collaboration, "Little Deuce Coupe," would appear on *Surfer Girl*, the Beach Boys's second album of 1963. Brian's partnerships with both Usher and Christian would provide songs for the Beach Boys, Jan & Dean, and other studio group projects on which they collaborated. In Brian's work with Usher, songs were built upon first-person narratives and everyday events, and each contributed to both music and lyrics. With Roger Christian, Brian composed the music while Roger penned lyrics that tended to anthropomorphize the mechanized power of the automobile. "Noble Surfer," the opening track on side two, is built on a harmonic progression similar to "Surfin' Safari" and might have been better suited on that album. It features one of Brian's least imaginative vocal arrangements, but one interesting feature is his use of the celesta in the instrumental break. Following their cover of the instrumental, "Honky Tonk," they provide another Wilson original, "Lana." While a solid, though less than remarkable tune, Brian delivers a confident falsetto and the celesta is used again, this time in unison with the lead guitar, which is more clearly heard in the stereo mix. Brian chose to perform the song at a brisk pace when it might have fared better at a slower tempo. Session documentation shows Brian worked on this song at three separate sessions. At a time when most of his songs were given no more than two days in the studio, a three-day investment indicates that Brian may have attempted to take this song in a direction that was different from what he eventually released.

The album concludes with "Finders Keepers," 1 minute and 40 seconds of muscle-pumped machismo in a cleverly constructed package and an appropriate closer to the band's most surf-centric album. What appears to be a straight-ahead boogie-woogie riff evolves into a song that sounds as if it was constructed from multiple sources. Brian would develop his skill with rapid and unanticipated shifts, first heard in "Finders Keepers," to greater effect in later songs such as "The Little Girl I Once Knew." Recorded at the last session for the album on February 12, 1963, a few sloppy moments show through in the rhythm section, but do not detract from this brief work. David Leaf maintains that the chorus of this song is modeled on the then current hit by the Four Seasons, "Big Girls Don't Cry." With the next album, Brian would make greater use of studio musicians in tracking sessions that would allow him to develop stronger instrumental performances with more complex arrangements. In the 1990 "two-fer" releases of the Beach Boys's 1960s catalog, bonus tracks were added from previously unreleased material, and the *Surfin*

Safari and *Surfin' U.S.A.* two-fer offered two new tunes. "Baker Man" is a Wilson pastiche on the Olympics's "Hully Gully" (1959) and was erroneously listed on an AFM contract from August 8, 1962 (as "The Baker"), when it was actually recorded on March 7, 1963, weeks before the release of the *Surfin' U.S.A.* album.[29] Leaf believes this song was recorded as a demo for Al Nevins and Don Kirshner, directors of Aldon Music, one of the most successful publishing concerns in New York's Brill Building.[30] At this same session, Brian recorded an instrumental, "Side Two," which remained unfinished and unreleased until 2014's *The Big Beat 1963.* Built on a boilerplate boogie-woogie riff, the most memorable part of this track is its prominent bass line that would later be incorporated into "Little Deuce Coupe." Another track recorded in winter 1963 and given a debut release on *The Big Beat* is "Ride Away." Credited to Bob & Sheri, this inoffensive song sounds like a template for songs Brian would compose with Usher and Christian for use in the Beach Party film series.

Between October 1962 and March 1963, when the Beach Boys released *Surfin' U.S.A.*, Brian entered into a pair of important collaborations. The first was with the Honeys, a trio of Jewish girls from Los Angeles's Fairfax neighborhood. Like the Beach Boys, the Honeys were a family group with sisters Diane and Marilyn Rovell and cousin Ginger Blake who, at the time, was dating Gary Usher. Brian met them in September 1962 during the Beach Boys's residency at Pandora's Box in Hollywood. The dates of the shows at Pandora's Box, the length of their residency, and exactly when Brian first met Marilyn Rovell cannot be definitively determined, but what is generally understood and agreed upon is that Brian and Marilyn Rovell (and by extension, the Honeys) met at this venue in August 1962.[31] Brian and Marilyn would marry two years later, but not before he produced and/or authored a handful of singles for the Honeys.[32] The other important collaboration was with the duo of Jan Berry and Dean Torrence. Jan & Dean were an established act when the Beach Boys opened for them at the Reseda Jubilee on August 25, 1962, which led to a genuine friendship between the two groups. Jan & Dean included "Surfin' " and "Surfin' Safari" on their album, *Jan and Dean Take Linda Surfing*, on which the uncredited Beach Boys performed and provided backup vocals. Over the next few years, Brian, both alone and with the Beach Boys, would collaborate with Jan & Dean on a number of tracks that include "She's My Summer Girl," "Drag City," "Move Out Little Mustang," "Ride the Wild Surf," "Surf Route 101," "Surfin' Wild," "Dead Man's Curve," "Gonna Hustle You" (later retitled "The New Girl in School"), and their biggest hit, "Surf City." Released in May 1963, "Surf City" featured Brian's distinctive falsetto and became Brian's first number one record in July 1963. Murry was furious that Brian "gave" a number one hit to Jan & Dean and believed the duo had stolen his song. Jan Berry and Brian had a good working relationship, but this too would also be short lived as the exclusive agreements each group had with their respective labels prevented them from being credited on each other's recordings. Brian's work with Jan & Dean would yield a number of hit records that ended with Jan Berry's near fatal car accident in April 1966.

The winter of 1963 was a period of experimentation for Brian, who expanded his work with artists other than the Beach Boys. We are unable to precisely date these activities as many of the AFM contracts from this period are believed to have been lost, so we are left to rely upon conflicting information and the memories of participants as to when much of this activity took place. One song with a complex gestation was Brian's "Gonna Hustle You." It is believed this Wilson-Norberg song was first demoed in fall 1962, before Jan & Dean recorded it in March 1963. Imperial did not want to release the song with its original lyrics, so with a new title and lyrics (most likely contributed by Roger Christian), "The New Girl in School" served as the B-side to Jan & Dean's "Dead Man's Curve." In an unexpected move, Imperial released the version with the original "Hustle" lyrics on Jan & Dean's 1966 album, *Fillet of Soul* (which featured the third version of "Dead Man's Curve"). On March 5, 1963, Brian produced the Honeys's debut single "Shoot the Curl" and "Surfin' Down the Swanee River." Though Nik Venet was listed as producer, this was Brian's project. The rollicking piano that propels "Shoot the Curl" was played by legendary Wrecking Crew member Leon Russell. "Surfin' Down the Swanee River" was inspired by Stephen Foster's "Old Folks at Home" set to new lyrics from Brian. This mash-up of surf themes and nineteenth-century Americana would be revisited when the Beach Boys recorded "South Bay Surfer" for the *Surfer Girl* LP. The arrangements of both songs are similar, though neither really succeeds.

Though Brian did not officially retire from the road until early 1965, he began to miss shows as early as April 1963. As a result, the band would perform as a four-piece, and on occasion Al Jardine would fill in for Brian. The six-man, Jardine/Marks configuration of the Beach Boys had a brief existence and is seldom mentioned, because David was out of the group before the year was finished. Sessions for the third Beach Boys album, *Surfer Girl*, likely began on June 12 at Western Recorders. This is the only album on which we get the six-man line-up of the Beach Boys, and with this album, the credit, *Produced by Brian Wilson*, would grace their records until 1967's *Smiley Smile*. A session on June 12 was spent at work on their next single, "Surfer Girl" and "Little Deuce Coupe." "Surfer Girl" was first attempted at the Hite Morgan session on February 8, 1962, but 15 months later Brian framed the song in an understated arrangement that stands as one of his first masterpieces. Brian's affection for Judy Bowles is constructed upon a melody inspired by the Walt Disney song "When You Wish Upon a Star," from Pinocchio (a song Brian would sing on his 2011 solo album, *In the Key of Disney*) into a wholly original work. Hickey makes note of what he perceives as sloppy double tracking in the middle-eight of the song, but I feel Brian consciously left this in. The hocket he creates on the words, "We could ride . . . (ride) . . . the surf together . . ." creates a sincere but pulsating tension that expresses longing in the heart of our teenaged narrator. Recorded at this same session was the Wilson/Christian car song, "Little Deuce Coupe." Aside from Christian's lyrics, which contain a comparable level of automotive vocabulary to "Shut Down," the song contains a number of memorable lines. One in particular makes no sense if you never owned a car in California. "I got the pink slip daddy" refers to the car's title, which, in California, was processed on pink stock. Full ownership of any automobile (and the attendant bragging rights) required one to possess the car's "pink slip."

Brian endured a punishing schedule both on tour and in the studio, but he continued to produce records with artists other than his band. One session on June 14, 1963, was at Gold Star where Brian's musical idol, Phil Spector, recorded many of his Wall of Sound hits. This was not the first session where Brian worked with musicians other than the Beach Boys, but it was one of the first times he used a number of musicians from the legendary Los Angeles studio band who would become known as "The Wrecking Crew" and with whom Brian would continue to work over the next four years. From this session came the songs "Back Home" and "Black Wednesday," neither of which would be released in their original form. Brian returned to "Back Home" a decade later and rerecorded it for the 1976 album, *15 Big Ones.* Though not a particularly strong track in its later iteration, the vocals in the chorus harkened back to Brian's earlier style. "Black Wednesday" would resurface as "Runaround Lover," the A-side of Sharon Marie's debut single.

The albums *Surfin' U.S.A.* and *Surfer Girl* are based on the simple themes of surf, sun, and cars. Where *Surfin' U.S.A.* was the band's best effort at creating an album of authentic surf music, with *Surfer Girl* Brian moved closer to the expansive symphonic textures he would begin to integrate into the Beach Boys repertoire. In mid-July, Brian recorded "South Bay Surfer," "The Surfer Moon," and vocals for "Catch a Wave." The latter, a Wilson/Love composition, opens with a cappella introduction and moves into a simple and effective vocal arrangement. The harp glissandi played by Mike's sister, Maureen Love, and the organ figure that closes each verse (and again borrows from Freddy Cannon's "Palisades Park") enable this track to stand out as something completely different from anything Brian had previously recorded. "The Surfer Moon" is an update of his May 9 recording of "The Summer Moon," and was the third iteration of the 1962 Bob & Sherri single, where Brian hit the sweet spot on this song. He used Jan Berry's string arrangement from the "Summer Moon" demo and sang all the parts himself to an absolutely charming effect. "South Bay Surfer" was Brian's second pass on the track he originally recorded with the Honeys as "Surfin' Down the Swanee River." The topical references to the surfers of Redondo, Hermosa, and Manhattan Beach are clever if one knows the area, but it is a harmless filler track and the mob-unison lead vocals are, for Brian, a mannered attempt at the ordinary. "The Rocking Surfer" is another instrumental surf tune that owes as much to German bandleader Burt Kaempfert (the reedy organ timbre and pizzicato strings in the last statement of the theme) as it would to any legitimate surf tune. One obvious feature of this track is the poor audio quality of the master recording. Tape hiss, much more audible in stereo than in mono, adds to the scratchy garage-feel of the piece. A throwaway piece, but a fun one at that.

Side two opens with the Wilson/Usher masterpiece, "In My Room." Brian has spoken about this piece on many occasions and its origins in his childhood and teenage years when he shared a room with his brothers in the house on 119th Street. The finger cymbals and harp glissandi in the introduction lift this song from the predictable into the very personal and private realm of Brian's inner world. His arrangement of the triplet accompaniment figure that runs throughout the song never becomes boring as he foregrounds and accumulates more colors that allow the richness of the song to climax in the final verse. The first of three Wilson/Love tunes, "Hawaii," is a clever number that highlights Brian's falsetto. "Surfer's Rule," like "Finders Keepers," from the previous album, is best remembered for its reference to Frankie Valli and the Four Seasons who, at the time, were the top vocal group in the country. The vocal in the final chorus states "Four Seasons, you better believe it," and is punctuated by Brian's falsetto in the style of the Four Seasons's hit, "Walk Like a Man." But this line has a second meaning in that four seasons can also refer to the fact that California surfers can surf all seasons of the year. "Our Car Club" gives Mike Love an opportunity to match Roger Christian in terms of car-specific lyrics though the most interesting features of this throbbing rocker are the fuzzy guitars and saxophone. The song is more convincing in mono, because the contrasting textures are separated and placed comparatively low in the stereo mix.

The album comes to its conclusion with two very different works. The first is a Wilson/Norberg ballad, "Your Summer Dream," a 1950s-style, breezy love song with jazz-inflected harmonies. As with "The Surfer Moon," Brian carries the lead vocal without any other Beach Boys. The triplet accompaniment in the acoustic guitar carries this touching love song from start to finish, and the wealth of minor seventh chords remind us of Brian's affection for the Four Freshmen. While this song carries a melancholy tenor similar to "The Lonely Sea," it has a far happier outcome. Brian's plaintive and heartfelt vocal captures the dreamy, soft, and slightly damp calm one experiences on Southern California beaches at twilight. This is the first of three songs Brian will record over the next year (the other two being "I Do" and "We'll Run Away"), which give voice to his romantic hopes and dreams. These songs likely have basis in the real-life romance that had begun to develop between Brian and Marilyn Rovell, whom he would marry on December 7, 1964. The final track, "Boogie Woodie," provides Brian with an opportunity to marry his piano chops with his love of boogie-woogie piano. While this album has many extraordinary moments, it is an uneven collection comprised of four classic songs that for decades have remained in the Beach Boys's live repertory and on countless hits collections, in addition to a pair of charming and stylized ballads, and six tracks of varying quality that deal with either surfing or cars. The sheer volume of material Brian composed, performed, or produced in the latter half of 1963 is remarkable, and it is astounding that he produced many of these songs in-between touring commitments. In summer of 1963, Brian watched Jan & Dean's "Surf City" climb the charts to reach the number one spot on July 20 and saw the single of "Surfer Girl" reach the top 20 in September. He also managed to produce strong tracks for both the Honeys and a new Wilson-Love directed artist, Sharon Marie.

Brian was in Capitol's studios with Nik Venet on July 24 to produce a new single for the Honeys, "Pray for Surf" b/w "(Oly, Oxen Free Free Free) Hide Go Seek." As with the previous Honeys single, the A-side was composed by the girls, while Brian composed the flip side. With members of the Wrecking Crew on the session, Brian produced an exciting single that made no mark on the charts.[33] It appears Capitol put virtually no support behind either of the Honeys singles, so it was no surprise when the trio moved to Warner Brothers Records. It is likely Capitol funded these projects to keep Brian happy while he continued to generate profits for Capitol via the Beach Boys. Brian missed selected dates of a Midwest tour at the end of July but was in the studio on August 5 with a trio of acquaintances, his old roommate, Bob Norberg, with Rich Arlarian and Dave Nowlen, who called themselves the Survivors.

Wilson produced three tracks for the Survivors at Gold Star Studio, "Witch Stand," "Girlie," and "Hot Harp" (with Maureen Love on Harp). This may have been another effort by Brian to establish himself as an independent producer/artist apart from the Beach Boys, but Capitol passed on all three songs, though a second Survivors submission, "Pamela Jean" b/w "After the Game" was released. Recorded on August 27, 1963, and released on January 6, 1964, the A-side was the preliminary version of "Car Crazy Cutie," a song the Beach Boys would record on September 2 for their third album of 1963, *Little Deuce Coupe*. The Survivors's take on "Pamela Jean" is stronger than the Beach Boys's version thanks to the Wrecking Crew's performance. It is an effective doo-wop tune and carries more than a scent of Dion's 1961 hit, "Runaround Sue." The vocals are washed in echo and this record, like many of Brian's extracurricular productions, pushed the production envelope ahead of his work on Beach Boys records. The B-side, "After the Game," is an instrumental that is distinct from earlier works and is a warm-up for "Summer Means New Love," on 1965's *Summer Days (and Summer Nights!!)*, which became a melody Brian returned to for "Somewhere Quiet," on his 2015 solo album, *No Pier Pressure*.

David Marks had grown tired of Murry's strong-arm managerial style, and in late August 1963, announced he would leave the band at the end of their tour (his last show was on October 5, 1963). This brought an end to the six-man studio Beach Boys, and allowed Al Jardine to resume his original role in the band both on the road and in the studio, which placed additional pressure on Brian to be a full-time member of the touring group. In one marathon session he produced eight new tracks for *Little Deuce Coupe*, an album Capitol released less than one month after *Surfer Girl.* On the band's first three albums there were filler tracks that were acceptable, but ordinary, songs, hastily written and recorded to fill out an album; under the continual pressure to produce new material, Brian could have tossed off a number of dispensable tracks for this album. He did, after all, have one of the band's most recent hits, "Little Deuce Coupe," and three previously released tracks to support this album.

Murry Wilson continued to involve himself in Beach Boys recording sessions, and the infamous argument that took place over a year later at the session for the single of "Help Me Rhonda" on February 24, 1965, provides some insight into the pressures Brian must have faced when producing the quantity of music that was demanded of him. In that argument, Murry chastised Brian for taking so much time to record a single and reminds him that "Chuck (Britz) and I used to make one hit after the other in 30 minutes. You guys take five hours to do it. . . ."[34] On a first listen it appears that Murry is all bluster and hyperbole, but when we look at the schedule Brian maintained throughout 1963, it is not a stretch to believe that he could turn out a hit every 30 minutes.

Of the new songs, none match the quality of "Surfer Girl," "Surfin' U.S.A.," or "In My Room," but neither are they throwaway tracks. There is one cover, "A Young Man Is Gone," a Four Freshmen-esque tribute to James Dean that placed new lyrics on Bobby Troup's "Their Hearts Were Full of Spring." There is the first version of "Be True to Your School," a song that in its single mix would demonstrate Brian's increasingly complex production values. A nostalgic car song, "Ballad of Ole' Betsy," is the first of five new Wilson/Christian songs on the album. It makes sense that an album focused on the automobile would be loaded with gender-specific, anthropomorphic prose, and from this perspective, "Ballad of Ole Betsy" takes the transference of female/mechanical affections to an awkward extreme. The production, as with many songs on this album, is a bit ragged, but not unexpected given the speed with which they were recorded at the conclusion of a two-week Midwest tour. The double-tracked vocals are sloppy at moments, and there is a discernable edit before the lovely a cappella tag.[35] The Four Freshmen-esque vocal arrangement is effective and is the saving feature for the song. Like 1965's "Help Me Rhonda," "Be True to Your School" exists in two very different arrangements now designated as the "single" version and the "album" version. The single was released on November 28, 1963, two weeks after the release of the *Little Deuce Coupe* LP. The differences between the two versions are startling and impressive. The album track is fine and is the most thematically juvenile song Brian would commit to disc. The single version is a fascinating transformation where Brian brings the electric ambience of a high school sporting event into the record. The Honeys provide cheerleader-like background vocals and with marching band colors of snares, tom-toms, piccolo, and flutes, it sounds as if a marching band and a cheerleader corps went out on the sporting field at the same time that a pop band was magically placed onto the 50-yard line. Not until *SMiLE* did Brian attempt to mix so many contrasting timbres as he did with this single.

"Car Crazy Cutie" was a rerecording of the Survivors's "Pamela Jean." With different lyrics, the Beach Boys version is cleaner and has stronger vocals with lyrics by Roger Christian. After the Hite Morgan recording of "Judy" and the as-then-unreleased "Land Ahoy," Brian used the best materials from those songs and ended up with "Cherry, Cherry Coupe." Roger Christian's lyrics are in top form for only he could take auto shop talk and turn it into pure pop poetry. This is followed by two older car songs, "409" and "Shut Down," good songs on their own, but after the more advanced production values of "Cherry, Cherry Coupe," they sound comparatively anemic. It is difficult to comprehend that barely a year-and-a-half had passed between "409" and "Cherry Chery, Coupe," but it demonstrates the speed at which Brian Wilson had developed, both as a songwriter and as a producer.

"Spirit of America" shares a little too much in terms of form and arrangement with the earlier "Ballad of Ole Betsy" but is a more satisfying work. The shuffle/doo-wop arrangement is beautifully layered under Brian's floating falsetto, and the parallel motion between the saxophones and background vocals is very effective. The subject matter was relevant at the time of this record's release since Craig Breedlove's land speed record of 407.45 mph had been set on August 5, 1963, and Brian's song pays tribute in a tasteful and sincere fashion. In "No-Go Showboat," Brian foregrounds the backing vocals, while his falsetto takes the melody behind them. This song was also recorded and released as a single in October 1964 by Jimmy Bowen for the Timers, on which Brian sang backing vocals. The final track on the album, "Custom Machine," is an enjoyable but unusual song. The ensemble performance is free of errors, the arrangement and harmonic shifts are clever, but the story of yet another fantastic car is by now tired and detracts from the complexity of Brian's harmonic choices and compositional structure.

In the months between the release of the *Little Deuce Coupe* LP and the arrival of the Beatles in America on February 7, 1964, the Beach Boys reverted to their original, pre-Capitol Records line-up. Brian would return to the touring band for the foreseeable future and would coauthor or produce a handful of outstanding records not only for the Beach Boys but also for Jan & Dean, the Honeys, Sharon Marie, and the Castells, with works that put him on par with, if not ahead of, the Beatles. Brian was in the studio with the Honeys on September 16 to record what would be their third, and final, Capitol single, "The One You Can't Have." On October 18 and 20, Brian and the Beach Boys also recorded their first holiday single, "Little Saint Nick."[36] Their holiday album would not be released until the following year, but this single with its Spector-esque rhythm bed remains a holiday classic 50 years after it was first released. It was backed with an unexpected selection, Brian's Four Freshmen-esque arrangement of Albert Hay Malotte's "The Lord's Prayer." On October 21, Capitol released the debut single for Brian and Mike's new "discovery," 20-year-old Sharon Marie Esparza, whom they met at a concert in June 1963.[37] The Wilson-Love tune "Run-Around Lover" was paired with George Gershwin's "Summertime," an early expression of Brian's love for the music of George Gershwin. The production values on Sharon Marie's record were not dissimilar to what he was doing with both the Honeys and the Survivors, but with the Wrecking Crew behind what is, for Brian, an average song, it comes off better than it should. Sharon Marie does not have a voice that grabs you, but her double-tracked lead vocal and the insistent backing vocals give the song an exciting edge.

Brian's work with Jan & Dean continued and on November 18 they released the Berry-Christian-Wilson hit song, "Drag City." On November 4 and 7, the Beach Boys recorded the stunning "I Do," which received an official release in 1990 on the two-fer CD of *Surfer Girl/Shut Down, Vol. 2.*[38] "I Do" (with a melody borrowed from 1962's "County Fair") is a beautifully constructed song composed by Brian in the vein of "Your Summer Dream." At Gold Star Studios on November 4, Brian and the band recorded a demo of "I Do" and a second version (for which only a backing track remains) of "Ballad of Ole' Betsy," which appeared one month earlier in its original iteration on "Little Deuce Coupe." Perhaps Brian intended to revise "Betsy" as he did "Be True to Your School," and would do, in 1965, with "Help Me Ronda." Since the backing track is all that exists, we do not know Brian's ultimate intentions for this song. Though it is similar in tempo to the original version, it is closer in feel to "Spirit of America."[39] At RCA Studios on November 7 with members of the Wrecking Crew, Brian recorded a faster and more fully realized version of "I Do."[40] Mike's lead vocal is assured and clear, the Beach Boys provide excellent backing vocals, Brian's falsetto soars over the choruses, and Hal Blaine's drum fills give this song a tight swing that comes to its conclusion far too soon. It is unclear as to why Brian did not include this song in *Shut Down, Vol. 2*, but the backing track from the session on November 7 would be used for a late-period single by the doo-wop group, the Castells.[41] The Castells version was produced by Brian on January 11, 1964, and featured a lead vocal by Chuck Girard.[42] It is still a great song, but much of the electricity is lost in this version. The chimes in the instrumental break of the Beach Boys version are all but obliterated by an overdubbed keyboard figure.

Brian and Mike composed "The Warmth of the Sun," one of the most remarkable songs in the Beach Boys's canon, in the wake of John F. Kennedy's assassination on November 22, 1963. The Beach Boys performed in Marysville, CA on the night of the president's assassination and it was Fred Vail, the band's promoter, who confirms that Brian and Mike composed the song in their hotel room after the show.[43] This extraordinary and majestic song appeared on *Shut Down, Vol. 2*, but did not appear on a single until October 1964 when it was relegated to the B-side of "Dance, Dance, Dance," the lead single from *Beach Boys Today!* On November 29, 1963, Capitol Records released the Beatles's "I Want to Hold Your Hand." This record marked the start of the British Invasion and ushered in one of the most exciting periods in music history. In response to these new challenges, Brian would compose some of the decade's most iconic songs. Before 1963 was finished, Brian would coauthor, lend his voice, and record Jan & Dean's "Dead Man's Curve." He also produced the Honeys's third single, "The One You Can't Have" b/w "Jimmy with Tears" (both sides produced by Brian, who also composed the A-side), which was released in December along with the Beach Boys's first holiday record, "Little Saint Nick."

I Want to Hold . . . . My Baby

The year 1964 was an important year for Brian and the Beach Boys. It was the last year he would continue to tour regularly with the band whose relentless schedule took them across North America, Australasia, and Europe and would end with the emotional breakdown that precipitated his retirement from the road. He produced two classic Beach Boys albums, *Shut Down, Vol. 2* and *All Summer Long*, while he produced, wrote, or performed on a range of singles by artists such as Jan & Dean, Annette Funicello, and others. He would fire his father, Murry, as the group's manager and, in December 1964, would marry 16-year old Marilyn Rovell.

Before the Beach Boys left on a two-week tour in Australia and New Zealand (January 13 to February 1, 1964), Brian was in the studio to produce songs for the Beach Boys's first album of 1964, *Shut Down, Vol. 2.* He also worked with the Castells on "I Do" and with teen television star Paul Peterson (*The Donna Reed Show*) on a new Wilson/Christian track, "She Rides with Me."

"Fun, Fun, Fun" was released in February 1964 and is one of the most irresistible songs from Wilson's early period. Lambert describes it as the ". . . ultimate Brian Wilson song of the early . . . era" and uses the song as a lens to look back at Brian's first two years as a songwriter.[44] This was the lead-off track on *Shut Down, Vol. 2*, an album that also included two of Brian's masterpieces, "Don't Worry Baby" and "The Warmth of the Sun." "Don't Worry Baby" was Brian's musical reply to the Ronettes's "Be My Baby," a song that has been embedded into the core of Brian's very being. What began as a work he hoped to give to Spector for the Ronettes turned out to be one of the Beach Boys's greatest hits. For all its wonderfully thick textures, the instrumental tracks are secondary to Brian's chorale-like vocal arrangement, which is the foundation upon which he constructed the timeless magic of this song. Still, *Shut Down, Vol. 2* is far from perfect, for it still has its share of filler provided by other songwriters or members of the band. The songs on which Brian is the lead author demonstrate a range of expression that was unexpected for a songwriter who was not yet 22 years old. The album featured songs composed by Wilson with Gary Usher, Roger Christian, Mike Love, and one with his old roommate, Bob Norberg (Norman). "In the Parkin' Lot" has unexpected qualities with an intro and outro that are up-tempo bookends to a song with a strong vocal arrangement. Lambert draws structural comparisons to both "Pamela Jean" and "Car, Crazy Cutie," but "In the Parkin' Lot" is a new level of writing for Brian. "This Car of Mine" ends side one and features Dennis's sturdy but less-than-perfect double-tracked vocal. I agree with Lambert, Doe, and Tobler, all of whom maintain that the song is "incomplete and uninspired."[45] "Pom, Pom Play Girl" is a brief 1 minute and 31 seconds that have not aged well, but if Gary Usher's recollections were true, then this early effort composed soon after "In My Room" can be excused. Carl (still a teenager at the time of the recording) delivers a confident performance and Brian's colorful juxtaposition of dissonant harmonies is effective.[46] "Keep an Eye on Summer" is an example of a lovely song that Brian cannot fully realize ("Sherry, She Needs Me" is another in this vein). Still, this sweet doo-wop ballad is understated and beautiful. He returned to this song for his 1998 solo album, *Imagination*, where the song withstood Joe Thomas's production but did not improve upon the sweet innocence of the original.[47]

While Brian worked on *Shut Down, Vol. 2*, he also produced a session for the Honeys on February 17, "He's a Doll" and the unreleased "I Can See Right Through You." The first track has a fantastic east coast girl-group sound and the Wrecking Crew deliver a fierce performance as Hal Blaine and Gene Estes provide an exciting and taut rhythmic bed upon which the wave of guitars and keyboards propel the Honeys into one of their most flirtatious and fun songs. The unison guitar and piano on the four-note sequence at the beginning of the song is absolute magic. The intended B-side, "I Can See Right Through You," is another of Brian's earliest "unrealized" gems. The song was left unfinished in 1964 and was later retitled "Go Away Boy." It was completed in 1983, with no further participation from Brian, for the Honeys's album, *Ecstasy*. Elements of this song hint at the heartfelt longing we would hear in songs such as "Kiss Me, Baby" "She Knows Me Too Well," and "Caroline, No." According to Ginger Blake, Brian wrote this song for Marilyn Rovell, to whom he was not yet married at the time, and it is easy to understand how he could not finish this very personal and intimate record. Unfortunately, this song would be shelved and replaced with a tune penned by the Honeys, "The Love of a Boy and a Girl."

Ride the Wild Surf

Following the Beach Boys's tour of Australia and New Zealand, February through March 1964 was an unusually prolific period for Brian. With Gary Usher and Roger Christian, Brian contributed songs to the movie *Muscle Beach Party*, which featured Annette Funicello, Frankie Avalon, and Donna Loren, while he continued to produce songs for the Honeys and Sharon Marie. Brian continued to collaborate with Gary on songs not only for the Beach Boys but also for Gary's solo single, "Sacramento," and for two of Gary's studio projects, the Super Stocks and the Hondells. Despite the different names, both groups, under Usher's direction, were comprised of members from the Wrecking Crew. For these projects Brian collaborated on "My First Love," "My Buddy Seat," and "Little Honda."

Though few in number, the songs Brian contributed to surf movies are an overlooked segment of his work. The Beach Boys, on March 2, 1962, played for the screening of an actual surf film at Millikan High School in Long Beach, CA, but in 1964, Brian contributed songs for movies in the successful AIP Beach Party franchise.[48] Les Baxter composed the scores for the majority of these films, though they featured a number of songs from pop stars of the era.[49] For *Muscle Beach Party*, the second film in the AIP series, Brian joined Usher and Christian and authored the title track, "Surfer's Holiday," "Runnin' Wild," "My First Love," "Muscle Bustle," and "Surfin' Woodie." Frankie Avalon, Annette Funicello, and Donna Loren released many of these songs in rerecorded versions on their respective solo albums, so these songs exist in both soundtrack and non-film versions. In the movie, Dick Dale provided guitar and vocals for "Muscle Bustle" and other songs. According to Beach Boys's historian and archivist, Brad Elliot, Brian and Usher produced the basic tracks and turned them over to Les Baxter who would then add the appropriate singer(s) for use in the movie.[50] Brian had no input into either the movie or the solo versions of these songs, which may account for the fact that these do not "sound" like Brian Wilson songs. Brian and the Beach Boys were involved in a surf film that was not a part of the AIP franchise, Paramount's *The Girls on the Beach*. The Beach Boys filmed their segments in April 1964 over a year prior to the movie's release and offered two new songs, "The Girls on the Beach" and "Little Honda" (both would appear in refreshed recordings on *All Summer Long*) and "The Lonely Sea" from *Surfin' Safari*. This movie had fewer stars but was a more polished production than the AIP films. Gary Usher provided the film score and former Capitol A&R man, Nik Venet, was the musical supervisor for the film.

The subjects of surfing and surf culture would no longer serve as primary subjects in Brian's songs after 1964. The ocean would continue to serve as an inspiration for songs such as "Surf's Up," "Cool, Cool, Water," and "Til I Die," but the subjects that provided Brian with his first song and others across his first four albums came to an end by mid-1964. With the next Beach

Boys album, *All Summer Long*, Brian entered his most prolific period as a songwriter and producer.

In the spring of 1964, Brian led five sessions for *All Summer Long*. In between sessions, there were filming dates for Paramount's *The Girls on the Beach*, and a new single by Sharon Marie, "Thinkin' Bout You Baby." The first session for the new album on April 2 is notable for two reasons. Brian directed the band on "I Get Around," a song that would become their first number one and would achieve this in the first rush of Beatlemania and the British Invasion. Secondly, Brian's relationship with Murry, while always conflicted, had become an intractable problem for him and the band, and it is believed that on this date, Brian fired his father as the Beach Boys manager. Murry devoted himself to the Beach Boys's career and had willed them to a major record contract.[51] His mantra of "sing from the heart" stuck with Brian, Dennis, and Carl, each of whom would, throughout their careers, project extraordinary emotion and sincerity in their music. His old-fashioned business manners opened many doors for the band in their early years, but his presence as a business manager, artistic advisor, record producer, and self-appointed guardian of image had become too much for Brian and he could no longer ignore Murry's unsolicited opinions in the recording studio, or his overbearing manner as manager/father. Brian was confident that "I Get Around" was going to be the hit he needed to place the Beach Boys above the Beatles who, since their arrival in North America, had sewn up the top five spaces on the charts. It has been reported that Murry, as before, challenged Brian's writing and production efforts while in the studio.[52] His patience depleted, Brian exploded and threw Murry against the wall and fired him from the band.[53] The already fragile father-son relationship was permanently damaged and would haunt Brian well after Murry's death in 1973. "I Get Around" was the hit Brian believed it would be, and its B-side, the extraordinary, "Don't Worry Baby," makes this single a timeless classic. If one could have read Brian's lyrics into the future, they might have heard, in the lyrics to "I Get Around," the disquiet in his head and the impatience that would lead to the next stage of his creative development, "I'm getting bugged driving up and down the same old strip. I've gotta find a new place where the kids are hip."

All Summer Long featured some of Brian's most developed songwriting and only one cover song, the classic Pomus/Shuman tune, "Hushabye."[54] There is one filler track, "Our Favorite Recording Sessions," and a fun 12-bar blues jam number, "Carl's Big Chance," while the remaining nine Wilson originals are a satisfying collection of songs. The album also features some of Mike Love's best vocal work to date, especially on "I Get Around" and "Wendy." The album's title track follows "I Get Around," and from the opening xylophone figure, it is clear we are in for something wonderfully different. In 1973, director George Lucas chose this song for use over the closing credits of his film, *American Graffiti*, which played no small role in the revival of the Beach Boys's popularity in the mid-1970s. "Little Honda" is one of Brian's best attempts at a dirty sound with its measured distortion, hard guitars, and insistent rhythm.[55] The chorus of the song is loaded with sexual innuendo. The call-and-response to Mike's counting up gears "first gear . . . . second gear . . . . third gear . . ." is punctuated with " . . . all right . . . . I'll lean right . . . . hang on tight . . ." and climaxes with Brian and Carl's explosive delivery of, "Faster, it's all right." It was one of three Beach Boys songs featured in the movie, *The Girls on the Beach*, where its sexual tension is allowed full rein in the visual accompaniment for this song. Capitol elected to not release this as a single, so Brian gave it to Gary Usher who recorded it with the Hondells. The 1990s' two-fer of *Little Deuce Coupe/All Summer Long* features an alternate version of the song that loses some of its suggestive punch, in part due to a different arrangement in the backing vocals.

"Little Honda" is followed by another Wilson-Usher ballad, "We'll Run Away."[56] Usher, in an interview with McParland, claimed he and Brian set out to write a sensitive song about a young boy and a young girl. In many ways, this song foreshadows the intimacy he captured in songs recorded for *Pet Sounds*, such as "Let's Go Away for Awhile." In "We'll Run Away," Brian revisits his earlier, 1950s-inspired, ballads such as "Your Summer Dream" and "Keep an Eye on Summer." "Carl's Big Chance," a jam built on a 12-bar blues, allows Carl an opportunity to expand upon some catchy solos in a work that bears more than a coincidental similarity to Marvin Gaye's "Can I Get a Witness."

"Wendy," one of Brian's most original songs on the album, opens side two. This upbeat song about regret and longing prepares us for the stop-time phrasing he would use the following year on "The Little Girl I Once Knew." In "Wendy," he opens with a chorus of Beach Boys vocals behind Mike and Brian's lead. The mono and stereo mixes of this song are easily identifiable, though I prefer the mono mix as it brings the arrangement into tighter focus and provides a more balanced view of Brian's aural canvas. In the stereo mix, background noise and chatter can be heard in the organ break, but the most obvious difference is a lack of blend between the vocal and the instrumental timbres. "Do You Remember?" could be considered a filler track except for Brian's clever arrangement and his liberal use of early rock n' roll tropes where he quotes many of the early stars of rock and roll. The opening figure sounds as if we all will hear a cover of Danny and the Juniors's "At the Hop" (another song featured in the soundtrack to Lucas's *American Graffiti*). Brian name checks Chuck Berry, Little Richard, Elvis, Dion, and earlier Beach Boys songs, which includes one with a reference to Frankie Valli and the Four Seasons. Brian was never shy in performing covers of classic rock and roll tunes and "Do You Remember," written barely a decade after the birth of rock and roll, demonstrates in less than two minutes how, from its earliest origins, rock was a rich and diverse genre. This song was first demoed as a Bob & Sheri song titled "The Big Beat." The irony is that Brian's music would inspire many artists in the decades that followed, and his would be held in as high (or higher) a regard as the artists he mentions in this song.

The third song on side two is one of Brian's most evocative songs of the period, "The Girls on the Beach." Its similarity to "Surfer Girl" has been addressed by other authors, but I find the opening phrase is closer in spirit to the work that is mentioned in regard to "Surfer Girl," the song, "When You Wish Upon a Star," from Walt Disney's *Pinocchio*. While Brian may have first heard this tune in the Disney film, the melody of this song served as the theme music for ABC's weekly television show, *Walt Disney's Disneyland*, first broadcast in 1954 and which served as Sunday night family fare in millions of homes across the country.[57] The vocal arrangement for "The Girls on the Beach" is far more elaborate than the simple figure heard in the opening bars of "Surfer Girl," and its rich arrangement has, for me, always connected this song to the Disney tune. "The Girls on the Beach" is extraordinarily evocative of place as the vocal arrangement and harmonies capture the unique sensations of the Southern California coast.

"Drive-In" is a paean to the nearly extinct social outing of the drive-in movie. The lyrics recount experiences that would be familiar to anyone who ever had a date at the drive-in. In the last verse, Mike does his mug-faced imitation of the Smokey Bear Public Service Announcement that was shown regularly in movie theatres, on television, and in print advertisements in the 1960s–1970s. Mike's delivery of this quote is the topper in a collection of teenage rituals that required one to pause the backseat fumbling of car sex in order to see enough of the movie to recount it when asked by your parents. This well-arranged and well-executed track is otherwise forgettable. The 1998 release of *Ultimate Christmas* gave Beach Boys fans a chance to hear an alternate version of "Little Saint Nick," set to the backing track of "Drive-In." Hickey proposed that Brian created two backing tracks for "Little Saint Nick" and ended up wisely choosing the version we all know, but the truth is a little more complex.[58] In the author's interview with Brad Elliot, it was explained that on the same day Brian cut "Little Saint Nick" (October 18), he cut two additional tracks, without titles, which he identified as "Track No. 1" and "Track No. 2."[59] Later, the first track was given the title of "My Bobby Left Me" and the second was titled "Drive-In." It is likely that Brian intended these for either Sharon Marie or the Honeys, but they were never executed with those artists.[60] When the band returned on October 20 to record the vocals for "Little Saint Nick," he also had them put a vocal track over what was "Track No. 2" with the lyrics from "Little Saint Nick." In spring of 1964, Brian came back to "Track No. 2" with the lyrics for "Drive-In" and completed the track with the Beach Boys. This is followed by the only filler on the album, "Our Favorite Recording Sessions." Given the amount of product Capitol demanded of Brian, he can be forgiven for this track, composed from excerpts of studio chatter and mock disagreements.

The closing track on the album, "Don't Back Down" is one of Brian's less well-known but more intriguing songs, and one of his last surf-themed works. The machismo required by surfers to take the big wave, as outlined in the song, can be read on another level. Given that fans, in mid-1964, could not have known Brian was at a breaking point, an alternate reading of the song can be appreciated now that we have seen Brian endure his many challenges in the years since this song was written, and in this light, the song offers an entirely different narrative. The 1990 two-fer of *All Summer Long* contained a second version of "Don't Back Down" with different lyrics and vocals. Brian had begun to wear under Capitol's pressure to create more hits in a formula that had proved so successful, while he wanted to expand his horizons beyond teen music and beyond the Beach Boys. If you compare the two versions, both are interesting and prophetic and reflect what must have been going through his mind as everyone wanted a piece of him just as he was about to come to a full stop at the end of 1964.

Nestled in-between sessions for *All Summer Long*, Brian produced a solo single for Gary Usher, "Sacramento" b/w "Just the Way I Feel." The A-side is a Wilson-Usher tune and while enjoyable, it is forgettable. Also released on June 1 was Sharon Marie's second Capitol single, "Thinkin' Bout You Baby" b/w "The Story of My Life." The A-side is wonderfully rich and romantic, but in the heat of Beatlemania, it was lost in the charts. "Thinkin' Bout You Baby" was transformed when its verses received a new chorus and retitled as "Darlin," which appeared on the Beach Boys's second album of 1967, *Wild Honey*. Brian felt the original song stood on its own strengths and returned to it in 1972 when he produced it for American Spring on their self-titled album. In that version, Brian gives the song a wonderful early-1970s AM radio-friendly twist, but like the Sharon Marie original, it faded into silence. The B-side of the Sharon Marie single is one of Brian and Mike's least memorable songs, "The Story of My Life."

In June 1964, Brian and the band finished an unusual project when they worked with Annette Funicello for the opening sequence of her last Disney film, *The Monkey's Uncle*. The band appears in the opening sequence where they perform the title song, "backing" Annette on a solid, Sherman Brothers song. More importantly, Brian was at work on the next two Beach Boys's albums, the Beach Boys's first holiday-themed album and the band's next studio creation, *Beach Boys Today!* With the success of "Little Saint Nick" in late 1963 and inspired by "A Christmas Gift for You from Phil Spector," it made sense for Brian to put his mark on an entire album of holiday music. Where Spector took traditional holiday tunes and arranged them with his signature Wall of Sound and used his stable of singers (the Crystals, Darlene Love, the Ronettes, and so forth) to deliver them in updated arrangements, Brian set out to create an album that would appeal to kids as well as adults.[61] Five of the tunes on side one were written by Brian, with Mike as coauthor on three, and the seven that remained were traditional holiday songs arranged for full orchestra by the incomparable Dick Reynolds whose earlier work as an arranger for the Four Freshmen made him the perfect collaborator for Brian. Reynolds would be called upon over a decade later to work with Brian on the aborted *Adult Child* album in 1977, but his work on the *Beach Boys Christmas Album* helped to make this record a timeless holiday classic. The previous year's hit song, "Little Saint Nick," was included in a different mix. The second and third tracks, "The Man with All the Toys" and "Santa's Beard," are the strongest works with stellar vocal arrangements that show two sides of Brian's creative world, one happy and upbeat and the other introspective and melancholy.

From July to the end of October 1964, the Beach Boys were on the road with performances in Hawaii, the Midwest, and the East Coast, and Brian was not back in the studio until August 5. While on tour, the *All Summer Long* album was released and peaked at number four on the charts. The band found time to appear on the Ed Sullivan Show and the T.A.M.I. show. With his few days off, Brian would work on *Beach Boys Today!*[62] Before the tour was over, Capitol released the band's first number one album, *Beach Boys in Concert.* Recorded at shows in Sacramento in 1963–1964, this album provides a window into the mayhem the band could inspire at their concerts.

Work with other artists received less of his time in the last half of 1964. It is believed the only session he produced outside of the band was a backing track for "Guess I'm Dumb."[63] This song, like others that would come from Brian over the next two years, is one of the most honest readings of Brian's insecurities, and it foreshadows his actions around *SMiLE*, just two-and-a-half years later. This song and others, such as "Go Away Boy" and "Don't Back Down," are the front guard of Brian's confessionals from *Pet Sounds's* "I Just Wasn't Made for These Times" and "That's Not Me."

Brian and the Beach Boys embarked on their first European tour in November 1964. In his 1991 autobiography, Brian recalled this tour as one of intense challenges. He was exhausted and it had been weeks since he had been in the studio on a regular basis. He missed Marilyn and was not at ease on this tour, their first in countries where English was not the first language. The 23-day trip was primarily for television promotional appearances, and since the band no longer traveled with Murry, their off-hours behaviors were what you might expect for a group of 20-somethings, and Brian, who was most at ease when at home or in the studio, was pushed to the breaking point on this trip. He had an unexpected opportunity to speak with Beatles manager Brian Epstein while their flight was delayed in Ireland at Limerick's Shannon Airport, while the band's exploits in Germany, France, Sweden, and Denmark were documented by journalist Earl Leaf. Rather than coming back to Los Angeles for some rest after this tour, the band flew to the east coast for concerts on November 25–29, 1964. They performed at Detroit's Olympia Theater on the Saturday after Thanksgiving and were relieved of about a half-dozen of their suitcases that contained many of the gifts they brought from Europe for family and friends. In a short break from November 30 to December 18 they taped their performance for the ABC television pop music show, *Shindig*, and recorded the extraordinary "Kiss Me, Baby" a song Brian composed while in Copenhagen. The footage from *Shindig* is fascinating as it shows the band in its last incarnation as the five boys from Hawthorne, CA.[64] They opened this holiday edition of the show with a performance of "Dance, Dance, Dance" on a festive party set filled with cast members, guest artists, and dancers. The Righteous Brothers Bill Medley and Bobby Hatfield dance with various girls, and amidst the festive decorations and balloons we see a band at the top of their game. At no point in any of the half-dozen songs the Beach Boys perform throughout the show could anyone know that everything was about to fall apart for Brian.

A one-off performance on December 19 in Tulsa was followed four days later with a 10-day tour that was to begin in Houston. On the flight from Los Angeles to Houston, Brian had his first major breakdown. Brian managed to play the show in Houston on December 23 but flew home the next day. A Christmas Day show in Jackson, MS was cancelled, and on December 26 Glen Campbell, an emerging solo artist, and member of the Wrecking Crew, stepped in for Brian. Campbell knew the band and had played on many Beach Boys sessions and was a perfect choice at the 11th hour. He continued to fill this role for Brian until the spring of 1965 since he simultaneously juggled his responsibilities as a studio musician and solo artist. When Glen joined the Beach Boys, he had already released three solo albums on Capitol, but would not have his breakout hit until 1967's *Gentle on My Mind*.

On January 7, 1965, Brian returned to the studio to complete tracks for *Beach Boys Today!* The drama that surrounded his breakdown en route to Houston would pale when compared to the crisis of mid-1967.

Serious Art at the Top (1965–1966)

2

Off the Road Again . . . and Again

Brian and the Beach Boys entered a new phase of their career when Brian retired from the road. Though he appeared with them in television appearances and at selected concerts, he would remain at home to compose and produce records for Capitol Records's second most profitable act. Brian and 16-year-old Marilyn Rovell were married at the end of 1964 and their home became a destination for the creative social set of young Los Angelinos. New friends, influences, and substances, when combined with Brian's suburban upbringing and emotional insecurities, would pose significant challenges for Brian, Marilyn, and the Beach Boys. Wilson's work with artists other than the Beach Boys began to decline in frequency as he produced three of the greatest albums of his career. Because the corporate marketplace was not ready for popular music as art, Capitol Records managed to undermine Brian's most personal and stunning album, *Pet Sounds*. In response to unsupportive and negative forces, and a label that did not know how to work with a new generation of artists, Brian went adrift during sessions for *SMiLE* that, had it been completed, would have resulted in one of the greatest albums of the 1960s.

"The Beach Boys have always been a sound and a feeling . . . ."[1] After his breakdown on December 23, 1964, en route to a concert in Houston, Brian retired from the road. Since late-1962, the band had been on an endless run of concerts, recording sessions, and promotional appearances driven by the sound of the Beach Boys's hit records that existed because Brian Wilson willed them into existence. The punishing schedule surely was difficult for all members of the band, but the stakes were significantly higher for Brian because he was expected to compose and produce hit upon hit. While the band learned to play his songs, Brian continued to create increasingly complex arrangements and produce all their records while also performing with them on tour. Brian began to miss shows in early 1963, which apparently had no effect upon the band's popularity, but by late 1964 it was clear the band had to find a more permanent solution. Glen Campbell was drafted to fill Brian's on-stage role and while he might have been a good stage replacement for Brian (he played on a number of Beach Boys sessions), he gave top priority to his own career and his tenure as a Beach Boy extended only through the winter of 1965. Between April 9 and May 19, Bruce Johnston began to take over Brian's stage duties by alternating, and at times sharing, dates with Campbell. He would become the de facto sixth Beach Boy, excluding the years 1972–1979.[2] Johnson was one-half of the Rip Chords, aka Bruce and Terry, and had been a fixture on the Southern California music scene since the late 1950s. He had played with Phil Spector and Kim Fowley, and proved to be an ideal yet mildly anonymous replacement for Brian, while also being a competent and integral member of the band.[3] Bruce sang on the session for "California Girls" on April 6 and made his official stage appearance with the band on April 9 in New Orleans, LA.

While Glen and Bruce were Beach Boys on the road, Brian was focused on the next Beach Boys album, *The Beach Boys Today!* Between the release of the *All Summer Long* in July 1964, and the March 1965 release of *The Beach Boys Today!*, Capitol, in October 1964, released the wildly popular *Beach Boys Concert* (their first number one album and last until the 1974 compilation, *Endless Summer*), and one month later released *The Beach Boys Christmas Album*, which successfully saturated the market with unit-shifting Beach Boys product, while Capitol's other star act, the Beatles, continued to dominate the Billboard charts. The eight months between *All Summer Long* and *Beach Boys Today!* was the longest stretch of time Brian had been allowed to compose new material, and it is from this period that we have some of his finest work as both a composer and a producer.

While Brian remained home in Los Angeles, he was introduced to a new and hip social circle whose presence and influence would sow divisions among the Beach Boys. Some of these people would become friends or future collaborators, while others were opportunists who only sought entrée into Brian's creative and personal scene. In *Wouldn't It Be Nice: My Own Story*, Brian mentions many of these new friends and hangers-on and the accompanying stresses they created among members of the band and Marilyn, but in *Catch a Wave*, Carlin provides a different picture of the people who entered Brian's creative and social scene in 1965. Some came from well-to-do families or were of independent means, others were college educated, literate, intellectually and artistically diverse, and more importantly were familiar with marijuana and other substances. Brian was easily impressed by this collection of people who clearly were not from the conservative, middle-class families he remembered in Hawthorne. The grandson of a migrant oil field worker from Hutchinson, Kansas, who was raised in the newly prescribed middle-class of mid-twentieth-century America, welcomed many of these people into his creative orbit if only because they came from a world so different from his own. Sixteen-year-old Marilyn Wilson was supportive of Brian's unique needs and his creative processes, and managed the immediate impact it brought into their home life and their marriage, but it was clear to her, and other members of the band, that Brian had begun to change in ways they were not comfortable. As an artist, he was hungry for new ideas and was willing to accept any and all options.

Popular music was in the midst of a transformational revolution by 1965, and Brian was at the center of this world along with Bob Dylan, the Beatles, and the Rolling Stones. Los Angeles was home to a cultural landscape where popular music flourished on West Hollywood's Sunset Strip, Hollywood Boulevard, and Santa Monica Boulevard. Once Brian was off the road, other influences began to inform his work with greater frequency. The British Invasion had, since February 1964, wrought an overwhelming influence upon American popular music, though the works of selected American artists remained equally popular in England as in the states. Artists on the Motown, Stax, Atlantic, and Chess labels were cultural staples among British groups who were influenced by, and borrowed from, the African-American blues and soul repertoire. Phil Spector and his signature Wall of Sound was an enormous influence, and both the Beach Boys and Frankie Valli and the Four Seasons were the established American vocal groups whose popularity endured amidst these changes. Newer bands such as the Byrds began to emerge from the burgeoning folk rock movement, though they too were influenced by the British Invasion. The hybridization of American and English styles created a new sound for the first wave of young American artists who would rule the airwaves into the late 1960s and beyond. In Brian's world, the Beatles and Spector's records were his greatest challenge and fueled his obsession to create unforgettable records.

The music Brian recorded in late 1964 and early 1965 was his most complex and richly produced work to date. While the Beatles charted three distinct forks in the road that enabled them to move from *Rubber Soul* to *Revolver* and to *Sgt. Pepper's Lonely Hearts Club Band*, Brian slowly developed a series of themes and emotional timbres that began in 1964 with *All Summer Long*, and concluded with the legacy he left unfinished, unreleased, and stranded, on *SMiLE*. When the Beatles retired from the road in 1966, the recording studio became their primary creative vehicle and their instruments were simply the tools they used to generate new and unfamiliar sounds. For Brian, it was a far more complex situation. Had he been allowed, like the Beatles, to rely solely upon the studio as his medium, he might have had an opportunity to develop as a contemporary artist and may not have faced many of the challenges and crises that serve as the centerpiece of his complex narrative. Brian and the Beach Boys had come to an agreement in early 1965 that would allow Brian to stay home and write music while the Beach Boys would continue to perform in concert. At that time, a year-and-a-half before the Beatles quit touring, it was impossible to imagine that a popular musician would not be a touring concert artist. The Beach Boys's need to have Brian Wilson's music to perform in concert was the tether that married Brian's creative vision to the Beach Boys's commercial enterprise. Though Brian's records remained popular with fans in 1965, the Beach Boys's public image was falling further out of sync with emerging styles, trends, and beliefs of the youth movement. Before long, they would fall further out of sync with the increasingly cerebral and imaginative compositional landscapes of Brian Wilson.

The Beach Boys's first studio album of 1965, *The Beach Boys Today!* was the first record from the "Brian-at-home" years. Brian displayed a maturity and technical expertise that demonstrated his music was at the vanguard of a new art form. Over the decades this album has ended up on various "Top Albums" lists and is regarded by many as a stylistic predecessor to *Pet Sounds*.[4] It appears Brian thought about this work as an "album," and not just a collection of singles and various sides. Their previous studio album, *The Beach Boys' Christmas Album* featured one side of new, Beach Boys holiday songs (with all but one penned by Brian), and a second side of traditional holiday songs backed by Dick Reynolds's orchestrations. Reynolds, an arranger for the Four Freshmen, was one of Brian's first collaborative mash-ups where he comfortably mixed older styles with a contemporary voice. On that album, Brian gave a rock side (side one) for the kids and a second side of traditional tunes with orchestra for the adults (side two).

Brian had released seven studio albums by the winter of 1965, but with *Today!* he set the Beach Boys on a new creative trajectory. He admired and, at times, imitated the sonic landscapes of Spector's Wall of Sound, but on *Today!* he achieved a balance where every instrument and vocal line was clearly defined within the mix. The background vocals on this album were his most elaborate to date and Mike Love contributed some of his most effective lead and backing vocals. The beautiful block harmonies on earlier classics such as "Don't Worry Baby" and "The Girls on the Beach," gave way to complex, contrapuntal arrangements that illuminated highly personal narratives. Though the Beach Boys performed their instruments on a majority of this album, Brian added a number of musicians from the Wrecking Crew to expand his timbral palette. Brian also called upon percussionist Julius Wechter who, with Hal Blaine, created what Beach Boys biographer David Leaf describes as Brian's "quirky percussion frame" that supported many of the album's tracks.[5]

"Don't Hurt My Little Sister" was recorded in June 1964 and was intended for one of Phil Spector's artists. Spector was disinclined to release a newly composed A-side where he was not credited as a coauthor, so he changed the lyrics and released the song as a public service announcement (PSA). Many sources claim this was written for the Ronettes but it was, in all likelihood, for Darlene Love, who fronted the Blossoms on "Things Are Changing (for the Better)," a PSA that addressed racial and gender-based inequalities in the workplace. Thankfully, Brian did not allow this song to disappear. His original lyrics provided listeners with a view into his then-current predicament in regard to his feelings for the three Rovell sisters. Brian would marry Marilyn Rovell on December 7, 1964, but during the extended period he lived at the Rovell home, he struggled with conflicted affections for all three sisters, Barbara, Marilyn, and Diane. In spite of its complicated gestation, this is one of the more exuberant songs on the album. The opening would have fit nicely on *All Summer Long*, but in the song's bridge it becomes clear that Brian was on a different trajectory with this album. The chorus, in response to Mike's pleas to get his girl, chastises him for the way he treats the "little sister." The key shifts on the chorus are not unfamiliar in Brian's work, but their angular and abrupt turns provide the song's arresting hooks.

In August 1964, Brian produced the next Beach Boys single, the ironically prophetic "When I Grow Up (To Be a Man)," and the heartbreakingly romantic, "She Knows Me Too Well." "When I Grow Up" opens with a decisive, five-part vocal introduction that shifts abruptly as the background vocals introduce new twists in both content and arrangement. Most notable is the count-up in age ("15, 16, 17") to the inevitable threshold of adulthood. Brian's falsetto soars throughout the song and provides an excellent bridge that connects lead and backing vocals. Brian arranged the song to sit high in the band's vocal register and it sounds somewhat strained, not unlike a male prepubescent voice that has not yet dropped but cannot easily find where it is supposed to sit. The use of the Harpsichord as a lead keyboard instrument is unexpected, but Brian may have picked up the idea through his work with Jan & Dean who used the instrument on an equally abrupt and rhythmically jerky track, "The Anaheim, Azusa and Cucamonga Sewing Circle, Book Review and Timing Association."[6] The single's B-side, "She Knows Me Too Well," is a stylistic change for Wilson and brings the listener into his romantic insecurities. Brian pleads for his girl's forgiveness and patience and delivers one of his most naked and emotional lead vocals. Again, the vocal arrangement provides an irresistible hook thanks to Brian's stylized doo-wop phrasing. The tune is wonderfully unmelodic and the instrumental track is spotless, as finger cymbals and electric guitar chords gently punctuate this heartfelt confessional. A number of songs on *Today!* afford us an intimate view into Brian's deeply ingrained insecurities, and the difficulties he faced in forming and maintaining relationships. Many of the songs on *Today!* can be read through a lens of the difficulties he faced in expressing his emotions to Marilyn. Earlier songs such as "Your Summer Dream," "We'll Run Away," and "I Do," are spoken from the heart of a young man for whom love is desirable and is easily acquired. The more personal songs Brian recorded less than a year later such as "She Knows Me Too Well," "Please Let Me Wonder," "Kiss Me,

Baby," and "In the Back of My Mind," unfold his maturing narrative just prior to, and following, his wedding to Marilyn.

"Good to My Baby" serves as a thematic preface to "Don't Hurt My Little Sister" as the singer is reminded in both songs that he needs to be better to his girl. Where Brian's earlier songs expressed more romantic, innocent, and idealized expressions of love, these songs imply that our protagonist has been selfish and cruel, and will need to change if he hopes to keep his girlfriend. The song's arrangement borrows gestures (the tambourine and background vocals) found in the girl-group song genre, but again, Brian demonstrates he can embody another artists' style into his own work, much as he did on "The Revo-lution."[7] Unlike his earlier song, these borrowings are not used as the framework for the song, but are wedded to a structure that is wholly his own. The guitar line winds its way around the first half of the verse and provides a wonderful preparation for Mike's entrance in the second half of the verse.

"Help Me Ronda," is one of Brian's best known songs, but this is not the more widely known version. Brian experimented with a range of ideas in multiple versions of this song, and in this iteration recorded in January 1965, it comes off as too many ideas with too little direction. This song was Al Jardine's second lead vocal on a Beach Boys record, and in the original "Ronda," the song carries a certain folklike workmanship. This is another example where Brian's original monophonic mix is superior its stereo sibling. In mono, Brian's "kitchen sink" arrangement holds nicely behind Al's vocal, though the most memorable feature is the outro where the background vocals of "Help me Ronda, help, help me Ronda" are phased in a near/far pattern that anticipates a false ending. The song's evolution to the superior "single" version, first recorded on February 24, is of note for a couple of reasons. In his autobiography, Brian claimed that Gary Usher expressed an interest in cutting the song, but McParland has disproved this.[8] The song was sought by another artist, but it was Terry Melcher who with future Beach Boy Bruce Johnston recorded as both the Rip Chords and Bruce and Terry, and cut a very effective arrangement of the song on February 26. The Beach Boys session on February 24 is of note because it was at this session that Brian and Murry had their explosive argument, which was captured on tape and has circulated on various bootlegs.[9] Melcher uses a rollicking piano ostinato as a rhythmic device, similar to the figure used in the Beach Boys's single, but the comparisons end there. The Bruce and Terry version was held back, ostensibly out of Melcher's respect for Brian, but it deserves a listen because it is, in many ways, superior to the version on *Beach Boys Today!*

"Dance, Dance, Dance" closes side one, is an exuberant conclusion to the "fast" side of the album, and was chosen for a single released in October 1964. A version recorded by the band one month earlier, while on tour in Nashville, shows the song as a work-in-progress. It is slower, is sonically muddy, and has different lyrics, where the October session produced one of Brian's most upbeat songs. Glen Campbell's guitar playing is central to the work as his insistent melodic line drives the song and provides a launching pad for the background vocals.[10] The Beach Boys (with Brian) performed this on December 14 at a taping for the groundbreaking music television program, *Shindig*! that was broadcast a few weeks later as their Christmas episode.[11] The Righteous Brothers, Marvin Gaye, and Donna Loren were among the stars on this episode, which is memorable for a couple of reasons. As the holiday-themed episode, the set was decorated for a holiday party and the Beach Boys opened the show with "Dance, Dance, Dance" while the other guest artists and *Shindig* dancers partied and danced around the set. Brian delivered a confident lead vocal and appears to be at the top of his game. This is the last time we see the original five-piece band with Brian as its uncontestable leader. A few weeks later he would suffer a breakdown en route to Houston. Other successes were to come, but they would occur with a different configuration of the Beach Boys.

The remaining Wilson compositions on side two, the album's slow side, "Please Let Me Wonder," "Kiss Me, Baby," and "In the Back of My Mind" are written in the same personal and emotionally daring tenor as "She Knows Me Too Well." "Kiss Me, Baby" was recorded on December 16, 1964, nine days after Brian and Marilyn's wedding. Brian claims to have written this song in Copenhagen when the lengthy separation from Marilyn inspired one of his most moving songs.[12] The melody, built on a descending four note pattern, is framed by guitars, piano, and percussion, which never intrude on this intimate confessional. Brian's vocal glides effortlessly above the instrumental track, Mike Love delivers one of his most tasteful vocals, and the background vocals are outstanding, yet subtle. The lyrics offer wonderful turns of phrase such as "I tossed and I turned, my head was so heavy." Even predictable teen fare such as "As I drove away I felt a tear" are shattering when punctuated with Hal Blaine's end-of-phrase snare flourishes, while the chorus patter of "kiss a little bit and fight a little bit and kiss a little bit . . ." is utterly magical. This is one of the few instances where the stereo mix is stronger than Brian's original mono mix. Brian's rich arrangement can be more fully experienced in stereo, where the horns and Leon Russell's keyboard have greater presence, but it is the descending four note pattern in the guitar that sounds as if it is drawn from the interior of Brian's sonic landscape. This mix also provides the song with a spacious canvas for the background vocals that were not as clearly articulated in mono.

"Please Let Me Wonder," originally titled "Don't Let Me Wonder," was recorded on January 7, 1965, in a 10-day stretch in which the Beach Boys were off the road and in the studio to record the remainder of the *Today!* album.[13] Brian claims his experiences with marijuana influenced his work on *Today!* that is not hard to believe given the sleepy and dreamy air that permeates this song.[14] Glen Campbell provides a simple and emotional guitar line that punctuates vocal phrases at their most critical junctures. Both Brian and

Marilyn have spoken in various interviews of how Brian was not a great husband because he was so obsessed with work and it appears this song neatly summarizes their challenges. He wants to be the husband Marilyn needs, but is incapable of being that person.[15]

The last proper song on the album, "In the Back of My Mind," is another dreamy-from-the-pot-haze gem. Lambert finds this song among the most daring of Brian's works as he ventures into new harmonic and orchestral territory.[16] While many of the songs on side two are focused on Brian's interpersonal relationships, this song is an introspective moment rather than a confessional. Dennis delivers a husky, wavering vocal that fits perfectly into Brian's orchestral canvas, which is a prelude to his work on *Pet Sounds.* There are no other Beach Boys on this song, so Dennis's solo outing makes a fitting conclusion for the album.

Stragglers

Though Brian would devote the majority of his time to the creation of new material for the Beach Boys, he did work on a handful of songs for other artists just prior to, and following, the release of *Beach Boys Today!* Throughout 1965, Wilson began to curtail his extracurricular work with Jan & Dean, the Hondells, and the Super Stocks, whose records continued to hit the market through 1964–1965, but songs that were not intended for the Beach Boys serve as a bridge to Brian's next studio album, *Summer Days (and Summer Nights!!).*

"All Dressed Up for School" was recorded September 16, 1964, under the title "What I'll Wear to School Today," as a potential single for Sharon Marie.[17] This song ultimately provided source material for two Beach Boys songs in 1969 and 1972 while Roger Christian provided two stories about the origins of this song for which neither can be verified.[18] We know the Beach Boys did record "All Dressed Up for School," but it remained unreleased until the 1990 two-fer of *Little Deuce Coupe/All Summer Long.* It is not difficult to imagine why the single was withheld given the rather questionable tone of the lyrics, especially with the repeated phrase of "ooh what a turn-on. . .she's so fine." Aside from this, the track was filled with strong hooks that would be recycled in later songs. Though "All Dressed Up for School" was held back, it demonstrated new and complex techniques that Brian would begin to incorporate into his work. He returned to the verse of this song for "I Just Got My Pay" recorded in the first months of 1970 and intended for the Beach Boys first, but rejected, record at Warners.[19] Two years later the band returned to this same material for "Marcella," one of Brian's few contributions to the Beach Boys's underrated 1972 album, *Carl and the Passions—"So Tough."* In this last version, Tandyn Almer and Jack Rieley, the Beach Boys's manager, shared authorship credits. By March 1972, the Beach Boys had officially added Blondie Chaplin and Ricky Fataar of the South African (and Brother Records) group Flame, and their inclusion on *Carl and the Passions—"So Tough"* brought a harder edge to the band's sound and helped to make "Marcella" a strong track.

A song Brian recorded with the working title "If I'm Dumb" became the Glen Campbell single "Guess I'm Dumb." It likely was intended for *Beach Boys Today!* but Brian gave the song to Campbell who had covered for him on tour in the winter of 1965, and who was still in search of his breakthrough solo record. "Guess I'm Dumb" was not that record, but it is a strong work and Glen's unique and effortless vocal style fit perfectly onto Brian's technically demanding melody. This song also marks one of Brian's first collaborations with Russ Titelman, who, as a Grammy winning producer, would work on hit albums by Randy Newman and James Taylor.[20]

"Sherry She Needs Me," another collaboration with Titelman, is the last of this group. First attempted in March 1965, early in the sessions for *Summer Days (and Summer Nights!!)*, as "Sherri She Needs Me," the song was put aside and would remain unreleased until 1998.[21] The instrumental track was recorded March 29, 1965, but Brian did not add vocals to the song until 1976, by which time his graceful tenor had been replaced by a hoarse and drawled vocal that somehow did not work for a song conceived at the height of his creative powers. This version was released on the 2013 compilation *Made in California*, but the first official release of the song was on Wilson's 1998 solo album, *Imagination*, where it received new lyrics by Carole Bayer Sager and a new title, "She Says That She Needs Me." The song is similar, and slightly expanded, and is one of the album's most effective and moving songs.

A little known Wilson-Usher song (their last collaboration until the mid-1980s), "My Buddy Seat," was recorded in September 1964 and released by the Hondells in November of that year. After the success of "Little Honda," Brian and Gary hoped to re-capture the electricity and kinetic excitement of "Little Honda." This song inherited the sexual tension of its predecessor, but the arrangement is dense and more complex than "Little Honda," and ultimately is not as strong a work.

". . . AND THEN THERE WERE SIX"

Released on July 5, 1965, Brian's ninth studio album, *Summer Days (and Summer Nights!!)* arrived one month prior to the Beatles's *Help!* and five months before *Rubber Soul*, the album Brian claims was his inspiration to compose *Pet Sounds*. It was the first album to feature new member Bruce Johnston (he would remain uncredited as he was under contract to Columbia), the sixth Beach Boy and Brian's on-tour replacement. *Summer Days* is frequently overlooked as it falls between the stunning excitement of *Beach Boys Today!* and majesty of *Pet Sounds*. In spite of the excellent songs contained on the record it has, over the years, been unfairly described as a sideways move for Brian instead of "the next great thing."[22] Briefly uneven at moments, it was a remarkable collection that demonstrated Brian's maturing aesthetic. The album has much to offer as it features two of the Beach Boys's classic hits, "Help Me, Rhonda" and "California Girls," and three underrated masterpieces, "Girl Don't Tell Me," "Let Him Run Wild," and the instrumental "Summer Means New Love." The latter work is in the vein of *Pet Sounds*, but the album's final track, "And Your Dream Comes True," is Brian's tender farewell to his Four Freshmen influences, and is a precursor to *SMiLE's* "Our Prayer." There is an effective Spector cover "Then I Kissed Her" and five additional Wilson originals of which one, "I'm Bugged at My Old Man," is a comedy track.

The album opens with an unexpected barnstormer, "The Girl from New York City," a slice of Beach Boys garage rock and an answer to a Lieber-Stoller produced hit from December 1964, "The Boy from New York City." Like "Dance, Dance, Dance," from *Beach Boys Today!*, this raucous opener leads us to believe we about to enter something special. Instead we are led to "Amusement Parks, U.S.A.," which takes us back to "County Fair," and references Freddy Cannon's "Palisades Park." The distinctive howl from the as-yet-unreleased "Punchline" is used to good effect and Hal Blaine's spoken contribution as the carnival barker is the real treat of this song. After a sterling cover of Spector's "Then I Kissed Her," the band delivers an unexpected work that praises the landlocked capital of Utah, "Salt Lake City."

In "Girl Don't Tell Me" we have the album's first masterpiece. Previous commentators refer to Brian's use of "wri-i-ite," "gu-u-uy," and "ti-i-ime," in the song's chorus, which is nearly identical to the Beatles's use of a stammering figure (which they likely borrowed from Motown) in *Ticket To Ride*.[23] The Beach Boys performed the majority of the instrumental track on this record, a practice that was becoming less common since Brian had begun to use studio musicians on a more regular basis. The guitars are prominent but not overwhelming, and the celeste provides a wonderful, rhythmic figure, a gesture of the kind we would hear two years later on the Velvet Underground's "Sunday Morning."[24] This is followed by the single version of "Help Me Rhonda," a song that has appeared on endless iterations of the Beach Boys greatest hits albums. The harmless campfire sing-along version that appeared on *Beach Boys Today!* had been transformed into one of Brian's tightest and most exciting productions. The brilliance of the song's arrangement did not happen overnight as another version released on the 1999 compilation, *Endless Harmony*, showed Brian at work with different background vocals that would have taken the song in a very different direction. The tempo is slightly slower than what Brian ultimately settled upon in the final version, and though Mike's "Bow-bow-bow-bow" is intact, Al's lead vocal is not mixed as prominently to the front. The final version is one of Brian's greatest achievements, and the arrangement is solid from the introduction to the final fade. Al's vocal, one of his finest, moves effortlessly between rhythmic figures while Leon Russell's piano and Glen Campbell's guitar provide the song's potent flourishes.

Side two begins with the majestic "California Girls." If *Beach Boys Today!* was Brian's first album on marijuana, "California Girls" was his first LSD song as realized in the spacious, sparkling, and crystalline introduction that descends from the ether as random textures enter from above and land onto Brian's "country and western shuffle."[25] Paul Williams, in his 1974 review of the Warners reissue of *Wild Honey* & *20/20*, believes the first 25 seconds of this song are rivalled only by the introduction of the Rolling Stones's "Gimme Shelter." Mike's vocal, even with somewhat sloppy double tracking, secures the song's hook. The background vocals are richly layered as Brian's falsetto soars over the chorus and we hear, for the first time on a Beach Boys record, a new color added to the band's vocal palette by Bruce Johnston. This song encapsulates Brian's compositional growth over the previous four years where he created rich panoramic and aural landscapes that he combined with the themes and production techniques he had developed since his first single, "Surfin'." "California Girls" was an instant classic for the band and has remained on set lists for both Brian Wilson and Beach Boys shows.

"Let Him Run Wild" is another underrated gem with a rich accompaniment that prepares us for *Pet Sounds.* In his autobiography, Brian considered this song as a tribute to Burt Bacharach, an often-overlooked influence upon Brian's work. The song posed issues for Brian because he did not like his vocal and denigrated his performance as sounding too girlish.[26] It was selected for the 1993 boxed set but he pulled it, citing dissatisfaction with his performance. In another interview, he would describe the song as a "sore spot" and was "real, real, real self-conscious," and critiqued his performance as "really, really lame." He claimed it was one of his least favorite performances and said his voice "sounds like a little girl . . . like a chick . . . a sick chick!"[27] The instrumental track shows how Brian can take a simple idea (a ham-fisted, quarter-note ostinato), add a Bacharach-like swing chorus, and make it all work as if no other option could have been as effective.[28] His arrangement captures a feel like no other of his works, and the tack piano and vibraphone playing in unison creates a color unlike any other in his work. This song along with "Girl Don't Tell Me" and "The Little Girl I Once Knew" (a single released in November 1965) point towards the future of Brian's work and each possesses a tone of intimate optimism. I love all three songs for their inability to fit anywhere else in Wilson's canon, and while they may be overshadowed on the album by "Help Me Rhonda" and "California Girls," they remain, half-century later, extraordinary and unique songs.

"You're So Good to Me" falls into the middle of side two and is one of the trickier songs on the album. Once again Brian uses a somewhat brutish garage-band arrangement with a dense mix of drums, organ, guitar, and repetitive backing vocals. The backing vocal stammer of *la, la, la, la* in phrases of eight predates the Beatles's use of *dit, dit, dit, dit* in "Girl" from *Rubber*

Soul; another indication of a subconscious symbiosis that existed between the two bands. Another "in advance of Pet Sounds" track is the instrumental, "Summer Means New Love." Where previous instrumentals were light, toss-away, fillers, or pastiche tracks, this work is miles ahead from those efforts and is one of Brian's most satisfying pieces. This piece is breezy, slightly melancholic, yet light and fun, with a simple instrumentation that features a wonderful guitar melody that is joined by French Horn and orchestra. Brian took inspiration from two of his earlier works, "Keep an Eye on Summer" and "After the Game," the B-side of the Survivors first single, to create one of his most unexpected and ingenious works. Brian came back to this theme on his 2015 solo album, *No Pier Pressure*, on the song, "Somewhere Quiet."

The album concludes with two unexpected works, "I'm Bugged at My Old Man" and "And Your Dreams Come True." These songs serve as a coda or farewell to Brian's youthful works as he prepares to take us into *Pet Sounds* and *SMiLE*. The clearly tongue-in-cheek humor of "Bugged . . . " has a basis in reality as Brian had fired Murry as the band's manager in 1964 but continued to deal with Murry's bullying until their very public argument in the February 1965 sessions for "Help Me Rhonda." Their unconventional and complex father-son, manager-protégé relationship would never be repaired or healed, and though intended as humor, the song's lyrics carry more than youthful annoyance at one's father. The band performed the song in their 1976 special, three years after Murry passed away, so its raucous goofiness is a little deflated when performed by men who, in 1976, were in their mid-thirties and were burdened with their own personal relationships, parenting, and substance issues. The album closes with the lovely "And Your Dreams Come True," a re-purposed "Twinkle Twinkle Little Star" arranged in a style reminiscent of the Four Freshmen. The virtuoso vocal calisthenics Brian would compose for *SMiLE* moved far beyond this simple and lovely tune, but "Dream" is Wilson's farewell to a style he had admired, emulated, and performed frequently in concert and on record, most notably in the band's performances of "Graduation Day" and "Their Hearts Were Full of Spring."

Make It Fast, Make It Faster

Capitol Records was slow to acknowledge that popular music was not a disposable teen fad. The corporation had become drunk on fast riches generated by sales of Beatles and Beach Boys records, but they continued to exert pressure upon Brian to produce new material. Label executives did not believe this music warranted the same respect and support they would accord to artists such as Nat King Cole or Frank Sinatra. The major labels were slow to acknowledge the core audience for rock and pop music, and Capitol, a younger label, was just as blind as the older, more established companies. Capitol A&R executive Dave Dexter Jr. had encouraged the label to pass on releasing the Beatles throughout 1962–1963, even though they were signed to Capitol

Records's corporate parent, EMI. He reasoned that with a successful domestic pop act on the label, the Beach Boys, another beat group, in this case, an English rock group, would not be the wisest use of label resources. Only when EMI chairman Sir Joseph Lockwood appealed to Capitol Records President Alan Livingston were the Beatles's records finally released on Capitol, which gave the label the two best-selling pop music acts of all time. Since Capitol neither owned, nor set the requirements, for the Beatles's recorded output, they could only release what EMI provided to them. They managed to wring every cent from each record through the reconfiguration of the Beatles UK albums (11 or 12 tracks on U.S. albums compared to 14 tracks on UK albums), and the practice of including previously released singles on albums, which created an entirely different catalog of Beatles records for fans in the United States. With the Beach Boys, they simply pressured Brian to produce multiple albums per year, per the agreement signed with Nik Venet in 1962 when the goal was to maximize profits with multiple releases before the band's popularity ultimately faded.

The Beach Boys's second long player of 1965, *Summer Days (and Summer Nights!!)* reached number two on the Billboard album chart, the single of "Help Me Rhonda" was a number one and its follow-up, "California Girls," reached number three. His progressive compositional and production styles were admired by industry peers, and with Phil Spector (whose own streak of chart success would soon begin its decline with "River Deep, Mountain High") and the Beatles, Brian was at the top of his game and was poised to climb even higher. Once *Summer Days* . . . .was finished, Brian took a break from the studio despite the fact that Capitol wanted new material for the holiday sales season. Not entirely sure of his next step, Brian began work in July 1965 on "Sloop John B." (b/w "You're So Good to Me"), added vocals on December 22, and released it as a single on March 23, 1966. "Sloop John B." would be placed as the closing track on side one of *Pet Sounds* and is the one song that does not quite fit in with the rest of the record. Still, this remains one of Brian's most popular records and has a long history with the band and is addressed by both McParland and Murphy in their respective books. The Bahamian folk tune exists under various titles, "The Wreck of the John B," "The John B. Sails," and "I Want to Go Home," among others, and was a hit for the Kingston Trio in 1958 (Al Jardine was familiar with this recording when he first sang the work with his high-school folk trio), and Brian performed the song as part of a vocal quartet he organized while at Hawthorne High School. It also was the tune Al and Brian first took to the Morgan's office in 1961 and which prompted the Morgans to ask if they had any original material they could audition for the couple.

While Capitol required more hit records from the Beach Boys, Brian was at work on an album he had not yet fully realized in his own mind, so in order to continue work at his own pace and on his own schedule, he considered stop-gap options such as another live album or a greatest hits collection.

The previous year's *Concert* album was an enormous success, and Brian came up with the idea to record the Beach Boys as if they were at a party, which created the live-at-home or "unplugged," record. It would require more in organization than in composition or production, so *Beach Boys' Party!* an unexpected option for one of the most progressive bands in popular music was released to great success on November 8, 1965. Live albums were nothing new, but an intimate "party" album expanded the genre of live recordings and worked to Brian's advantage when the album made it to number six on Billboard.[29] Recorded in August and September 1965, the album was a collection of casually performed, acoustic versions of the most diverse collection of songs ever heard on a Beach Boys album.[30] Brian added "party" effects provided by wives, girlfriends, and other friends, on top of the band's takes, and this slap-dash collection managed to hit big with fans who bought it in quantities. "Barbara Ann," the single drawn from the album, landed at number two on Billboard.

As soon as Brian finished work on *Party!* he continued work on three new studio projects. These included the next Beach Boys single, a session of standards recorded with orchestra, and sessions slated for the next, but as-yet-unnamed, album. The next Beach Boys single, "The Little Girl I Once Knew," was recorded in mid-October and released on November 22, two weeks after the release of *Party!* This song was problematic from a commercial standpoint as it only reached number 20 on Billboard, though it is one of Brian's most innovative works of the period.[31] In some ways, it is a continuation of "Let Him Run Wild," but with a richer instrumental and vocal arrangement. An alternate mix was released on the 2001 compilation, *Hawthorne, CA* and features an a cappella break in the final chorus that was not used in the final version of the song. This is notable because Brian would use the same a cappella break in the final chorus of "Sloop John B.," a work that had been tracked that July, but whose vocal sessions were recorded over a month after "The Little Girl I Once Knew."

Two days after the first session for the new single, Brian convened a three-hour session at United Recorders for which he contracted a 40-piece orchestra.[32] This session produced three tracks, none of which have seen an official release though they have appeared on various bootleg recordings. They include "Stella by Starlight," "How Deep is the Ocean," and an unlisted third work, "Three Blind Mice."[33] These standards were arranged and led by Dick Reynolds (the arranger with whom Brian worked on *Beach Boys Christmas Album* and would later work on the aborted *Adult/Child* album), who also provided a guide vocal with the orchestra. Two weeks later Brian was back in the studio to record the instrumental "Trombone Dixie" and "In My Childhood." The former would have no further reference until its release on the 1990 CD issue of *Pet Sounds*, while the latter would be transformed (with Tony Asher lyrics added in early 1966) into "You Still Believe in Me," which marks the true beginning of *Pet Sounds*.

Pet Sounds

Brian did not exist in a bubble of creative isolation and understood the impact of the British Invasion on American popular music and heard many of the new sounds coming from clubs on the Hollywood strip. While the Beatles were his primary, and admired, rivals, Brian was aware of newer bands such as the Byrds, Buffalo Springfield, and others. He saw the music world changing, and with an abundance of creativity expressed in every aspect of his life, he had no intention of relying upon past successes to chart the future of the Beach Boys.

On December 6, 1965, Capitol released the Beatles's *Rubber Soul*, the first, non-soundtrack, Beatles album composed entirely by the group.[34] Lennon and McCartney composed every song but one, which was written by George Harrison.[35] Brian recalls that he heard *Rubber Soul* and that, "It really blew me out."[36] He refers to the Capitol version of the album that removed four tracks from the UK, Parlophone edition and included two tracks that appeared earlier in the year on the non-film side of the UK version of *Help!* While the Parlophone version of *Rubber Soul* bore an electric, mod, Carnaby Street sensibility, the reconfigured Capitol edition conveyed a tone that could be described as folk-rock, a style very popular at that time in North America with groups such as the Byrds and the Mamas and Papas. Though Robert Freeman's cover image and Charles Ford's graphics were used in both the UK and U.S. versions of the album (a first for a Beatles album), Capitol selected a different level of color saturation for the cover image, and used brownish, golden tones in place of the orange and greenish tones used on the UK edition.[37] It was the Capitol version that Brian heard in December 1965 and that inspired him to create a fully unified album. He set himself to "go in there and experiment with sounds" and felt "challenged to do really good."[38] This is more than a bit ironic given that Brian was always developing his aural palate and had recorded some of the most progressive compositions in popular music, but he clearly took the Beatles's album to heart and was inspired to create something entirely new. The Beatles set a path in their progression from *Rubber Soul* to *Revolver* to *Sgt. Pepper's Lonely Heart Club Band*; as each album built upon the work that preceded it and allowed listeners to approach each release as something wonderfully new. For Brian, his most recent hit single was the *Party!* track, "Barbara Ann." As a result, *Pet Sounds* would be released to a market that continued to see the Beach Boys in their striped shirts, singing songs about fun-in-the-sun.

In his 1991 autobiography, Brian stated "*Pet Sounds* represented the maturing of my talent, the single-minded pursuit of a personal vision . . . I was speaking directly to them, directly from my heart." *Pet Sounds* is, quite deservedly, one of the most written about and analyzed albums in popular music and represents Brian's artistic maturation. For a thorough review of both the making of this album, and its impact upon popular music, the generous notes provided in *The Pet Sounds Sessions* boxed set provide multiple perspectives on the album from the many participants involved in its creation.[39]

We have never known a world where one could not acquire a copy of *Sgt. Pepper's Lonely Hearts Club Band*, *Aftermath*, or *Blonde on Blonde*, but *Pet Sounds* has not always been in print. In 1969–1970, Capitol pulled the Beach Boys's albums from their catalog, and made many of Brian's original albums unavailable to the public until the 1980s.[40] His songs were repackaged on countless "Greatest Hits" and "Best of . . . " collections and were licensed to a variety of subsidiary and budget labels, but Brian's original album configurations and mixes of Beach Boys albums from 1962–1965 would be unavailable for over a decade.

In the period between the second and third Warners albums, *Surf's Up* (August 1971) and *Carl and the Passions—"So Tough"* (May 1972), the Beach Boys had acquired from Capitol, a temporary license for their catalog from *Pet Sounds* through *20/20*. Capitol had intended to reissue *Pet Sounds* in 1970, most likely in its duophonic mix, but this never came to pass, so once the Beach Boys licensed their post-*Pet Sounds* catalog, it is likely that Warners planned to release a 1966–1969 era album along with every new release from the band, in effect, a double album package for the price of one.[41] When the band came to release *Carl and the Passions—"So Tough,"* an album with minimal involvement from Brian, it was paired with the mono mix of *Pet Sounds.*[42] Warners reissued it as a single disc in 1974 with the original cover photo and different graphics, and this edition was available until their Warners contract expired in 1978. With the rights transferred back to Capitol, the label reissued the monophonic mix in 1980 on their "green dome" reissue series, though the cassette edition retained the muddy duophonic mix.[43] The album was remastered in 1990 for its debut on compact disc and included three previously unreleased tracks.[44] The 1997 release of *The Pet Sounds Sessions* offered a true stereo version of the album (authorized by Brian and prepared by Mark Linett) and a refreshed mono mix, in addition to a number of tracking sessions and alternate versions for many of the songs on the original album.[45] Since then, Capitol has released a 40th-anniversary edition of the album with the 1997 mono and stereo mixes plus a bonus DVD with videos and Hi-Res PCM and Dolby 5.1 Surround Sound mixes.[46] Multiple configurations of the album were released in summer 2016 as part of a 50th-anniversary edition. This includes a vinyl edition, a two-CD set with the mono and stereo mixes in addition to the instrumental tracks and a series of live recordings. For the completest, there is a deluxe four-CD plus Blu-Ray Audio edition that combines mono, stereo, live, the hi-res editions, and selections from the 1997 *Sessions* set. For some, the obsession and quest for the best "sounding" version of *Pet Sounds* can become an overwhelming quest for an intangible moment of sound in time.[47] For an album that was hastily passed over by Capitol on its original release in favor of a "Best of . . ." collection, many fans have sought to acquire the "best" version of an album that has become one of the most repackaged and reissued masterpieces in the history of popular music, and provided a profitable legacy for Capitol Records.

Though *Pet Sounds* was conceived as a whole work (more of a concept album than a song cycle), Capitol released three singles from the album that made *Pet Sounds* the only Beach Boys album to produce four, top 40 singles. The first "Caroline, No," was released on March 7, 1966, as a Brian Wilson solo single.[48] This emotional and touching love song spent a mere seven weeks on the charts, three of those in the top 40, where it reached number 32.[49] Perhaps this was due to its striking originality, but just as easily could have been a result of the decision to market the single as a Brian Wilson solo record rather than as a Beach Boys record. On March 21, Capitol released "Sloop John B." that spent a month-and-a-half in the top 10 and peaked at number three. The third single, released on July 18, paired two of the most loved and recognized songs from the album, "Wouldn't It Be Nice" and "God Only Knows." The album was released on May 16 and peaked at number 10 in Billboard in a 39-week run on the charts. The perceived failure of this album may lie in the fact that when released, it was their first album, since the debut of *Surfin' Safari*, that did not earn a gold record on its initial run.[50] The five albums prior to *Pet Sounds* had all charted in the top 10 (*Beach Boys Party!* was the lowest charting at number six), and when *Pet Sounds* could climb no higher than number 10, it was described as a "weak" performer in their catalog. In England, the album reached number two, and for weeks it remained in the top 10. The accounting for this album had been poorly tracked from its original release through its multiple reissues. It did not earn gold record status on its first, second, or third release cycles, but once the compact disc was made available in 1990, sales for this album were finally reconciled, which pushed it to earn both Gold and Platinum status.[51]

When Capitol Records released *The Pet Sounds Sessions* boxed set on November 4, 1997, they included two booklets that provided comprehensive documentation on the making of the album. The collection was an archival gem for fans and offered pristine mixes of an album that helped to chart a new direction for popular music in the decades that followed its release. This set was originally slated for release in May 1996, the 30th anniversary of the album, but the Beach Boys's internal politics delayed its release for over a year because some parties felt the project perpetuated the legacy of Brian as the sole visionary behind the album. Negotiations between Capitol and the Beach Boys resulted in a compromise where an essay from Mike Love would preface David Leaf's introductory remarks in the booklet, "The Making of Pet Sounds."[52] Mike posited a narrative that the Beach Boys were always behind Brian, and he emphasized the contributions of each member of the band.[53] Additional documentation included David Leaf's essays, Brian's essay and interview, an interview with lyricist Tony Asher, and memories from Carl, Al, Dennis, and Bruce, and a number of the musicians and engineers who participated in the creation of the work. Also included were interviews with former Capitol A&R producer Nik Venet and Karl Engemann, the Capitol Records executive, who was Brian's most sympathetic supporter at Capitol. Contributions from Paul McCartney, Sir George Martin, Danny Hutton, and Audree Wilson rounded out the collection, but a thoughtful and loving essay from Marilyn Wilson Rutherford is one of the highlights of the set. More than anyone else present at the creation of *Pet Sounds*, Marilyn was Brian's closest confidante in addition to her role as the wife of popular music's most celebrated artist.

Another valuable resource was recording engineer Mark Linett's essay that provided a wealth of information about the source tapes that have been used in the many editions of *Pet Sounds*. The evolution of recording technology in the mid-1960s provided Brian with access to three-track, four-track, and eight-track recording hardware, which played an important factor in Brian's organization of his aural canvas. Wilson's extraordinary development in his use of instrumental textures for this album and his complex vocal arrangements were informed by the studios and recording hardware he elected to use.[54] Linett's painstaking efforts to provide high-quality masters to serve both mono and stereo editions of *Pet Sounds* has corrected mastering missteps from prior releases of the album. *Pet Sounds* was originally released in North America on compact disc in its monophonic mix in 1990, and while celebrated, the standard application of noise reduction in the mastering process resulted in an aural canvas that was weightier and flatter than what had been captured on the original vinyl album. The 1997 release included an authorized stereo mix of the album (prepared by Linett under Brian's supervision) and a "corrected" monophonic mix. In addition to a remaster of the complete album there were numerous tracking sessions, preliminary versions that preceded Brian's final mix, and vocals-only tracks. The various takes of each song illustrate Brian's ability to develop and shape ideas through the verbal directions he gives to the musicians.[55] With multiple versions for many of the songs, we are provided entrée into the possible directions Brian considered for these songs.

Pet Sounds was composed in collaboration with Tony Asher, an advertising man for the Carson-Roberts Agency, who was introduced to Brian through Loren Schwartz at a recording session a year prior to their work on the album. Mike Love had collaborated with Brian on the majority of his songs since the July 1964 release of *All Summer Long*, so Asher became Brian's first significant outside collaborator since the departures of Roger Christian and Gary Usher.[56] Tony's lyrics allowed Brian to express unusually mature themes with a depth of narrative sophistication, and while he was Brian's primary collaborator on the album, he was not involved on every track. When Asher was brought on board, Brian confessed that he was under pressure from Capitol to deliver new product, and though he had worked on a few songs, he had not found exactly what he wanted to say, and he looked to Asher to help him bring this work to fruition. Marilyn has said that Brian looked for collaborators who were interesting and unusual and whose minds were different than his. As a musician who understood the importance of economy and organization with words, Asher was an ideal partner on *Pet Sounds*. Brian set out to make an artistic album and "wanted to combine pop music with orchestral music."[57] The results were, and remain, breathtaking in their intimacy and honesty. Stebbins describes the album as "the most intimate grand production ever, the saddest hopeful sentiment of all time, the most comforting confession of loss . . . "[58] It was the expression of the internal feelings and thoughts of a complex controlling consciousness through "sophisticated-feeling music."[59]

Though "Sloop John B." was recorded in July 1965, before Brian recorded the *Party!* album and before he had formed his ideas for what would be *Pet Sounds*, the first proper sessions for the album were held in November 1965.[60] On the first of the month, Brian tracked "Trombone Dixie" and "In My Childhood," and two weeks later recorded what would become the album's penultimate track, "Pet Sounds." Titled at this time as "Run James Run," this was Brian's personal homage (or tongue-in-cheek effort) to create a tune that could have been a title song for a James Bond film.[61] He recorded this a month prior to the release of Eon Production's fourth issue in their James Bond franchise, *Thunderball* (December 1965), and he would have been aware of the excitement that surrounded this film as the Sean Connery-era Bond films were at their peak following the release of *Goldfinger* in September 1964. This instrumental is easily overlooked and often is dismissed for its unstructured "lounge" groove. It is a fun and quirky piece and a reflection of Brian's grand sense of humor while it also provides an emotional release prior to the album's concluding, and heartbreaking final track, "Caroline, No." Another instrumental, "Let's Go Away for Awhile," is a striking work with a slightly confusing history behind a story that will never be decided upon since both Asher and Wilson's memories of the song have never been in agreement. It has been documented that Asher composed lyrics for this song that Brian chose to not use, though Asher does not recall providing lyrics.[62] Brian acknowledges the influences of Burt Bacharach and Phil Spector on this work, and in 1967 stated this work is "the most satisfying piece of music I've ever made." The remaining non-Asher songs "I'm Waiting for the Day" and "I Know There's an Answer" come from very different points in Brian's creative trajectory. The former, composed with Mike Love and first registered in 1964, is closer in style to Brian's work of the *Today!* era. The arrangement is understated and well-constructed, though Love's lyrics are less sophisticated than Asher's. "I Know There's an Answer" was one of the more difficult works from the sessions. Brian composed this song with the Beach Boys former road manager and latter-day hanger-on, Terry Sachen, as "Hang On to Your Ego." Mike refused to sing the song unless the lyrics were changed, so the title was duly changed and excluding the chorus the remainder of the lyric was changed only slightly from the original.[63]

Speaking a decade later, Tony found it difficult at first to accommodate to Brian's working methods, and expressed his distaste for Brian's taste in "an ever-changing array of philosophies, what (Asher) called the 'marshmallow mystics,' " or what could be described as Brian's singular focus on making music that came at the expense of everything, and everyone, else.[64] Asher's first assignment was to put lyrics to Brian's track from November 1965, "In My Childhood," and on the following day he delivered a new melody, lyrics, and a new title, "You Still Believe in Me." Sessions for the album resumed on January 18, 1966, with Brian's second instrumental for the album, "Let's Go Away for Awhile." The Beach Boys were on tour in Japan throughout January, performed in Hawaii on the January 29 and began to add vocals for Brian's new tracks in the first days of February. Work on the album continued into the middle of April. Assembly of the record began on April 16 for a release exactly one month later.

"Feeling" was central to the creation of *Pet Sounds*, but Brian also ventured into spirituality and prayer, subjects often ignored but of importance in any study of his work. Brian felt the songs on *Pet Sounds* were the result of a full range of emotional experiences from "sadness and pain . . . . or joy, exultations in nature and sunshine."[65] "Feels" were particular "rhythmic patterns, fragments or ideas," that served as points of departure in his work. While Brian's working methods with Usher and Christian were quite distinct from each other, his methods with Asher combined elements developed in his earlier collaborations, but also delved into mature and thoughtful themes. Following a day of work, Asher would go home to refine his text and when he returned the following day, Brian would be free to edit his words. Asher has stated "The general tenor of the lyrics was always his. . . . I was really just his interpreter."[66] The songs reflected concerns the both of them shared as young men who stood at the edge of a cultural and social revolution, but with the same insecurities, worries, and fears that had been faced by earlier generations of young men. He admits to a great deal of procrastination in their writing sessions, but said that Brian would work to come up with a "feel" that he loved, and once a certain emotion found him, the two would develop a song around that "feel." The topics of women and relationships with women (past, current, and future) were a central theme on the album. Prior to their work on *Pet Sounds*, they knew each other only as acquaintances, so as they learned of each other's lives, experiences, and feelings, women were continually at the center of their conversations. "Emotion" and "Feeling" were, in Asher's opinion, the source behind every work on the album. Brian would enter the studio to record instrumental tracks with no melody, and would take the recordings back to the house for him and Tony to complete. Songs were created with a certain level of spontaneity, which left them with a series of options they could use to complete the song. The lyrical thread for any song was nothing more than "a reflection of what was going on in Brian's mind."[67] While the music on this album sounds so natural and organic, its gestation was far from natural. Asher would attest that for "every four hours we'd spend writing songs, there's be about forty-eight hours of . . . dopey conversations about some dumb book."[68]

The Beatles, Bob Dylan, and the Rolling Stones also displayed a sophisticated maturity in their work from this period with, respectively, *Rubber Soul, Blonde on Blonde,* and *Aftermath*; but Brian expressed every song from *Pet Sounds* in the first person. Optimism and a faith in love and coupledom is expressed in "Wouldn't It Be Nice," which is followed by repentance and a request for his girl's forgiveness in "You Still Believe in Me." "That's Not Me" is Brian's declaration of an identity that is not what his family, friends, and fans would prefer to believe, where the next two songs, "Don't Talk (Put Your Head on My Shoulder)" and "I'm Waiting for the Day" are an attempt to console and reassure, an admission that perhaps what he believes is real is actually unrealistic and unrequited affection. "Let's Go Away for Awhile" is the most confident and mature work on the album. "God Only Knows" is both a confessional and an acknowledgment of his love. The opening statement, "I may not always love you, but as long as there are stars above you. . ." may be the most moving and intimate declaration of love ever expressed in popular music. The next three songs, "I Know There's an Answer," "Hang on to Your Ego," and "Here Today," are Brian's self-centered moments, and while each song is as strong as any other on the album, they express an emotional immaturity and highlight his selfish, inward focus. "I Just Wasn't Made for These Times" follows on themes of earlier songs ("Guess I'm Dumb" and "Don't Back Down") where Brian simply admits that his insecurity and inability to "fit-in" are not his imagination but an honest admission to what he knows about himself. "Pet Sounds" is the album's final blow-out of unbridled fun and enthusiasm while "Caroline, No" can be read through multiple lenses. Is it an expression of sadness to a love who has moved on from him, or, as Bruce Johnston posits, is it Brian telling his own story, of a sweet innocence that has disappeared, and will never return. The final word of the song "No" stands in direct opposition to the cautious but irrepressible optimism of the album's opening track and concludes our excursion through Brian's most honest and emotional work.

The nakedly personal nature of *Pet Sounds* can be seen by some as a Brian Wilson solo record, but it is the band's contributions and unique vocal colors that complete the work and demonstrate that *Pet Sounds* could never have occurred without them. There was a great deal of strain within the group by early 1966 because the Beach Boys needed Brian far more than he needed them. Carl, whose voice would become the central color in the band's vocal blend, delivered the stunning lead on "God Only Knows," and the rest of the group provided the flawless backing vocal textures that wove golden timbres across the album. This came at a great cost, as many accounts recall Brian's obsessive quest for perfection that would manifest, to the irritation of the band, in take-upon-take-upon-take.[69] Brian could sing all the parts exactly as he wanted them and he recorded his demos in this way, but he wanted the Beach Boys to perform at a level that was higher than anything they had done before. Brian's relationship with Carl, while always close, grew deeper through the process of making the album as he relied on him for creative and personal support. While Lambert describes this album as having "... unsurpassingly beautiful melodies over haunting chord progressions ....," the impact of this album cannot simply be attributed to its unique orchestrations and arrangements, or the maturity of the songwriting, but as a result of the whole, and that included the Beach Boys.

In recording *Pet Sounds*, Brian wanted to "... create something that I thought would bring an adequate amount of spiritual love to the world."[70] While this has often been quoted and referenced in descriptions of the album, the deeper meanings of this statement have only recently become part of the dialogue in the analysis of Wilson's work. Brian attempted to bridge sacred and secular art with *Pet Sounds* and would continue the following year with works such as "Our Prayer." At the Beach Boys's 1988 induction into the Rock and Roll Hall of Fame, Brian said "Music is God's voice. I've often felt that I was on a musical mission, to spread the gospel of love through records."[71] Brian has spoken about holding prayer sessions during *Pet Sounds*, praying for guidance to make healing sounds, and to this day he ends his concerts with "Love and Mercy," a deeply spiritual song that conveys the intentions he first expressed on *Pet Sounds*.

Marilyn Wilson was married to Brian from 1964 to 1979 and was his companion through his most creative period and through some of his most difficult and unhappy years. As articulated in her essay included in *The SMiLE Sessions*, "... (she) had the fortunate blessing of loving him, marrying him, and living the music experience by his side." She has sat for numerous interviews over the decades and always has spoken of Brian with honesty and affection. As a singer whom he had produced with the Honeys, Marilyn had a musical connection with Brian that enabled her to support him and fully appreciate the depth and emotion of his work. She also has claimed their marriage "wasn't much of a relationship," and there was no typical day in their life, and they only "really ever related ... musically." She accepted the fact that she was not the number one priority in his life because music was always first. With a resigned, but non-accusatory acceptance, she has said "I was never number one, I was always two or three ... I just wanted to be number one as a mate and in his love life. Music was who he was."[72] His humor was attractive to her, but the bond from their very first meeting was music, and it remained such through their marriage.[73] Marilyn said Brian loved to do fun things, was unpredictable, and that one simply had to go along with it. She would "hear Brian with his music when there was nobody else there .... ."

While millions of fans continue to experience the intense beauty of this album, Marilyn's memories of this work are consistent with what we accept as the creative process and the "artists' need to make art." Honesty is at the center of Brian's creative voice, and *Pet Sounds* was a story he had to tell even though audiences and the commercial market might not know what to make of it. Marilyn believes Brian's songs on this album "came from a tortured person" because "he was in self-turmoil, unhappy about his life and his feelings, and he just was never happy with himself."[74] According to her, Brian let everything out, never held anything back, and loved to "express things like that." The songs on *Pet Sounds* were an expression of the frustrations he felt in his life. When he wrote music, he wrote for himself and wanted to share what was coming from inside of him. "I Just Wasn't Made for These Times" is perhaps the purest expression of Brian's frustrations. This intense level of exposure and sensitivity led to his emotional breakdown that followed the cancellation of *SMiLE*, but before these experiences became debilitating, he could, with Asher's assistance, express feelings in ways that no other rock musician had considered, or dared, to try. So many of Brian's songs from *Beach Boys Today!!* are confessionals and expressions of love to Marilyn. On *Pet Sounds*, the comfort, stability, and importance of this relationship was expressed in songs such as "You Still Believe in Me," Don't Talk (Put Your Head on My Shoulder)," and "Let's Go Away for Awhile." Marilyn has also spoken of how Brian could be a sweet, romantic husband, and recalls the night he came home with the acetate of the entire album and they listened to the whole album in the near dark. She said the experience was "so beautiful, one of the most spiritual times of my whole life ... this was his soul in there . . . ."[75]

Popular music had not yet arrived to a place where artists could express intimate, personal emotions in their work. Brian wanted to move the soul of teenage America with "music so passionate ... so majestic ... shazam—Instant Epiphany."[76] Marilyn has also stated that music was the only thing that mattered to Brian. His personal hang-ups were intertwined with his creative voice, "Everything was always just one. The music was the good feeling part, and the other part didn't feel good."[77] For all of the emotional turmoil Brian must have experienced in the creation of this album, Marilyn believes that simplicity was always at the core of his best work, and the fact that *Pet Sounds* was not an immediate success "really destroyed Brian."[78] He could not understand why, if he put his heart and soul into this record, people would prefer something mediocre. Once the album was accepted as a milestone in the field, its delayed successes only served to further destroy Brian. She recalls that when people would want to talk about it later and tell him how great it was, he "didn't want to hear about it, it reminded him of failing" (we can place this scenario into his years at Warners and the "Brian's Back" period, in addition to *SMiLE*, and in this light it becomes all the more painful), "... and then he was more tortured. It never stopped. It just got layered on."[79] By the time the rest of the music world caught on, Brian had already let go of his masterpiece. She has said that all Brian could do was to live and breathe music, but after the perceived failure of this album was followed by *SMiLE*, he simply wanted to hold back. The market for rock music was not ready for an album with the emotional, spiritual, and expressive depth of *Pet Sounds*. Sufficient blame can be placed on Capitol Records's marketing team whose decisions helped set into motion the indifference that greeted *Pet Sounds*, the first "failure" of Brian's career.

Brian's relationship with Murry, while never healthy, became increasingly brittle while recording *Pet Sounds*, as his envy of Brian's extraordinary creativity grew to greater heights.[80] It was known that Murry resented Brian and went behind his back, talking to each of the guys in the band to get them at each other's throats in order to make himself appear as the solid, responsible beacon of light amidst the constructed madness. Brian had the respect and enthusiasm of his studio musicians, all of whom were seasoned veterans of the Los Angeles studio scene, and the dedication they showed Brian surely rankled Murry.[81] While Murry's many faults are easy to identify, he can be given credit for one specific decision in the production of "Caroline, No." The original recording was one half-step lower than what is heard on the album and Murry suggested that the tape be sped up so the song would play back one pitch higher, which would give Brian a younger sounding voice.[82] He used this technique on their first single, "Surfin'," because he felt the "younger" sound would be more appealing to record buyers. Brian's sweet tenor sounds more vulnerable in the higher key, but on *Sessions*, we have mono and stereo mixes of the song at its original speed and key, and while it feels different from the song we have known, the longing and sadness in Brian's voice expresses loss in a way the more familiar version does not. The family's resistance to the album, especially with the lyrics, is a theme that would continue into Brian's next project, but all the support he had from Marilyn and others could not erase the pressure he felt from his immediate family.[83] The political machinations that occurred among these players would temporarily subside, but return en masse by mid-1967.

Karl Engemann had approved numerous recording sessions for Brian and the Wrecking Crew, and may have been Brian's strongest ally in the company.[84] He was at the label when the band moved from Candix to Capitol, and had witnessed Brian's explosive growth and the influence he had upon the field.[85] Brian trusted Karl and liked his "normal" personality, while Marilyn described Karl as "a really nice person."[86] He is on record stating that Nik Venet was always supportive of Brian's growth and activity as a producer, contrary to other narratives that have tried to frame the Nik/Brian dynamic as one of conflict.[87] Capitol was accustomed to receiving three albums per year from Brian, but as he continued to bring depth and real creativity to popular music, it became more difficult for him to meet Capitol's demands. Brian made them wait, but they always were happy to get their product from him. Brian previewed his most personal and emotional album for the executives at Capitol in the latter part of April 1966, and found them to be unimpressed. There was a brief discussion about shelving the album, but they finally agreed to release it the following month. Engemann knew that marketing reps at Capitol were not enthusiastic about the album because it was so different from Brian's previous records. They wanted more "fun" hits, as Brian was about to deliver one of the greatest works of his career, though Engemann claims to have recognized its "musical worth" and its "originality."[88] Though it cannot be proven, he believes that any chance for the album's success was thwarted by sales representatives who were not excited by *Pet Sounds* and requested other Beach Boys product. He believes this lukewarm reception led to Capitol's decision to move up in the calendar, an already planned for "Best of . . ." collection. Al Couri, then head of promotion at Capitol, justified the marketing failure of the album by acknowledging that Brian was someone whom they did not understand. He said, "You've got to understand that Brian was so impulsive, compulsive, you never knew what was coming next."[89] Nik Venet, who no longer worked for Capitol at the time of *Pet Sounds*, defends the label in saying "There were (salesmen) out there that could sell Beach Boys product and the (customers) were asking for it. The *Pet Sounds* album was supposed to be ready a long time before, and it wasn't going to be ready. The whole company was geared up to the 'best of' package."[90] Sir Joseph Lockwood, the chairman of EMI, was learning to acknowledge that popular music could be art, but at the Capitol Tower, the label had one view of Brian, and art did not fit into their picture.

Best of the Beach Boys is now regarded as Capitol's great misstep in their handling of Brian and the band. Less than two months after the release of *Pet Sounds*, Capitol released the first of many compilations albums they would release over the next five decades. This 12-track album featured their classic hits, but managed to exclude the recent hits, "Help Me Rhonda" and "California Girls." This album managed to sell in numbers well above *Pet Sounds*, and was the record that Capitol elected to put into motion with their publicity machine.[91]

On August 1, 1966, a month after the release of *Best of the Beach Boys*, Capitol released a third *Pet Sounds* single with two of the album's most beloved songs, "God Only Knows" and "Wouldn't It Be Nice," which reached number eight on the Billboard charts within the month. In spite of the label's passive vote of no confidence for the Beach Boys's new sound, this single managed a top 10 chart showing, but for the label, the die was cast and it would be eight years before another Beach Boys record would grace the top 10 on Billboard.[92]

Pet Sounds received a far different reception in England than in the United States, thanks to advance publicity on the part of Bruce Johnston, who travelled to England in May 1966. The album had not yet been released in the UK, so Beach Boys (and former Beatles) publicist Derek Taylor along with Kim Fowley, a Sunset Strip scene maker who happened to reside in England at the time, arranged for Bruce to do some interviews to promote the album while he was in town. Bruce was set up at the Waldorf Hotel and caravans of the English music press were ushered in for steak dinners and champagne to accompany their preview of *Pet Sounds*. Johnston's professional manner had been cultivated at a young age, and his early work with Spector and other acts provided him with a confident and articulate manner, so a preview of the album presented by Bruce meant that journalists would be engaged in friendly but businesslike conversation.[93] Tony Rivers, a member of the Castaways and a seasoned studio singer, invited Keith Moon to the Waldorf where he and Bruce hit it off. Thanks to Moon, Bruce would host a number of English pop artists including Lennon and McCartney, who came by to hear the work.[94] Artists such as Cream and the Rolling Stones were early adopters of the album, and Stones manager Andrew 'Loog' Oldham referred to *Pet Sounds* as the "*Scheherazade* of pop." Mick Jagger also gave his support for the album by getting pirate radio stations to play Beach Boys singles in advance of *Pet Sounds's* official release.[95] The buzz among English musicians was significant and reportedly pushed the UK release from November to late June. Once released, it held the number two spot and stayed in the top 10 for six months, far outpacing and outselling its U.S. counterpart.

Johnston's recollections of the period provide a very different interpretation of "Caroline, No." He believes the song is not about a person, but is Brian expressing an awareness that "(the) special door that had been open to him was closing, where he'd do special things naturally."[96] He also believes that Brian did not lose his fans with *Pet Sounds*, but its lack of sales was a result of the label having lost faith in Brian. Record labels were willing to give their serious artists the room to grow and develop, but pop music was too young and in the minds of older record executives it was not a genre that would have staying power and would soon come to an end. So a *Best of*... compilation was the first step for a label who were about to express their indifference for one of their top-selling artists.[97] In some karmic fashion, Capitol would never be a leader in rock music and would miss out on every major development in popular music, in spite of having a number of top artists on their roster.[98]

In spite of the label's indifference to Brian's masterpiece and the disappointing sales numbers of *Pet Sounds*, Brian managed to move forward. The myth of Brian Wilson began to flower, in part because of the Beach Boys's new publicist, Derek Taylor, who birthed the narrative of "Brian Wilson is a Genius," but also because *Pet Sounds* was being reviewed and critiqued by more mature audiences who saw it as an extraordinary milestone in popular music. Brian preferred to downplay the hype in interviews by saying "No, I'm not a genius. I'm just a hardworking guy."[99]

Once *Pet Sounds* was released, Brian returned to work on "Good Vibrations." Sessions for this song stretched from February 17 to September 1, 1966. Six-and-a-half months over three studios (Gold Star, Western, and Sunset Sound), and reported to have cost over $50,000 to record, made it the most expensive single ever recorded at the time. Brian composed this song using smaller units, modules, instead of through-composed phrases, as one might typically do in a traditional song. Modular compositional methods are not notoriously difficult if one reads music notation or works with digital audio hardware, both of which provide the efficient means needed to organize thematic materials. But in the pre-digital era, Brian recorded, arranged, and selected his modules through a painstaking process of recording, cutting, and splicing his various modules into place. Where *Pet Sounds* had arrived with a quiet ecstasy, "Good Vibrations" was a smash hit both in the United States and in England. The scope of this song was unlike anything that had come before and unlike any single that scaled easily to the top of the charts. For Brian, it was a vindication of his creative vision and leadership and should have been the start of a new, long, and successful era for both Brian and the Beach Boys. This would collapse within the year and when faced with an opportunity to pursue his artistic vision, he understood that leaving the Beach Boys was not an option, so he "abandoned his art rather than break from the security of his life as it was."[100]

Good, Good, Good, Good . . .

October 10, 1966—"Good Vibrations" is released (b/w "Let's Go Away for Awhile").

October 21, 1966—"Good Vibrations" enters the Billboard top 100 at number 81.

October 22, 1966—The Beach Boys premiere of "Good Vibrations" live at the University of Michigan's Hill Auditorium. Both sold-out performances were recorded, and photos of Brian on the stage of Hill show him coaching the band through their most complex song to date.

October 23, 1966—On Brian's request, Marilyn Wilson and Diane Rovell convened a number of Brian's friends, relatives, and members of his then-current circle to greet him upon his return from Michigan, at Los Angeles International Airport. The group was captured, in a series of now-legendary photographs, against the Charles Kratka-designed mosaic walls in the old LAX terminal. In the photos are Brian and Marilyn, Diane and Barbara Rovell, Annie Hinsche Wilson, Jules Siegel, David Anderle, June Fairchild, Van Dyke Parks, Danny Hutton, Mark Volman, and a number of others. These photos show Brian surrounded by a selection of the many supporters and collaborators he had attracted over the previous couple of years and, as Jules Siegel would report in *Goodbye Surfing, Hello God,* most of those people would be gone within a short time. In less than a year, *SMiLE* would be withdrawn and the family would close ranks, which, for Brian, would initiate an extended period of isolation. But in these last moments, Brian was at the top of his game, at the top of the field, and conceivably could have scaled ever greater heights.

December 10, 1966—"Good Vibrations" hits number one on the top 100.

January 20, 1967—"Good Vibrations" exits Billboard with a final showing at number 50.

November 4, 1988—Twenty-one years, eleven months later, and for the first time since "Good Vibrations," the Beach Boys take the top spot on the top 100 with "Kokomo," a song written and produced with no participation from Brian.

As Brian worked on "Good Vibrations" he also began work on *Dumb Angel*, a working title for his next album. "Good Vibrations" began life with a set of lyrics composed by Tony Asher, but over the course of its development, Brian and Mike expanded upon these to create one of their most remarkable works.[101] If not the first psychedelic record, it was, along with the Beatles's two-sided single "Strawberry Fields Forever"/"Penny Lane," the expression of an entirely new and utterly original form of popular music.[102] From May through September 1966, Brian was on a journey of discovery while he acquired, discarded, and drew from an endless well of ideas. He described this work in its early iterations as an R&B track and had considered giving it to another artist and label when the Beach Boys's frustrations became too great a distraction. He reconnected with Van Dyke Parks, a year after first being introduced to him by David Crosby, and the two began work on songs for *Dumb Angel*. About a third of the way through sessions for "Good Vibrations," Brian realized that he had to develop a different approach to construct this work. The traditional through-composed form with alternating verse/chorus/bridge sections would not work for this song, and instead he began to develop individual harmonic, melodic, and timbral sections without making a final determination as to how these sections would fit into the song. Though he had limited formal music training, Brian instinctively adopted an approach to composition where, through the creation of smaller and self-contained sections, he could organize them into a complete narrative. This method was unheard of in popular music, and while the Beatles would use less problematic collage techniques in works such as "Being for the Benefit of Mr. Kite" and "Revolution 9," it would be a few years before rock music caught up to Brian in the use of modular construction. Pink Floyd's "Echoes" from *Meddle* (1971) is perhaps the best example of a work composed in this manner.[103] In spite of its complexities, the song retains elements of a verse/chorus structure, but Brian's transitions and timbral interpolations resulted in a work that was unlike any other of the period.

There exists, thanks to the various reissues that began with the 1990 *Smiley Smile/Wild Honey* two-fer and the various compilations released in the two decades that followed, multiple versions of the song, from Brian's first tracking sessions, to the various components he incorporated over the course of the seven months he worked on the song. The 3-minute-and-38-second single edit, the most widely known version of the song, is related to a hybrid version included on *Brian Wilson Presents SMiLE*, where on *The SMiLE Sessions* there is a 4-minute and 15-second version that offers an expanded bridge, what Lambert refers to as "the meditation half of the 'dream sequence' " prior to the third iteration of the chorus. While the Beach Boys had always been an extraordinary vocal ensemble, Brian created an exquisite vocal fugato after the third chorus that displayed their talents to stunning effect. The band's otherworldly sound once more brings the listener towards a spiritual experience in Brian's music. He claimed to have composed this song after his third and final LSD trip and had stated that this song converged song-writing and spirituality. Brian's evolution from "God Only Knows" to "Good Vibrations" to the upcoming "Our Prayer" placed him on a path that no other white, popular music artist had dared to tread.

Brian kept discovering additional paths towards completion, and on April 9, he came to what he believed was his "finished" version, but on June 18, he arrived at what could be described as another "final" version, which still retained Asher's lyrics. He asked Van Dyke Parks to work on the lyrics, though he wisely declined, and ultimately Mike and Brian expanded upon Tony's original text. Brian left the song on the shelf and did not return to the studio until July. In the interim, Capitol released *Best of the Beach Boys*, which further stymied the sales of *Pet Sounds*, and released the stunning double-sided hit single, "Wouldn't It Be Nice"/"God Only Knows" on July 18.

Brian returned to the studio in early August and resumed work on *Dumb Angel*, (which had begun on May 11 with a preliminary session for "Heroes and Villains") to record "Wind Chimes" and "Look." By mid-August, Brian completed "Good Vibrations" and began to devote his attention on the new album. The single was ready by the end of September and once finished, it qualified for the most expensive single yet recorded, but also the longest in terms of its production. Released in early October, its immediate success silenced all doubters. This stunning and phenomenal song proved that Brian Wilson was, in fact, a genius.

SMiLE (1966–2011)

3

For over three decades, *SMiLE* was the Beach Boys's mythical "lost" album; an album that, had it been realized in 1967, could have expanded the field of popular music beyond what was experienced in the wake of the Beatles's *Sgt. Pepper's Lonely Hearts Club Band*. It also represents a lost history because for four decades the rock music canon has been framed around *Sgt. Pepper's*. Connected with the loss of Brian's masterpiece was the loss of Brian's authority within the Beach Boys, the loss of his position as a leader in the field, and ultimately the loss of Brian Wilson's very self. The tempered corporate and market response to *Pet Sounds* and the battles he faced in the effort to complete *SMiLE* ultimately broke his spirit and broke his creative heart. *SMiLE* was "a culmination of Brian Wilson's musical genius, as a story that entails loss and gain in grand measure."[1] He poured every ounce of his being into the work only to have his vision rejected. Over succeeding decades, bootleg recordings of the album were shared among collectors, and the few pieces from *SMiLE* that were reconfigured for *Smiley Smile*, or hijacked and cobbled for inclusion on various albums between 1969 and 1971, simply enhanced the loss of what might have been, and thus, the cult of *SMiLE* was created. David Anderle maintains that *SMiLE* was not just an album, but an extraordinarily rich and creative period for Brian where *SMiLE* was just one, though a primary, work among a number of works, in a period he described as "... (when) there were many different interchangeable concepts floating around."[2] There are numerous books written just on this work alone, and if one attempts to construct a picture of what actually happened between late summer 1966 through July 1967, it might appear the era was one of cacophonous, exuberant, near-anarchic brilliance, or an extended decline accompanied by an amphetamine-fueled despair.[3] The 1993 release of *Good Vibrations: Thirty Years of the Beach Boys* offered over 30 minutes of *SMiLE* and whetted appetites that a long-hoped-for release of the original album would finally come to pass. Over the decades, while Brian insisted that *SMiLE* never existed, the desire to see its release blinded fans from the fact that however many *SMiLE* pieces were recorded and stored in the vaults, Brian never settled upon a final running order, so while it existed as individual segments, many of them complete, *SMiLE* could not exist because Brian never compiled a final sequence for the album.

With the support of his band, the editorial assistance of guitarist Jeffrey Foskett and multi-instrumentalist, Darian Sahanaja, orchestrations by Paul Mertens, and critical links provided by Van Dyke Parks, Brian presented his fans with a resolution to one of the greatest mysteries in popular music. Wilson and his band presented a complete performance of *SMiLE* to rapturous acclaim at London's Royal Festival Hall in February 2004, and Nonesuch Records released *Brian Wilson Presents SMiLE (BWPS)* that September. The album, recorded in the aftermath of the London shows, presented the work as a cohesive and complete experience. It was as if the work had always existed in this form, and in truth it existed for over three decades, except that Brian had chosen to keep it for himself and deny its existence at every opportunity. For many who were close to the making of the original album, such as Diane Rovell, who served as a session contractor in 1966–1967, the 2004 recording was a revision of the original work because however close Brian may have been to its completion in 1967, there was no final track order, and for many songs there had been no final determination as to the exact sequence of thematic modules. Given the disappointment and criticism that was heaped upon Brian in its wake, he had every right to keep it for himself. When his bandmates expressed their reservations and could not process Van Dyke Parks's wonderfully expressive and surreal lyrics, Brian refused to let it go forward in 1967, which may have been the only means by which he could save its' purity. If, as Sellars argues, Brian's abandonment of *SMiLE* was "an act of innocence," this was the only means by which he could insure that the integrity of the work would stand as he intended.[4] If *Pet Sounds* was an album with "all good songs" then *SMiLE* was an experience like no other in popular music. *SMiLE* was grounded with a powerful, pulsating heart with "Heroes and Villains," whose multiple motifs and rhythmic gestures were interspersed throughout the album. While it sounded like any "normal" song, its construction was anything but typical as it was composed in fragments or modules that Brian arranged into a complete work.[5] In this way, he was able to extract smaller gestures that could be interpolated throughout the album. But *SMiLE* also had a soul. "Surf's Up," described by Diane Rovell as "Brian's swan song," is perhaps the most breathtakingly beautiful and poignant song he ever composed, and its kaleidoscope of colors and emotions were at once intangible but utterly embracing.

Between the 2004 recording and the tracks released in 1993, we could grasp the full scope of this work, for while *BWPS* was complete, the original tracks provided us with sections and musical fragments as he may originally have envisioned them, and proved that the 2004 iteration required very little new material because it was reconstructed on the template of a nearly completed work. Generally lauded by fans and critics, the surviving Beach Boys were somewhat reserved in their response, which was not surprising when we consider the work also represented their legacy. But it also served to confirm the role they would have played in the cancellation of the original project in 1967. In Carlin's post-2004 interview with Mike Love, the Beach Boys leader inferred that Brian may have infringed on the copyright of the original work because his new recording featured reconstructed arrangements borrowed from the original sessions. It was a ludicrous argument that relied upon a very liberal interpretation of copyright laws, but it may have laid the groundwork to finally bring *The SMiLE Sessions* into existence just prior to the band's 50th anniversary. Still, Brian's newly reconstructed masterpiece was a splendid statement, 37 years in the making, a bold moment of creative agency, and a supreme act of intentionality on the part of its composer. Brian would not see it to completion in the 1970s when both Warners and CBS expressed interest (and cash) in the "completed" album, and instead he chose to allow the work to remain stillborn. Perhaps it was the 2004 release combined with Mike's steadfast belief that the Beach Boys had sustained the legend of *SMiLE* over three decades (we should not underestimate his desire to profit from its legacy) that the narrative was allowed to come full circle. With the approval of all parties, Capitol Records released *The SMiLE Sessions* in November 2011 in a multi-option, multi-format set of releases that gathered all of Brian's 1966 and 1967 *SMiLE*-era recordings, and presented them in a track order that was based largely upon Brian's 2004 reconstruction.

I've Been in This Town So Long

Brian stated, "We wanted to achieve something completely different, we were trying to create musical artistry."[6] Although *SMiLE* was a myth, at its core was a truth extraordinary in its beauty, remarkable in its construction, and honest in its kaleidoscopic story about the United States. While neither preaching or self-righteous, Van Dyke's narrative could be read as a critique of four centuries of American expansionism to remind us we were small players on an enormous stage populated with pilgrims, farmers, animals, cowboys, American Indians, Mexicans, Chinese, Hawaiians, surfers, sons, daughters, fathers, and mothers, all of whom were embraced by the elements of earth, water, air, and fire.[7] Like Marvin Gaye's 1971 masterpiece, *What's Going On*, it is a tale about a world that should have tipped out of balance into mayhem, and the lesson was that we had the power to exchange the hand of cards dealt to us by history and the legacy of those who came before us.[8]

SMiLE was Brian's "Teenage Symphony to God," and is a continuation of Brian's expression of the spiritual being in song.

The period from *Pet Sounds* to *SMiLE* was the last time Brian would fully engage with outside collaborators until he embarked on his solo career in 1988. In spite of all its dysfunctional players, Brian's devotion to his family would remain a mystery that no one from the outside could ever understand, and it was this devotion and the need for familial harmony that helped to derail *SMiLE*, Brother Records, and numerous others of Brian's creative aspirations. New members of Brian's circle of friends and associates unknowingly drove a wedge between him, the band, and his family, and once Brian shut the door on *SMiLE*, his authority and leadership had been challenged for the last time and he no longer had the interest or will to create with the same passion or energy that had fueled his creativity over the previous six years. The months from *Pet Sounds* through "Good Vibrations" to *SMiLE* were Brian's most creative and extraordinary months, "the beginning of the moment . . . a period of creativity that burned and died with supernova brilliance."[9] But the speed at which Brian could generate and create ideas simply became too much for the group, who, while they had been together since 1961, were not comfortable with many of Brian's ideas and did not approve of his circle of friends, advisors, and collaborators. So many things happened to Brian, to the Beach Boys, and to all involved in the making of *SMiLE*, that a brief timeline of events can help us to better understand this period.

February 1966—Work begins on "Good Vibrations."

May 1966—*Pet Sounds* is released, work continues on "Good Vibrations," and the first session for "Heroes and Villains" is tracked.

June 1966—Additional work on "Good Vibrations."

August 1966—Work on four pieces for *Dumb Angel* (the original working title of *SMiLE*), David Anderle works with Brian to organize Brother Records.

September 1966—Further work on "Good Vibrations" and two new works for *Dumb Angel.*

October 1966—"Good Vibrations" is released, *Dumb Angel* is retitled *SMiLE*, and work begins on over a dozen new pieces.

November 1966—Over half-a-dozen works are recorded for *SMiLE.*

December 1966—Five new works are recorded for *SMiLE*, Beach Boys are voted "Most Popular Vocal Group" in Britain with the Beatles coming in second in the New Musical Express poll, Capitol begins their promotion for *SMiLE.* CBS films Brian for the *Inside Pop* TV special.

January 1967—Numerous sessions for "Heroes and Villains."

February 1967—Continued work on "Heroes and Villains"; Beach Boys file a lawsuit against Capitol Records.

March 1967—Van Dyke Parks leaves the project over conflicts with certain members of the band. This, in combination with emerging business issues around Brother Records, distract Brian from his work in the studio.

April 1967—Van Dyke briefly returns to the project, but leaves once again and numerous sessions are recorded for "Vege-Tables"; CBS airs *Inside Pop: The Rock Revolution*.

May 1967—Work on *SMiLE* slows to a crawl, yet Brian records a new work, "Love to Say Da Da." Beach Boys publicist Derek Taylor announces to a British music magazine that *SMiLE* has been scrapped and he terminates his employment with the Beach Boys. Beach Boys tour of the UK receives mixed reviews.

June–July 1967—Songs from *SMiLE* are rerecorded for a new project, *Smiley Smile*. Beach Boys withdraw from their spot at the Monterey Pop Festival.

September 1967—*Smiley Smile* is released.

While some observers continue to treat *Pet Sounds* and *SMiLE* as works from distinct periods in Brian's creative trajectory, there was a significant overlap between the two albums that were linked by the extended gestation of "Good Vibrations." The freedom with which he experimented on *Pet Sounds* instilled in him the confidence he needed to create an album wholly on modules or "feels." Everything was intended to be interchangeable, individual ideas were no longer wedded to one or other "song" and could be borrowed and combined with any other module.

When Brian retired from the road at the end of 1964, he had to adjust to a new life that no longer was structured around travel, concert stages, and hotels, and could focus solely on making records. He and Marilyn were married at the end of the year and their house on Laurel Way became a destination for people who wanted access to Brian. Friends from the business, such as Terry Melcher, David Crosby, and Roger McGuinn were friendly associates, others like Loren Schwartz would introduce Brian to a range of new and (to him) exciting people who were so different from the people he knew in Hawthorne. Of course, the nobody hangers-on, who Marilyn described as "The Users," slid into his world but were minor players when compared to those Brian invited into his orbit.[10] When Tony Asher began work on *Pet Sounds,* he learned to adjust to a undisciplined world where Brian stayed-up late, slept-in late, ate enormous meals, and dawdled around before he ever sat down at the piano. Like a school kid in the first weeks of vacation, Brian kept to a schedule that was entirely his own. This would evolve into a more fluid and highly constructive set of routines as he created *Pet Sounds* and moved away from non-Beach Boys productions. By the time he arrived at *SMiLE*, it was clear that Wilson had so much to say, yet he required a structure that could provide him with the creative freedom needed to express his ideas, and would need skilled professional guidance to help him realize these goals.

The first step was the Beach Boys's hire of Nick Grillo as their manager. They had attempted, with mixed success, to work with temporary solutions after Murry had been fired, but Nick would help them to organize their expansive financial and personal needs; for in him they had a lawyer who understood responsible accounting practices as well as personnel management, and he attempted to bring a level of organization and fiscal responsibility to the Beach Boys's business activities. Murry was still in the picture, as he continued to wrest full control of Sea of Tunes from Brian, and would be seen at occasional recording sessions. Through Loren Schwartz, Brian met David Anderle, one of Hollywood's hip, young agents, who was an ideas man with savvy business skills. Through him, Brian met Danny Hutton, a rising figure in the Los Angeles music scene, Michael Vosse, another manager/organizer, and would become reacquainted with Van Dyke Parks, whom he initially met through David Crosby in mid-1965. Anderle understood Brian's relentless curiosity and could see that he had more ideas and plans than could be realized through the traditional arrangements the Beach Boys had with Capitol Records, so he helped Brian to create Brother Records and was appointed the first president of the company. Derek Taylor, a recent transplant from England and the Beatles former publicist (he would later return to work with the Beatles at Apple Records), was hired to help the Beach Boys update their stale, unhip, and conservative image. Brian understood that music had moved beyond the candy-striped shirt era, and the band needed to reflect the period instead of holding on to a now-vanished Kennedy-era wholesomeness. Taylor met the Beach Boys when they moved into the office across the hall from his at 9000 Sunset Boulevard. Brian hired him because he saw in Derek someone who could help the Beach Boys and knew Taylor would have the imagination and vision to bring the band into the present day.[11]

The creation of Brother Records was concurrent with Brian's work on *SMiLE*, and was just one facet of this extraordinarily creative period. While the Beach Boys remained with Capitol, Brother Records would allow Brian to express his ever-expanding creative palate and enable him to record acts and pursue non-Beach Boys projects that might otherwise have a limited or noncommercial appeal. Humor albums, improvisational comedy, and nature sounds were some of the ideas Brian had in mind for Brother Records.[12] It was a similar model to what the Beatles would attempt after 1967, with limited success, through Apple Corps. Brother Records also served to distract Brian from *SMiLE* in the winter of 1967, at the very time he needed to focus on the record. Anderle also became a point of conflict within the Beach Boys family as the band would return from tour to find new people, agendas, and plans, in which they may or may not have been involved. They were suspicious of many in Brian's new circle, and when he explained that his ideas would be beneficial to everyone in the group, it only served to widen the gap that would lead to his breakdown in mid-1967. The band voiced their mistrust for Brian's associates, which spilled into their mistrust of Brian's business agendas, his musical vision, and his leadership. It may have appeared to the group that as the touring band that performed his music in concert, they were responsible for the business end of things and Brian was only required to write accessible, hit music for the group. Anderle admitted that he was not sure that the Beach Boys should have been a part of Brother Records because it was designed to serve Brian's creative voice.[13] He also maintains he was not out to break-up the Beach Boys, and worked to include everyone and keep it together because he learned that hassles with the family would have horrendously unhealthy consequences for Brian, and he was already aware of the resistance the band members had shown towards *SMiLE*. He tried to encourage Brian to go on with the project as a solo album because he understood that it was his personal vision and not the band's idea of who they were.

As with *Pet Sounds*, Brian composed "feels" to create *SMiLE*, and "feels" poured out of him as he recorded dozens of ideas and snippets of ideas that would be added to his perpetually evolving composition. On previous albums, Brian came into the studio with ideas mapped-out, either on paper or in his head, but with *SMiLE*, he came in with little more than a "feel" or "module," and was open to how that might develop in the studio. This approach was just one point of friction between Brian and others within the band. Anderle wanted to keep Brian believing that "... everything is possible, nothing is impossible. Nothing is so silly that we can't pull it off, nothing is so serious that we can't pull it off."[14] While he was there to assist Brian in realizing his ideas, he clearly wanted Brian to feel completely at ease to create *SMiLE*. "Happening quickly" is how Brian described this period. The music was serious, the lyrics were important, and the sounds were very different from anything he had done previously. He was interested not only in music and film but in all forms of communication.[15] He wanted to create a new kind of radio, with no format save for humor and gentleness. Anderle acknowledged that all of Brian's ideas "struck our ears as totally insane ... anything he said was right, no matter how outlandish it seemed ... he never had one idea that was simple."

To create *SMiLE*, Brian engaged with a progressive and challenging collaborator, whom he described as someone who "knew about everything."[16] Van Dyke Parks provided the colorful prose that was unlike anything heard in popular music, and "dragged Brian away from the familiar territory of romantic love towards a new style of writing ..."[17] Parks, as a precocious youth, had acted in films and was now a musician and lyricist who made the rounds on the coffeehouse circuit. He was the foil who would provide Brian with the most dynamic narratives of his songwriting career. In their first sessions they composed "Heroes and Villains," "Wonderful," "Cabin Essence," and "Surf's Up," which became the primary themes of the album. *SMiLE* was not so much a story, but a historical travelogue of the country's westward expansion. Because this was Brian's work, Van Dyke's lyrics could never possess an air of pretension. Even in its most surreal moments, the prose was sincere and straightforward. Where *Pet Sounds* was a concept album, *SMiLE* was a song cycle in a model not terribly different from Franz Schubert's *Winterreise* (Winter Journey).[18] As with Schubert's late opus (he died at the age of 31, the same year he completed *Winterreise), SMiLE* was not simply a collection of songs, but a single monologue and an expression of the artists' deepest and most visceral emotions.

We are fortunate to have documentation of the events that occurred when Brian was in the process of making the album. Jules Siegel, writing for the *Saturday Evening Post*, and Paul Williams, founder of *Crawdaddy*, each had access to Brian over an extended period of time and documented events between fall 1966 and the early summer of 1967. In the years that followed Brian's decision to shelve the work, interest in this unheard, purported masterpiece only increased, and thanks to the writings of David Leaf, Brad Elliott, Domenic Priore, and others, fans were provided with guides that helped to unpack a work that officially never existed. By the 1980s, a variety of *SMiLE*-era recordings had begun to circulate on bootlegs. Through these unofficial releases, fans could begin to envision the scope of Brian's historical panorama, and only then did the cult of *SMiLE* take on a life of its own. Jules Siegel, in his 2011 afterword to *Goodbye Surfing, Hello God*, claimed that "if it weren't for me there would be no cult of *SMiLE*." While the writings of Siegel and Williams provided the initial impetus from which further research could be undertaken, the cult of *SMiLE* developed from decades of shared research, shared bootleg recordings, and discussions among hardcore fans of both Brian and the band. To give him his credit, especially now that Williams has passed away, Siegel was privy to so much of Brian's process, that his recollections can be accorded serious consideration as he provides a dark, complex, and at times, sad picture of an artist on the threshold of something magical that ultimately became intangible and unattainable. For all of the beauty one can construct around Brian's desire to create spiritual music, Siegel also addressed the other, equally complex, side of this equation stating that "Brian was creating emotional, religious, spiritual music, and there was no room for everyday reality."

The now voluminous research on *SMiLE* stands on the thorough and exhaustive inquiries undertaken by engineer Mark Linett, Wilson biographer David Leaf, Beach Boys archivist Alan Boyd, and multiple lines of research by Brad Elliott, Craig Slowinski, Peter Reum, Domenic Priore, and others. Domenic Priore, regarded as one of the world's leading experts on *SMiLE*, published *Look! Listen! Vibrate! SMILE!* under the auspices of the *Dumb Angel Gazette*, which has been the primary, single-volume collection of articles and interviews about *SMiLE*. While the composition was finished with the release of *Brian Wilson Presents SMiLE* in 2004 and *The SMiLE Sessions* in 2011, Priore's book serves as an important key to follow three-and-a-half decades of information about this work. This collection, part discography, part collage, and part biography, may look like an amateurish scrapbook, Priore's decision to present the materials in this manner allowed him to eschew traditional editorial processes in order to provide readers with an opportunity to construct their own conclusions about *SMiLE*.[19] While his unstructured editing may have been in response to limited financial resources, it managed to preserve the tenor of the period in which Wilson created this work. The book contains facsimiles of original press materials that lend an air of authenticity to the collection, as they would have been encountered in 1967, when it was just another Brian Wilson-produced Beach Boys record.

SMiLE was a period of extraordinary creativity for Brian as much as it was the album slated to follow *Pet Sounds*. Before Leaf and Priore published their research on *SMiLE*, fans knew of the music through the following sources:

> ***SMiLE*** (Capitol T 2580, unreleased)—The back cover slick for the unreleased album listed 12 songs with the caveat, "See label for the correct playing order." This list was copied in the order of Brian's handwritten note (with the misspelling of Villains as "Villians") to Capitol with a partial list of the tracks that would appear on the album. This was prepared in late 1966, before Brian had begun to consider any track order. Mark Linett's notes in *The SMiLE Sessions* highlights the fact that the 12-song list on the album jacket totals approximately 50 minutes of music. This would have required a commitment from Capitol to expand to a double-album release, or to cut 15 to 20 minutes of music from a single-disc release. None of the existing documentation of the period addresses the possibility of a two-album release.[20] The two-column list offered the following songs:
>
> "Do You Like Worms"
> "Wind Chimes"
> "Heroes and Villians [*sic*]"
> "Surf's Up"
> "Good Vibrations"
> "Cabin Essence"
> "Wonderful"
> "I'm in Great Shape"
> "Child Is Father of the Man"
> "The Elements"[21]
> "Vega-Tables"
> "The Old Master Painter"
>
> ***Smiley Smile*** (September 18, 1967)—Many of the songs created for *SMiLE* were re-worked with new and radically stripped-down arrangements for *Smiley Smile* and bore little in comparison, save for song titles, to their original versions:
>
> "Heroes and Villains" (Used the original verse and chorus backing tracks with newly added sections)
> "Vegetables" (New, except for the use of two brief sections from the end of the original Vega-Tables)

"Fall Breaks and Back to Winter" (Material borrowed from "Fire: Mrs. O'Leary's Cow" in a simplified arrangement)

"She's Goin' Bald" (From the *SMiLE*-era track "He Gives Speeches")

"Little Pad" (Related to "Love to Say Da Da" that would later be used as a source for "Cool, Cool Water" and finally on "In Blue Hawaii" on *Brian Wilson Presents SMiLE*. In each of these four instances, these tracks are believed to represent the "Water" component of the "Elements.")

"Good Vibrations" (unchanged from official "single" mix)

"With Me Tonight" (created in the transition from *SMiLE* to *Smiley Smile*)

"Wind Chimes"

"Wonderful"

"Whistle In" (from a fragment related to "Heroes and Villains")

Wild Honey (December 18, 1967)

"Mama Says" (Coda from the original "Vega-Tables")

20/20 (February 10, 1969)—Carl secured two works from *SMiLE*, both of which appeared in as near to an original state as Brian had intended for *SMiLE*.

"Our Prayer" (Doubled vocal tracks were added to Brian's original track)

"Cabinessence" (Originally "Cabin Essence")[22]

Sunflower (August 31, 1970)

"Cool, Cool Water" (Brian composed this based on an extended fragment from "Love to Say Da Da." Brian's first attempt at "Cool, Cool Water" occurred early in the sessions for *Smiley Smile* and resumed in October 1967 sessions for *Wild Honey*. It remained unfinished until label executive Lenny Waronker convinced Brian to complete the work for *Sunflower*).

Surf's Up (August 30, 1971)

Jack Rieley and Carl "pressured" Brian to help them complete the already legendary track for their new album. After the disappointing sales of *Sunflower*, Warners wanted a surefire hit, and Rieley, in his function to bring the Beach Boys into the current, counter-culture mainstream, wanted Brian to complete this track. Carl, with Brian's suggestions, cobbled together the nearly finished pieces of Brian's stunning late-1966 work that were first heard on the *Inside Pop* documentary in spring 1967. Carl would add instrumental support and new vocals to Brian's original 1966 tracks.[23]

No one but Brian knew how *SMiLE* was supposed to fit together, and when pressured, he could deny he ever knew because his modular construction techniques did not predicate a prescribed narrative and everything was in-process when he ceased work on the album. There were rumors of multiple versions of "Heroes and Villains," in addition to the many short works that shared this title. This would only confuse matters because a narrative emerged to support the belief that "Heroes . . ." existed in substantially longer edits that topped out at over six and seven minutes in length. "Do You Dig Worms" is one of the more interesting pieces of the *SMiLE* puzzle. It received an official release on the *Good Vibrations* boxed set, but McParland documented the process used to create this work. Recorded over a five-and-a-half-hour session, it began with Brian asking Chuck Britz to roll the tape, over which he continued to improvise a series of parts using the "Heroes . . ." motif and unrelated themes until he filled all available tracks on the tape.

Bootleg recordings of *SMiLE* were more widely disseminated throughout the 1980s, and fans debated about the song order of the album and tried to re-create what Brian "might have done." This led to a fan culture where people would create their own mix tapes/CDs and share them among other collectors who also made their own *SMiLE* mixes.[24] The inclusion of 30 minutes of previously unreleased *SMiLE* materials on the *Good Vibrations* boxed set allowed us to hear, in sonically superior mixes, many of the tracks that had circulated on bootlegs, but with the release of *BWPS*, it became clear Brian used elements of "Heroes and Villains" as an "idée fixe" or "fixed melody" throughout *SMiLE*.[25] The melodic figure that underscores the text "Heroes and Villains" was used in multiple variations throughout *SMiLE*, as was an eighth-note, broken-chord accompaniment figure that was used to support numerous melodic figures. While these elements may not meet the formal requirements of an idée fixe, they function in a similar manner. The melodic motif is built around scale degrees 2, flat-2 and 6 (which alternates with scale degree 5 at the end of the phrase), and its corresponding rhythmic gesture of long (2)-short (2)-short (flat-2), long (2), long (6 or 5) in the chorus under the text "Heroes and Villains." This dissonant melodic line, paired with an accompaniment that implies a sense of continuous momentum, allowed each musical section to unfold into unresolved transitions. The smaller phrases built on "Heroes and Villains" were simply iterations of the idée fixe that were used to affix Brian's song cycle into place.

The "idée fixe" is most frequently associated with Hector Berlioz and his *Symphonie Fantastique*. Composed in 1830, this Romantic-era symphony is a central work in the orchestral repertoire. In an episode of Leonard Bernstein's *Young People's Concerts* that aired on May 25, 1969, titled *Berlioz Takes a Trip*, he describes *Fantastique* as the first psychedelic symphony. Berlioz's own program notes at the 1830 premiere of the symphony read:

> A young musician of a morbidly sensitive nature and a feverish imagination poisons himself with opium in a fit of lovesick despair. The narcotic dose, too weak to cause death, plunges him into a heavy sleep accompanied by the strangest visions, during which his feelings, sensations and memories are translated by his sick brain into musical thoughts and images.

Elements of Berlioz's text (morbidly sensitive . . . feverish imagination . . . sensations and memories . . . translated . . . into musical thoughts and images) could just as easily describe Brian at the time of *SMiLE's* gestation. He had already experimented with LSD and had sought to compose a work of great sacred and spiritual import, equal to what Berlioz sought to express in his sensual and profane symphony. Two years prior to the *Young People's* episode, Bernstein provided commentary for a CBS news special hosted by David Oppenheim, *Inside Pop: The Rock Revolution*, in which Brian was a featured artist. Oppenheim introduced "Surf's Up" in Brian's now-legendary solo performance recorded at his home on December 17, 1966. It was first recorded for the cameras two days earlier at Columbia studio, and though that version was not aired, it would serve as the core of Carl Wilson's 1971 reconstruction of the song. This CBS clip was the only "original" fragment of *SMiLE* to have been aired to the public and was the first time Brian's music was deemed worthy of comparison and analysis with "serious" art music.[26] Brian sought to incorporate two qualities that, in other settings, might be seen to be mutually exclusive, humor and spirituality. He believed humor could be a solution for man's ills and viewed humor and spirituality as two sides of the same coin. While he wanted to infuse laughter and humor into his music, he wanted to make sincerity into something that was "hip" and to create white spiritual music, something he knew would be difficult for many people. Brian wanted to create "music people will pray to." Michael Vosse would later describe it as a "Southern California non-country-oriented gospel album . . . Brian was going for . . . his own form of revival music."[27] He believed in the spiritual power of laughter, and *SMiLE* was "American Gospel" from the perspective of a native Southern Californian.

SMiLE addressed the effects upon both man and nature from 300 years of American expansionism across North America and the Western Hemisphere, and asks us to consider a shift in the arrangement of the then-current world order. In conversation with Jules Siegel, Brian used the lyrics of "Surf's Up" to articulate his ideas:

> . . . the audience, playing their roles . . . so far away from the drama, from life . . . "Columnated ruins domino." Empires, ideas, lives, institutions—everything has to fall, tumbling like dominoes . . . Reality is gone; he's creating it like a dream. "Dove-nested towers." Europe, a long time ago . . . "While at port adieu or die." . . . A kind of Roman empire thing. "A choke of grief." . . . his own sorrow and the emptiness of his life, because he can't even cry for the suffering in the world, for his own suffering . . . And then hope, Surf's up . . . "'I heard the word'—of God . . . the joy of enlightenment, of seeing God . . . the song of God, hiding the love from us, but always letting us find it again . . . "

This was a reflection of Brian's concerns with ecology, culture, family, and God. Siegel concludes by saying that after Brian's sincere explanation, he went into the kitchen and squirted Reddi-Whip from the can into his mouth, and ate a couple of candy bars. Brilliance, the id of a child, or creativity in its purest form?

From the opening of "Heroes and Villains," Brian and Van Dyke take us on a 5,000-mile tour of the "American Experience" as traced from Plymouth Rock, Massachusetts to the Hawaiian Islands. Wilson associate Tom Nolan described *SMiLE* as "an intimate epic, a vision and history of America . . . as experienced via the mind, the memory, the consciousness of a two-minded pilgrim in progress through time and inner space." Hawaii was granted statehood in 1959 as the 50th state in the union, in the same year Brian entered his final year of high school. Schoolkids of that generation were encouraged to embrace a sense of national pride in their country's extraordinary topographic footprint as Plymouth Rock and Hawaii represented two bookends of this nation's successful occupation of North America. Brian may have had no desire or intention to make a political statement, but a worldly and well-read Van Dyke could express politically and socially charged themes through his lyrics. The text for *SMiLE* could be considered a call for his generation to reevaluate the havoc wrought upon the continent, upon Native American populations (including the native inhabitants of the Hawaiian Islands), whose cultural footprint had been compromised and often decimated with every expansionist opportunity. The story also addressed the natural world that greeted our forefathers and fueled their singular desire to acquire and tame all that lay before them. By the time Brian composed *SMiLE*, the phrase "Surf's Up" was an acknowledgment that this call to action evoked a past that could never be recaptured. *SMiLE* was a young man's story, just as the story of the United States was the story of a young nation built on youthful confidence, ingenuity, and ambition. The story Brian and Van Dyke created asked us to stop, look, and consider where we were headed, to laugh at the madness, to find humor wrought by the modern world, and to allow ourselves to reconnect with some higher power, experience, or belief system.

In the first session for *SMiLE* on May 11, Brian tracked "Heroes and Villains," before he had finished "Good Vibrations." He continued to work on "Good Vibrations" through May and June before he took a month-long break. When he returned to the studio early in August, he began work on "Wind Chimes," "Look (Song for Children)," and continued with "Good Vibrations," which he finally completed in late September. Brian forged ahead with "Holidays" and "He Gives Speeches," the latter of which would be resurrected on *Smiley Smile's* "She's Goin Bald." From October 3 to 20, Brian tracked the "Home on the Range" section for "Cabin Essence," "Our Prayer," "Wind Chimes," "Wonderful," "Child Is Father of the Man," "Look" and the "I'm in Great Shape" section for "Heroes and Villains," "Vega-Tables," and "Do You Like Worms." Brian took a break while the band filmed (in their one off day before travelling to Michigan) the promotional video for "Good Vibrations." The Beach Boys performed a pair of shows in East Lansing on October 21 and in Ann Arbor the following day, where they premiered the live version of "Good Vibrations." Brian flew out to coach the band on their performance and returned home. Upon arrival at Los Angeles International Airport, the now famous series of photographs were taken that feature Brian and Marilyn with a number of friends, relatives, and associates. The next day, the band travelled to Europe for their second official European tour.

Before the end of October, Brian resumed work on "Heroes and Villains" and tracked "Surf's Up." He continued work on "Vega-Tables," and began work on his arrangement of "You Are My Sunshine." He resumed work after the Thanksgiving holiday to focus on vocal tracking sessions. In December 1966, he began sessions for "The Elements," "I Wanna Be Around," "You're Welcome," and the "Iron Horse" section for "Cabin Essence." In the midst of this, Brian was filmed by David Oppenheim for the "Inside Pop" documentary where he performed his solo arrangement of "Surf's Up." In spite of this extraordinary activity, Capitol could not get Brian to deliver *SMiLE* for the 1966 holiday sales season. In the new year, the entire project would become more difficult, complex, and emotionally damaging to Brian as 1967 promised to be a period of unrivaled creativity in the field of popular music.

In anticipation of a record they believed would be delivered for a mid-January release, Capitol hired Frank Holmes to create the unique cover art as well as an elaborate booklet that would include lyrics and pictures of the band. Van Dyke Parks met Frank Holmes at the Insomniac Café in Hermosa Beach (where Van Dyke once performed in his coffeehouse days), introduced Holmes to Brian, who commissioned from him the cover and lyric booklet for the album.[28]

When the Beach Boys returned from their European tour in November 1966, they were at the top of their game. They had been voted the top group in Britain, over both the Beatles and the Rolling Stones. They had a massive hit single with "Good Vibrations" but returned to Los Angeles to find Brian at work on music that made little sense to some members of the band. Anderle described the Beach Boys upon their return as "triumphant heroes" with their awards and their latest hit, but "...found the town had changed."[29] They came back to find unfamiliar faces, none of whom had any history with the Beach Boys except for Brian, so it was natural they would want to reassert their position and reclaim his attention. Van Dyke was the first to come under criticism at vocal sessions in December, which soured his relationship with Brian. While Brian already had countless pieces of the "Heroes and Villains" puzzle in the can, his inability to find a direction for the work led him back into the studio to create even more music. The humorous Jasper Dailey sessions occurred in the midst of this and demonstrate that Brian was still thinking "outside" of his Beach Boys duties.[30] February led to March and "Heroes..." gave way to "Vege-Tables" as the next single.

As with "Heroes . . . ," Brian had become lost within his mass of musical modules and could not decide upon definitive versions for either song.

In the first two months of 1967, Brian had focused everything on "Heroes and Villains."[31] As productive as he had been in late 1966, he fell into an obsessive, repetitive pattern in response to mounting pressures, which ultimately slowed momentum on *SMiLE* and caused him to second- and triple-guess every decision he made for every section of every song.[32] With dozens of vocal and instrumental sections now recorded and the increasing number of possible directions in which Brian could take his songs, he could no longer retain control of the process.[33] Van Dyke left the project in late winter, returned briefly, but left for good in April. Mike Love continually questioned Parks as to the meaning of his lyrics, for which Parks maintained that his lyrics had no specific meaning. These conflicts served as the primary impetus for his departure from *SMiLE*.[34] Van Dyke's presence, and the closeness he had developed with Brian, did not set well with the band. He was a flamboyant, elfin character who could hustle his career as easily as he could make music. Once he left, the supportive and protective support team upon whom Brian had come to rely over the previous year began to break down. With Van Dyke no longer there, Brian's "creative spark began to wane . . . he obsessively rearranged the pieces of the *SMiLE* puzzle . . . trying to form a coherent picture."[35] In mid-March, the band was out for a brief Midwest tour, and upon their return, Brian ran them through 10 dates of vocal sessions for "Vege-Tables," which he announced to Capitol would be their next single.[36] That too would be withdrawn as Brian was unable to bring it to completion. The new business opportunities provided by the nascent Brother Records would slow all activities and become an additional distraction for Brian. This convergence of events gave the band more reason to express their frustrations with an album that was not yet complete. Brian's mounting paranoia and artistic indecision presented an opportunity for the Beach Boys to reassert their influence and control over Brian's work and by the end of 1967, Parks, Anderle, Vosse, and others were gone from Brian's circle.

The final sessions for *SMiLE* occurred between May 16 and 19, when Brian recorded "Love to Say Da Da." Rather than serving as the "nail-in-the-coffin" for *SMiLE*, this work served multiple functions and would likely have been the "Water" component of the "Elements," but it also provided material from which Brian would create "Little Pad," on *Smiley Smile*, and *Sunflower's* "Cool, Cool Water." In the 2004 production of *BWPS*, we heard "In Blue Hawaii" as the logical conclusion to ". . . Da Da," with new lyrics by Van Dyke Parks that tied the "Water" element into the final tableau of the album.

What came between Brian and his creative team? Most sources point to the Beach Boys and the family.[37] He had challenged himself to compete with the Beatles and single-handedly dealt with ongoing pressures from Capitol to produce their next hit record. He faced a band that was resistant to *SMiLE's* lyrics, unsure of its very concept and structure, and all the while the group and the label were in litigation over royalties. His only choice was to stop, but to do so, *SMiLE* had to stop. He felt it was killing him and had it continued on, it might have ended the Beach Boys. How close was Brian to the completion of *SMiLE*? There are many opinions on this but as a nonfamily member of group, Al Jardine, is afforded a slightly more objective view of Brian and acknowledged in conversation with Elliott, "It's not far from completion." Bruce Johnston who, as the true outsider within the group, would have the most objective and extended view of the dynamic within the band and would also admit that he too believed it was pretty close. He stated "... with Brian, you were almost overdubbing as you went to the lathe to cut the parts so just don't know until it's out."[38] He understood this work was completely different than what anyone might have expected from Brian Wilson and felt the album should have been released on Angel Records, the classical music imprint for Capitol/EMI in North America.[39] Whatever his reasons, Brian stopped all work on *SMiLE*. On June 3, two weeks after his last session for "Love to Say Da Da," Brian began tracking sessions for *Smiley Smile*.

In the first years of the new millennium Brian and his band wowed audiences around the globe with live shows that included the complete *Pet Sounds*, but he was notably less active in 2003, except for the sessions that became his next studio album, *Gettin' In Over My Head*. If it appeared that much of the year was spent in the wings, the real excitement was in response to an announcement in May 2003 that Brian and his band would premiere *SMiLE* in concert at London's Royal Festival Hall in February 2004. The process behind *SMiLE's* reconstruction was captured in the David Leaf-directed documentary, *Beautiful Dreamer*. The journey Brian had traveled to complete this work was made possible; for while he had Parks, Anderle, and Vosse to support him in 1966, he now had the support of Melinda with Darian Sahanaja, Jeffrey Foskett, his entire touring band, and Van Dyke Parks. Sahanaja and Foskett served as repetiteurs who learned the individual parts and taught them to the other band members, not entirely dissimilar to how Brian communicated his ideas to the studio musicians who recorded the work over three decades earlier. The album was recorded over the spring and early summer of 2004 and released in September of that year.

The 2004 edition of *SMiLE* was the reconstruction of a nearly complete work and not a revival of a formerly shelved or unreleased work. Wilson's band had, in the early years of the new millennium, begun to integrate songs from *SMiLE* into their live shows as a means to comfortably engage Brian with the works that for so many years represented his greatest failure and unhappiness, but as he became more comfortable with the material, he agreed to present the entire work in concert. What remained was for him to connect the pieces and complete the few links left unfinished upon Van Dyke's departure in winter 1967. Fortunately, Parks was willing to join the project and complete the work. For those who felt *SMiLE* was so close to completion in 1967, Sahanaja confirmed it when he constructed an order of works for Brian's approval.

The earlier work of Boyd, Linett, and Elliott brought integral source materials to light that helped Sahanaja to construct a template from which Brian could move forward to finish the song cycle. Parks, upon his return, completed lyrics that fit into the existing narrative for a pair of structurally critical works, "Do You Like Worms" (which was transformed into "Roll Plymouth Rock") and "Love to Say Da Da" (now transformed into "In Blue Hawaii"). In 1966, Brian incorporated sections of four cover songs within *SMiLE* to serve as musical links and retained them in the 2004 version. The first, "Gee," is an early doo-wop tune originally recorded in 1953 by the Crows. This piece helped to bridge the spiritual air of "Our Prayer" to the electric energy of "Heroes and Villains."[40] He merged two mid-century, popular standards and used the melody of "The Old Master Painter" in tandem with Paul Rice's "You Are My Sunshine."[41] This medley served as a link to the album's two most "Americana"-themed works, "Barnyard" and "Cabin Essence." The last borrowed work Wilson included was the 1959 Johnny Mercer tune, "I Wanna Be Around."

One significant feature of this reconstruction was its organization into three sections or movements. Neither bound by the 12 titles listed on the back cover of the unreleased album, nor by the physical limitations of a two-sided vinyl album, Brian was able to order the songs in a way that supported his and Van Dyke's narrative of a journey across three centuries of the American Experience. The band's arrangements were prepared by Sahanaja, and while not exact transcriptions, they were modeled on Brian's original arrangements and are strikingly similar to the timbre and feel of the 1966–1967 recordings. Wilson's reeds player and orchestrator, Paul Mertens, led the Stockholm Strings "n" Horns and Brian's multi-instrumentalist band were able to create both on record and in concert, Brian's elaborate and technically demanding instrumental tracks.

While fans filled concert halls to hear Brian and his band perform *SMiLE* and purchased the compact disc in healthy quantities, his work was recognized with a number of Grammy nominations that yielded one win, Best Rock Instrumental Performance for, of all pieces, "Mrs. O'Leary's Cow."[42] The compact disc was presented in a slipcase with a booklet that included the lyrics, notes by David Leaf, and Americana-inspired artwork that mashed nineteenth and early twentieth-century images informed by Parks's lyrics. The bright, sunny graphics were loosely reminiscent of Frank Holmes's original artwork.

With the 2011 release of *The SMiLE Sessions*, we heard a complete album that was based on the track list of *BWPS*. Included was a wealth of tracking sessions that showed Brian's compositional methods and allowed us to understand why no one but Brian could have any idea how the entire work would fit together. The 2004 reconstruction of *SMiLE*, in combination with the tracks from the 1993 boxed set, closed the door on this work and reflected the artists' decision to present the work in the order we heard on record and in concert. So while the 2011 release provided an engaging and fascinating view of Brian's process in the creation of the work, *The SMiLE Sessions* did not offer anything new beyond what had already been presented in 1993 and 2004.[43] In no way does this detract from the extraordinary effort that went into preparing . . . *Sessions*, a herculean effort that began nearly two decades earlier. Both Alan Boyd and Mark Linett remarked on the challenge of constructing Brian's masterpiece in the order presented on *BWPS* from the hundreds of hours of musically interchangeable fragments Brian recorded in 1966 and 1967. They also reported that the earlier loss of many session tapes required them, in certain instances, to rely upon inconsistent source materials of different generations to construct individual pieces.[44] Reum's essay in the accompanying booklet quotes a source who succinctly addresses the release of *Sessions*, saying "There's nothing more that needs to be said about it. Forget everything—the legends, the psychodrama, the delays. Forty-five years after Brian created . . . the most beautiful, singular, and original collection of compositions of the twentieth century . . . (the) music speaks for itself." After decades of fan-driven sleuthing over "what" exactly constituted *SMiLE*, we had, within the span of seven years, Brian's final word on the piece. While it may have added nothing new to our understanding of the work, the 2011 edition served an aesthetic and commercial need in that we were allowed to hear how the Beach Boys originally performed the work, and they were finally compensated for work they recorded over four decades earlier. After 37 years, we heard *SMiLE* as a wonderful, pure, but bittersweet experience. While Brian may have emerged from the shadow of this work in 2004, we also know so much of his suffering and psychic scarring can be traced to *SMiLE*.

Though *The SMiLE Sessions* borrowed a track order from *BWPS*, there were minor differences between the two. In 2004, Brian placed "I'm in Great Shape" at the opening of the third movement in a nostalgic, old-time band arrangement that served as a fitting introduction to the final section of the work. In constructing the 2011 edition, Brian chose to place this piece in the first movement, between "Roll Plymouth Rock" and "Barnyard."[45] This arrangement is not as fully realized, but is similar in feel to the version on *BWPS*. Van Dyke left the original sessions before he could produce the lyrics for "Holidays," so we heard the work in a purely instrumental arrangement, whereas on *BWPS* "On a Holiday" receives Van Dyke's lyrics and an interpolation of the text from "Roll Plymouth Rock" that prepares us for "Wind Chimes." "Love to Say Da Da," the bulk of which was recorded after Van Dyke's departure, was very much a work-in-progress when Brian closed the project in May 1967. On *BWPS*, the "Cool, Cool Water" motif is provided with a text that sets the stage for a more fully realized treatment on "In Blue Hawaii."

David Anderle, speaking about the enormous differences that exist between *Pet Sounds* and *SMiLE*, describes *Pet Sounds* as Brian's blue period and *SMiLE* as his cubist period. Brian felt that nothing else he recorded has topped the music he made with Van Dyke. Leaf, in the liner notes to *BWPS*, stated "This music was created by him not to cause pressure, but to ease it. He believed then and still believes in the spiritual power of laughter."

An Intermittent Genius (1967–1973)

4

Low Tides

While Brian ascended ever greater heights with "Good Vibrations" and his prolific creativity during sessions for *SMiLE*, he wanted to expand his creative imprint beyond the Beach Boys in ways that would involve more than producing other artists, something he had done regularly from 1962 to 1965. He hired David Anderle to set up a record label that would allow him to "vent his creative spleen."[1] The band's manager, Nick Grillo, ran an audit of Capitol's books and found an underpayment of royalties to both Brian (for production duties) and the band, which led to the Beach Boys filing a quarter-million-dollar lawsuit that enabled the band to hold *SMiLE* until the matter could be resolved. Additional stresses delayed the completion of the album when Wilson's collaborator, Van Dyke Parks, left the project after Mike Love and others questioned his surreal, alliterative prose. Brian and Van Dyke's working relationship was broken, and with it, so was the momentum he needed to complete *SMiLE*.

In April 1967, Carl Wilson was detained by FBI agents for his refusal to report for his military call-up. He claimed status as a conscientious objector and was eventually allowed to resume his work with the group, but the band reportedly was shaken by Carl's arrest. That May while in London to collect their New Musical Express award of "World's Top Vocal Group," they were prohibited by the British musician's union, from using four backup musicians who helped to enhance their stage sound. Without their supporting musicians, the quality of the band's live set suffered and they received less than glowing reviews.[2] In addition, publicist Derek Taylor announced to the

British press in *Disc and Echo* that *SMiLE* had been scrapped, though it is unlikely that Brian knew of this since he was in the studio a few days after Taylor's proclamation at work on a new *SMiLE* track, "I Love to Say Da Da."[3] Perhaps it was the poor reviews overseas where critics questioned the validity of a live band that could not faithfully reproduce the songs heard on their increasingly elaborate records, but the measured disintegration of *SMiLE* and the transition into new sessions for its proxy, *Smiley Smile*, compounded already existing problems that surrounded the band in light of Carl's arrest.[4] In the face of these challenges, Brian pulled the band from their slot at the Monterey Pop Festival on June 17, 1967, and with it, he removed an opportunity to claim their spot in the "new" music of their generation. This was the first step in the Beach Boys's irreversible fall from grace, and while Brian, who remained the de facto leader of the band, was responsible for this miscalculated decision, it was just one in a series of events that hastened his emotional decline.

Brian's world imploded in the first half of 1967 in response to a sequence of events that consisted of corporate pressures, interfamily struggles for power, excessive use of various substances, and ill-timed legal actions. In the first half of the year, while the world awaited *SMiLE, Are You Experienced, The Velvet Underground and Nico, Surrealistic Pillow,* and *Sgt. Pepper's Lonely Hearts Club Band* were released to an anxious and maturing youth market. In the three months that followed the fall release of *Smiley Smile*, three distinct, but equally important albums, *Disraeli Gears, The Who Sell Out*, and *Days of Future Passed,* were issued. Each of these albums represented a radical shift in the genre, and the period in which they were created occurred as Brian Wilson withdrew as leader of the Beach Boys and entered the "eccentric" phase of his career. Brian had given every ounce of his being to create some of the most timeless and extraordinary music of the decade, but the deafening rejection of his vision and the abuse of trust in his leadership surely led to his decision to retreat from his role as the guiding voice of the Beach Boys.

The end of *SMiLE* marked the end of an era where Beach Boys albums read, "Produced by Brian Wilson." Beginning with *Smiley Smile,* the credit, "Produced by the Beach Boys," reflected a democratically directed band where production duties were handled by the primary songwriter of a given work, or left under Carl Wilson's oversight. Brian would continue to provide a majority of the group's songs until *Friends*, with Mike Love as his primary collaborator, but he began to include other band members and a select group of new "outsiders." Asher and Parks followed a path not dissimilar to one followed by Usher and Christian just a few years prior, so nonfamily members with whom they collaborated were restricted to secondary roles and the band once again became a "family" concern, and Brian was encouraged (or bullied) to focus his creative energies on the Beach Boys. David Leaf maintains that Brian was by this time more of a benefactor than an artist to the family.[5] Brian could have broken up the Beach Boys but for reasons known only to him, he was unable to resolve the conflict of whether to break away (a prophetic title for their 1969 single) from the family to move forward on his own, or to stay in a familiar, but unhealthy, series of relationships. In spite of this, Brian remained active in the studio and produced a number of excellent songs with strong arrangements and production values. When he chose to work with other artists, they inevitably were pushed out of the picture by either Mike or Carl, who continually pressured Brian to give his time, his work, and his physical self, to the Beach Boys. They may have rejected *SMiLE*, along with Brian's visionary leadership and creativity, but in doing so they also destroyed Brian's spirit. Whether it was jealousy, greed, or irritation, by late 1967, the group acted as if they owned or, more importantly, were owed the creative capital that was Brian Wilson. In response, Brian would retreat further and further from the center and by 1972–1973, he would produce little, if anything, for the band that, just one decade earlier, he led to fame and success.

As *SMiLE* ceased to exist, *Smiley Smile* entered the audio sphere of the Brian Wilson canon. Lambert defines the period that covers the four albums from *Smiley Smile* to *20/20*, as Brian's period of "re-definition."[6] Carl Wilson's legendary critique of *Smiley Smile*, " . . . it was a bunt instead of a grand slam," may have been intended to ease fans into the 11-song collection released in the fall of 1967, but the first two of four new studio albums that concluded the band's relationship with Capitol did not look distinctly different, at least not on the surface, from the albums before *Pet Sounds*.[7] Brian composed a majority of the songs, but the credit "Produced by the Beach Boys" replaced "Produced by Brian Wilson." Though Brian produced his songs (often in partnership with Carl), he opted for simplicity over opulence and would no longer direct the band's sonic aesthetic.

Fans who were left waiting for *SMiLE* would find ways to justify Brian's diminished creative activity in the years that followed, but the magical word, *SMiLE*, would never be erased from either Brian's or the band's narrative. The myriad challenges Brian faced in the Beach Boys's early years continued as before. Conflicts with Murry, conflicts with other members of the band, and his bottomless well of self-doubt were more present than ever. The non-release of *SMiLE* created the legend of the greatest "lost-album" in the history of popular music and would haunt Brian's career for more than three decades. Every Beach Boys album that followed *Smiley Smile* would be compared, often unfavorably, to Brian's unrealized, and largely unheard, masterpiece.

Sessions for *Smiley Smile* began on June 3, 1967, at Hollywood Recorders. For the first sessions, Chuck Britz was at the mixing board, and on the surface it appeared Brian had chosen to drop one project to pick up an entirely new project.[8] Within a week, sessions would be moved into Brian's house, where Jim Lockhart would engineer the remaining sessions in a hastily constructed home studio. Though *SMiLE* had been withdrawn, the projected single of "Heroes and Villains," the song that provided the core and idée fixe throughout *SMiLE*, held one last opportunity for Brian to reclaim his position as one of the field's leading artists. Wilson had worked obsessively on this track, and multiple versions of varying lengths were known to exist, in addition to a number of the related musical links that were intended to connect Brian's and Van Dyke's surreal Americana travelogue.[9] He had a substantial amount of material from which he could create a single, but he continued to record additional material for the song even though eight months had passed since the release of "Good Vibrations." Brian held the record back until July, when he decided to release it as an unannounced exclusive to local radio station, KHJ-AM, where just nine months earlier, he and Van Dyke had given a live, in-studio preview of the song on "Humble Harve" Miller's show. Brian, the band, and their entourage drove to KHJ in the late hours of July 11, talked themselves past security into the station, and offered the late-night DJ an exclusive airing of the single. The music world had changed since "Good Vibrations" had topped the charts, and a Brian Wilson single no longer warranted immediate attention. When the DJ said he could not play records that were not on the playlist, he was bullied into calling his program director. It was reported the disc jockey received an earful from his boss and finally aired the single. Still, the damage was done. Brian's normally fragile state had been exacerbated by months of amphetamine and hashish use, and the station's initial indifference to his latest masterpiece was one more reminder that maybe his father had been right all along. Perhaps he really was a failure.

"Heroes and Villains" was released at the end of July with "You're Welcome," a remaindered track from the now-abandoned *SMiLE* on the B-side.[10] Built on Brian's obsession for vocal rounds and chant-like mantras, "You're Welcome" is a gentle recording from December 1966 that served as a barometer for the sweet simplicity we would hear in Brian's newer music. The echo-drenched atmosphere of "You're Welcome" could have been a success with the new, hip music audiences, but the damage to the band (and Brian's) reputation was already fixed into place.

Smiley Smile was released upon the Beach Boys return from Hawaii where they (with Brian) had performed a series of concerts that were recorded for a proposed live album, *Lei'd in Hawaii. Smiley Smile* reached no higher than number 41 on the Billboard charts and it initiated the Beach Boys's seven-year string of underperforming albums. In the decades since, *Smiley Smile* has been accorded a kinder reputation in place of the initial indifference it suffered upon its first release. Reissued by Warners in October 1974, the album began to acquire a fan base that heard magic in Brian's lo-fi production at a time when progressive rock and bloated arena bands filled the airwaves. In the 2000s, it began to appear on various lists of must-hear albums, and is now considered an important work in Brian's catalog. In a world that embraces lo-fi art, the album is considered a masterpiece. *SMiLE* provided source material for eight of the album's 11 tracks, and Van Dyke Parks's lyrics, which originally presented issues among certain of the band's members, remained on *Smiley Smile.*[11] Brian's Baldwin organ, pictured in both stills and film footage from their Hawaiian concerts, provided the central timbre of Brian's stripped-down, minimalist arrangements on *Smiley Smile.*

A less well-known but equally telling response to *SMiLE's* replacement came from Bruce Johnston, who said, "very spacy, weird album, but it is so subtle and so damn innovative."[12] The only tracks that arrived relatively unscathed from their origins in *SMiLE* were the album's opening track, *Heroes and Villains*, in a contracted and partially rerecorded version that dispensed with the various surreal landscapes that supported Brian's "idée fixe" and "Good Vibrations," the hit single that was intended to bridge *Pet Sounds* to *SMiLE.* "Vegetables" was a drastic revision on "Vega-Tables." The original song featured one of Brian's most rhythmically complex arrangements, but in its revised form it sounds like a skiffle or campfire song.[13] This was followed by "Fall Breaks and Back to Winter (Woody Woodpecker Symphony)," a short, innocuous instrumental that borrowed material from *SMiLE's* most infamous track, "Fire (Mrs. O'Leary's Cow)." When Brian spoke about his abandoned masterpiece, he often referred to the negative vibes he believed had been generated by "Fire," so it is ironic that a significantly simplified version was created for *Smiley Smile.* The next track, a cabaret-comedy tune titled "She's Goin' Bald," was sourced from a *SMiLE*-era track, "He Gives Speeches." Side one ended with a straight-up stoner song, "Little Pad," which is obliquely related to "Love to Say Da Da," recorded at the final sessions for *SMiLE.*

"Good Vibrations" opened side two of *Smiley Smile*, but if any song encapsulated the opposite of the extraordinary production aesthetic of "Good Vibrations," it was the album's next track, "With Me Tonight," a work created in the transition away from *SMiLE.* Described in the 1990 liner notes for the *Smiley Smile/Wild Honey* two-fer as "do it yourself acid casualty doo-wop music," its calm simplicity makes it one of the album's more enjoyable works. "Wind Chimes," another *SMiLE* centerpiece, was originally arranged on a bass-and-marimba rhythm bed that floated into a Spector-on-acid mass of sound and would have segued into "Fire (Mrs. O'Leary's Cow)." On *Smiley Smile*, Brian rearranged the darker qualities of the song into a haunting, pointillist soundscape.

The last half of side two features one of the "new" songs, "Gettin' Hungry," a persistent, though indifferent, boogie-woogie riff about two of Brian's greatest passions, women and food. "Wonderful," a simply gorgeous song with some of Van Dyke's most elegant lyrics had been, in its original setting, a beautiful slice of baroque pop with an exquisite arrangement and backing vocals. On *Smiley Smile*, its elegance is veiled in grey with low, droning organ chords. The vocals, though barely audible, are beautiful and the calm strength of the new arrangement is interrupted by a doo-wop passage not found in the original version of the song. While this appears to be another watered-down work from *SMiLE*, it is one of the most "arranged" songs on the album and conveys a different angle on Van Dyke's narrative. In both versions, the accompaniment figure borrows a gesture used in "Heroes and Villains." With this interpolated section, Brian's intended idée fixe was allowed one brief appearance in this minimal, but complex, arrangement and is one of Brian's best efforts on the album. The final track, "Whistle In," is drawn from a whistling section created for one of the many "Heroes and Villains" links and is nothing more than an extended A-section that leads into the album's run-out groove.

In *Look, Listen, Vibrate, SMiLE*, there is a Capitol advertisement for *Smiley Smile* that reads "Why Not Put out a Smile? The Beach Boys Have." While *SMiLE* garnered so much attention in the press, Capitol wanted to sell its replacement as a legitimate sibling to the unreleased original. Brother Records, not unlike *SMiLE*, had met an ignominious end with Anderle's departure, and with it, Brian's creative ideas for the label simply came to an end. The name, if not the intention, of the label lived on while the Beach Boys and Capitol agreed that *Smiley Smile* would be released on Brother Records and distributed by Capitol. In addition to this album, the Brother Records label appeared on the singles of both "Heroes and Villains" and "Gettin' Hungry."[14] These would be the only Brother Records releases in the first Capitol years. The label was dormant once *Wild Honey* was released as Capitol ST 2859, and did not reappear until the band's move to Warners where their albums were released on Brother/Reprise Records. Brad Elliott has acknowledged a memo circulated by Capitol's Karl Engemann dated July 25, 1967, where he directs that the elaborate booklet prepared for *SMiLE* would not be included in *Smiley Smile*. He also alludes to discussions with Brian (and others on the Capitol team) that the booklet would not be included in *Smiley Smile*, but would be included in a 10-track *SMiLE* album. The album would leave "Heroes and Villains" and "Vega-Tables" off of the album, in spite of their lyrics being included in the booklet and suggests "some word of explanation could be included in the liner notes of the second album." Elliott points to this as a possibility that the 10-track *SMiLE* would have been released as Brother Records ST-9002 and *Wild Honey* as ST-9003.[15] None of this matters today since we have a complete and authorized collection of music created around *SMiLE*, but this points to the horse trading that continued between Brian, Capitol, and the Beach Boys. Andrew Doe offers a theory that any discussion of a 10-track *SMiLE* may simply have been Brian " ... being his usual agreeable self and telling people what they wanted to hear ... or a simple misunderstanding." As the Beach Boys moved into *Wild Honey* and beyond, we would see a diminution of Brian's influence as 1967 led to 1968 and the years that would follow.

A review of *Smiley Smile* appeared in a column review with *The Piper at the Gates of Dawn*, the debut long player of Pink Floyd (with founding member, Syd Barrett) released on Capitol's subsidiary imprint, Tower Records.[16] The review of *Smiley Smile*, though neutral, is politely supportive and closes with "We still like *Pet Sounds* better."[17] The pairing of the two reviews is prophetically ironic as Barrett would suffer a breakdown halfway through the making of the Floyd's second album and would be replaced by David Gilmour. As Barrett was the primary songwriter and front man for the band, his departure was explained by various of the group's members as an arrangement where Barrett would not tour but instead would stay in London and compose music for the band.[18] In the immediate aftermath of Syd's removal from the road, Barrett was described as "Pink Floyd's Brian Wilson."

Music for Brian . . .

Brother Records was transformed into a holding company and an imprint that would be used on selected Beach Boys albums.[19] Though *Smiley Smile* was released as Brother Records T-9001, the 10-track *SMiLE* album, referenced in the Capitol Records memo, was scrapped, and the next Beach Boys album, *Wild Honey* was released in December 1967 as Capitol ST 2859.[20] *Wild Honey* is considered by many fans as the Beach Boys's R&B album, and while the album's sparse production aesthetics and stripped-down sonic palette are deceiving, the album is arranged with an attention to detail and tonal clarity. With the exception of *Love You* and *That's Why God Made the Radio*, *Wild Honey* is the last album to feature Brian as the Beach Boys's primary composer, and it is here that the "Brian-is-the-Beach Boys" era comes to a close. With the exception of the two aforementioned albums, Brian would never again be at the center of the band, and he later would describe this album as "Something to clear my head out." As another indication of change within the Beach Boys's hierarchy, *Wild Honey* is the last Beach Boys album to be mixed in monophonic. As with *Smiley Smile*, the group provided a majority of the instrumental tracks with minimal contributions from studio musicians. After *Wild Honey*, the Beach Boys were no longer Brian's creative vehicle, in spite of what the band might have preferred that their fans, the press, or their successive record companies, to believe. Carl Wilson had been featured as a lead vocalist on Beach Boys songs as early as 1964, but he begins to take a more prominent role on *Wild Honey* and becomes the band's primary singer until his premature death in 1998. While the band recorded a majority of *Smiley Smile* in Brian's newly constructed home studio, *Wild Honey* had the band at Wally Heider's studio, in addition to Brian's home studio. With the exception of "Mama Says," based on a fragment of the coda from the original "Vega-Tables," *Wild Honey* borrowed nothing from *SMiLE*.

The album opens with the punchy title track led by Carl's bluesy vocal and a Theremin counter-melody that informs us that America's once-favorite band was back on solid ground after the orchestral sweep of *Pet Sounds* and the surreal, lo-fi proxy that replaced *SMiLE*. "Aren't You Glad" is a catchy tune with a deceivingly tight arrangement. "Country Air" follows with a wonderful, floating rhythm and lovely group vocal over a sustained accompaniment. Much has been made of the track's sonic "imperfection" in which sustained organ notes crackle as if the signal into the board was faulty, but I find this detail to be quite charming regardless of whether it was intentional or unintentional (the more likely scenario). The first side ends with "A Thing or Two," which offers a catchy boogie-woogie riff, but is a less appealing sibling to the previous album's "Getting Hungry," with a chorus that presages the upcoming single, "Do It Again."

Side two begins with one of Brian's best "recycled" songs, "Darlin." This song originated in "Thinkin' Bout You Baby," the 1964 single Brian and Mike produced for Sharon Marie. In its original form, the spacious and beautifully arranged ballad was delivered with a solid dose of longing and desire in Sharon Marie Esparza's lead vocal. Brian returned to this song with new, though less sophisticated, lyrics and produced "Darlin" for Redwood, a band led by Brian's friend Danny Hutton, whose group he had hoped to sign to Brother Records. Carl and Mike did not approve of Brian giving quality work to artists other than the Beach Boys (the same battle Brian had endured with Murry over his work with Jan & Dean), and they pressured him to drop Redwood and give "Darlin" to the Beach Boys. Brian also turned over a second Redwood song, "Time to Get Alone," which Carl and Mike placed on their last Capitol album, *20/20.*[21] The Beach Boys took the nifty backing track Brian produced for Redwood, added their vocals, and instantly had one of *Wild Honey's* strongest and most fully realized songs. The Beach Boys exerted their influence upon Brian to cease work with Redwood in October 1967, barely five months after the band rejected *SMiLE.* The events, as they unfolded in the studio when Mike, Carl, and Al confronted Brian and forced him to drop Redwood, are recounted in painful detail in Chuck Negron's memoir, *Three Dog Nightmare.* While the larger narrative of these events has appeared in various sources, Negron provides a first-person account that describes how easily the trio bullied and manipulated Brian.[22] These painful interactions would be repeated in slightly different situations throughout the 1970s–1990s, but always came back to the same issues. The Beach Boys needed Brian's music but when it was offered to them they were just as likely to accept it as they were to reject it if they felt (for a variety of unarticulated reasons) the work did not meet their standards. So whether it is *SMiLE*, Redwood, "Mount Vernon and Fairway," the *Love You/Adult Child* era, or the aborted entente cordiale of the mid-1990s, Brian would continue to suffer rejection upon rejection from both the family and the band.

The remainder of side two captures a range of emotions and styles and in some ways is an indicator of the schizophrenic tenor that would mark many of the band's later albums. "I'd Love Just Once to See You" is one of Brian's "a-day-in-the-life-of" songs where he describes the mundane but pleasurable activities of his daily life. This is not brilliant work, but is lighthearted and imbued with Brian's cheeky humor. "Here Comes the Night" had the misfortune to have been recycled in 1979 for the Beach Boys's first (and only) disco song, which was reviled by fans of all stripes. In its original form on *Wild*

Honey, it tries to be a cool R&B track, and almost succeeds, but is a pleasant song. The last two of Brian's songs on the album "Let the Wind Blow" and "Mama Says" are among my favorites on the album. The former is a gentle waltz with lovely vocals that recall the album's title ("let the bees make honey . . . "), and the latter is the delightful, and aforementioned, snippet excerpted from *SMiLE*. It has been proposed that *Wild Honey* was slated to be the third album on Brother Records and featured a different track lineup with four songs that have never appeared on a Beach Boys album. The record's move from Brother to Capitol and the change in the track line-up has never been explained and will remain for now, another of the mysteries that surround the Beach Boys's extensive archive of unreleased songs.

As with *Smiley Smile*, time has been kinder to *Wild Honey*. The Warners reissue in 1974 had a hand in the album's reevaluation among fans and critics. Both albums have endured and are loved by many Beach Boys fans.[23] Their simplicity, charm, and sheer nerve have been interpreted as another facet of Brian's brilliance as a songwriter and innovator. *Crawdaddy* founder, Paul Williams covered this album when it was initially released and again with the Warners reissue, and his perspective helped to give both of Brian's 1967 albums a stronger shelf life. In addition to the music the Beach Boys released in the aftermath of *SMiLE*, the band's image had been a stumbling block in regard to the perception that they were completely out of touch with social issues of the period. At the end of 1967 they dispensed with their Kennedy-era, clean-cut concert wear, and in its place adopted a stage uniform that, while it was contemporary in one regard, was just as out-of-touch with current styles. The ensemble of white, polyester suits that resembled those of a Las Vegas show band, or an upscale version of Gary Puckett and the Union Gap, were introduced to audiences in Detroit in November 1967.

Peace and a Maharishi

The "Baby Boom" kids who, just four years earlier, screamed at the Beatles and sang to the Beach Boys's "Surfin' U.S.A.," took to the streets and college campuses after 1967, so the gentle songs and upbeat messages of the late 1960s-era Beach Boys would not connect with contemporary audiences. The social unrest, protests, and riots that occurred across the country were miles from the tenor of the late 1960s Beach Boys. This generation saw the final nail driven into the country's cultural, social, and ethical coffin after the assassinations of Robert Kennedy and Martin Luther King Jr. The Beach Boys singing Bobby Troup's "Graduation Day" might just as well have come from another century, and the neo-psychedelic artwork on the cover of their first album of 1968 did nothing to convince anyone that the Beach Boys were in touch with anything in particular.

From late February into early April 1968, the Beach Boys recorded their next album, a peaceful, quasi-unplugged album, *Friends*. While the two preceding albums managed to break the top 50, *Friends* was an unmitigated failure that landed in Billboard at number 126.[24] In spite of the album's miserable commercial performance, it remains a fan favorite and is a personal favorite of Brian's, who has stated " . . . *SMiLE* had potential. But *Friends* has been good listening no matter what mood I am in."[25] While Brian is listed as a cocomposer on nine of the album's 12 tracks, there are more and varied collaborators on *Friends* than are found on any prior Beach Boys album. Brevity is a central feature on this record, as only two of the 12 tracks last over three minutes and the majority of songs barely break the two-minute mark. This was the first Beach Boys album to be offered in true stereo, and the first album recorded with their new engineer, Stephen Desper, who would go on to engineer Beach Boys sessions through *Surf's Up*. From 1968 to 1972, Desper was as invaluable to the Beach Boys as Chuck Britz had been to Brian in the years at Western, and the albums on which Desper worked all share a cohesive, consistent, and warm sound.

The album opens with "Meant for You," a 38 seconds prelude that provides an entrée for the title track. While short, the original 1 minute and 50 seconds track from which it was drawn was released on *Made in California*. I wish Brian had selected, if only for its simple beauty, the full version for *Friends*. The title track is an optimistic, upbeat triple-meter song where each member of the group, except for Mike Love, received a songwriting credit. The harmonic shifts in this song are wholly Brian, but as another sign of his growing disinterest in making music with the Beach Boys, everyone who had a hand in the recording received a credit. Brian had begun to compose with Al Jardine, and between 1968 and 1971 they would create a handful of absolutely charming songs. "Wake the World" is one such piece, and at a minute-and-a-half is one of the shorter songs on the album. This is another of Brian's "a-day-in-the-life-of" songs, and his childlike fascination with the sky and stars would be mined further on "Solar System" and "There's So Many." For all of its simplicity, it contains lovely touches with shimmering strings on the bridge and a tuba on the choruses. This is followed by another waltz, "Be Here in the Morning," composed by Brian with Carl, Al, and Mike. Though he chose to not resurrect the perfectionist auteur of the pre-1967 Brian, all songs on which he is the primary author bear evidence as to the possibilities that could have been realized had he been allowed to create work on his terms. Still, the songs are Brian's and they bear his familiar hooks with unprepared harmonic shifts, descending stepwise progressions, and unusual phrase structures.

On earlier albums, such as 1965's *Beach Boys Today!* Brian sang openly of his affections and insecurities for Marilyn, whom he married in December 1964. Three-and-a-half years later on *Friends*, Brian speaks to Marilyn through songs such as "Be Here in the Morning" and "When a Man Needs a Woman," where he expresses the comforts of their daily life. The next track, "Passing by," is an enjoyable instrumental composed solely by Brian. Though he initially intended for this song to have lyrics, it was offered as a wordless solo over an addictive riff. Brian is listed as the primary author on the next song, but based on its subject matter we might assume the song is Mike's. "Anna Lee, the Healer" is a simple ditty about a masseuse Mike met while at the Maharishi's retreat (with the Beatles) in Rishikesh, India.[26]

The last three songs on side two are the most dissimilar works on the album. Brian's solo composition, "Busy Doin' Nothin," another "a-day-in-the-life-of" song is constructed over a clever bossa nova arrangement. "Diamond Head" is an unusual instrumental for a Beach Boys album and is an unstructured jam (Brian lists three studio musicians who played on the track as coauthors) that is part exotica lounge a 'la Martin Denny, and part open jam in a Pidgin-Hawaiian style. For all of its square-peg-round-hole qualities, it would not have been terribly out-of-place on *SMiLE.* At 3 minutes and 39 seconds, it is the longest track on an album mostly comprised of two-minute-and-under works. "Transcendental Meditation," the album's noisiest and most raucous track is a completely unexpected conclusion for their most peaceful and calm long player. Though Brian is listed as a coauthor for this song, I would guess that Mike and Al, the band's two dedicated meditators, composed the bulk of the song, with minimal contributions from Brian.

From fall 1967 into the summer of 1968, Brian worked on another of his minimalist vocal rounds, in this case, a fragment known both as "Been Way Too Long" and "Can't Wait Too Long." It was never completed, so a number of takes of this song were edited to create a "complete" work that first appeared on the 1990 two-fer of *Smiley Smile/Wild Honey.* A fragment titled "I Believe in Miracles" was released on the 2013 boxed set, and was credited as having come from the *Smiley Smile* sessions. It has shown up on various bootlegs, often attached to one of the many mixes of "Can't Wait Too Long." It may be related to that work or simply may be a random vocal riff of the sort Brian was known to toss off. One of his often overlooked collaborations from this period was with Ron Wilson (unrelated), drummer in the early 1960s surf outfit, The Surfaris, who is forever enshrined into music history for his unmistakable drum-solo on "Wipe Out." He and Brian composed "We're Together Again," which Brian directed in the studio with the Beach Boys over May and September 1968.[27] On June 28, Brian produced Ron's solo single, "I'll Keep on Loving You," backed with the Jagger-Richards ballad first recorded by Marianne Faithful, "As Tears Go By." The single was produced under their new partnership, Ron-Brian Music Productions, and released on Columbia in September of that year, where it faded without a trace.

Brian's next non-album single for the Beach Boys, "Do It Again," is a fantastic track composed with Mike Love that looks back to their earlier works. Though the Beach Boys are given the production credit for this song, it is Brian's work. Recorded late in May and in the first part of June, the song is loaded with a number of familiar rhythmic and textual tropes. It is relatively simple in terms of structure but its tight arrangement and strong hooks make the song. The record had a respectable domestic showing, where it reached number 20 in Billboard, but was a number one in the United Kingdom. While this may have been some of Brian's strongest work of the period, it did nothing to reverse the band's decline in popularity. Capitol had given up on them as they continued their practice of releasing "Hits" compilations. A third volume of greatest hits was released on August 5, which was followed two weeks later by *Stacks-O-Tracks*, a 15-song collection that featured Brian's instrumental tracks without the vocals. The gatefold album was originally packaged with a lyric sheet and chord charts so one could play and sing to the Beach Boys's instrumental tracks. Similar to products produced since the 1950s by New York-based, "Music-Minus-One," this release demonstrated that Capitol continued to have no idea how to market popular music. Such a package might have been a hit in 1964, but in 1968 it was a painful misfire from Capitol's marketing department. When reissued in 1990 (on a two-fer with *Beach Boys Party!*), the instrumental tracks provided a fascinating look into the development of Brian's production style, and the album is appreciated today far more than it could ever have been in 1968. It had the lowest sales of any Beach Boys album of that period and went out of print after its first run.

In the summer of 1968, Brian recorded demos of "Sail Plane Song (Loop de Loop)," "Old Man River," and "All I Wanna Do." The first two tracks would wait decades for an official release, but "All I Wanna Do," which Brian first demoed during sessions for *Friends*, would be polished into one of his most ethereal works, with Mike Love's lyrics and lead vocal on *Sunflower*. "Sail Plane Song (Loop de Loop)" was composed with Al Jardine and remained in creative limbo for close to three decades. It was recorded in late 1968/early 1969 and included on a track list prepared for Warners (on Capitol Studios stationery) dated August 1970 for a follow-up album to *Sunflower*.[28] When released on *Endless Harmony* (August 11, 1998), it was an Al Jardine-completed track. Prior to this it survived a number of permutations, that included an unreleased holiday song, "Santa's Got an Airplane," prepared in late 1977 at Maharishi International University in sessions intended for their proposed second holiday album.[29] In its original mix, it is a wonderfully noisy and busy song, a veritable "calliope-on-acid-merry-go-round," while Al's late 1990s mix tempers some of the song's charm in exchange for a taut sonic production.

Life Anew with the Brothers Warner

Brian's (and by extension, the Beach Boys) history from 1968 to 1971 has been presented in multiple, and often conflicting accounts. From *Friends* (1968) to *Surf's Up* (1971), purported albums with names such as *The Fading Rock Group Revival, Reverberation, Add Some Music,* and *Landlocked,* exist in various narratives by members of the band and other biographers and are working titles for albums released under different names between 1969 and

1971, but are not "lost" records as has so often been suggested. The albums from this era, *Sunflower, Surf's Up, Carl and the Passions—"So Tough,"* and *Holland,* provide only a fraction of Brian's story. A chronology of his activities from 1969 to 1973 (and in Chapter Five, into the early 1980s) will better reflect the development of his work based on dates of production rather than album releases dates. It was not unusual for Brian to begin a song at one point in time, only to let it sit for a month or longer before he would choose to either finish or abandon the track. It might end up on the next Beach Boys album, on one a year or more later, or remain unfinished. The 1970s is when the cult of "Brian-as-burned-out-casualty-case" began to take hold among fans and detractors of the band. The years of near inactivity (1972–1975) were followed by the first serious attempt at therapy and recovery, a few years of creative (if not necessarily commercial) activity, and a second period of an even greater decline that nearly brought Brian to a premature end.

In "Busy Doin' Somethin': Uncovering Brian Wilson's Lost Bedroom Tapes," Brian Chidester's addresses a purported collection of unreleased, incomplete, or unfinished songs Wilson recorded in the 1970s. Brian's reticence to produce a substantial body of work for the Beach Boys resulted in the belief that any musical scrap Brian committed to tape might in fact be the hook that could inspire him to become a fully functional member of the band whose fortunes had fallen dramatically in the years that followed the non-release of *SMiLE.* Chidester argues that "Bedroom Tapes" are not limited to the years of Brian's home studio (1967–1972), but encompass the entire decade of the 1970s when Brian struggled with (or was coerced into) periods of productivity. While it would be exciting for both fans and scholars to discover an unheard cache of songs composed by Brian Wilson, it should not imply that anything of import awaits discovery in these tapes as these are sketches that can inform our understanding of Wilson's methodology, but are not keys to lost or unrealized works. The Beach Boys were known for their nonlinear approach in compiling their albums, and it is a challenge to trace the chronology for many of Brian's songs. The band was often required to submit albums with a specific percentage of his songs, and they would often take his fragments or half-ideas and develop them into complete works.

The last Beach Boys studio album of the 1960s, *20/20,* is the final studio album from the band's first period at Capitol Records and the first where Brian serves as a minor contributor. Though five songs on the album were composed by Brian and his pieces constitute a majority of album's best material, his active participation beyond those works was negligible. In need of material, Carl was able to take *SMiLE*-era songs, "Our Prayer" and "Cabinessence" for the album. The photos on the album jacket featured the Brian-less touring band, a sign that the group was determined to forge their own identity without their founding architect. It is strangely symbolic that they recorded most of their new material for the album at Capitol Studios, nearly six years after they had, on Brian's request, decamped from the Tower to Western. Their most recent hit single, "Do It Again" served as the album's opening track, except they tagged an unrelated coda that was absent on the original single. An excerpt of Brian's musique concrète from *SMiLE's* "Workshop" was lifted for this purpose and was Brian's only contribution to side one.

Side two opened with Brian's production of Leadbelly's, "Cotton Fields" as a vehicle for Al Jardine, but it is the next two songs that are minor gems in Brian's catalog. The first, "I Went to Sleep" was recorded in the summer of 1968, just after *Friends.* Like a number of Brian's songs from this era, it is another of his triple-meter "a-day-in-the-life-of" songs, with Brian and Carl's vocals layered over a wonderfully cloudy track that foregrounds a soaring flute line. This is followed by "Time to Get Alone," a track Brian originally produced for Redwood in October 1967. The final two tracks were poached from nearly completed and previously off-limits *SMiLE.* On November 17, 1968, the Beach Boys took the gorgeous, a cappella, "Our Prayer" into Capitol's studios with Stephen Desper to add additional voices onto Brian's original mono track. This was followed by "Cabinessence," a nearly finished work when Brian shuttered *SMiLE* that was completed at Capitol on November 20.

A close listen to the late 1967 tracks originally intended for Redwood show that Brian continued to produce music at a level that was consistent with the work he created just prior to the end of *SMiLE.* He had limited his work with "outside" artists after 1964, but Redwood provided an irresistible opportunity, just as (American) Spring provided in 1972.[30] Brian produced a pair of cover songs for the Honeys in December 1969, nearly five years after their last collaboration. The Honeys had continued to work through the 1960s, primarily as background singers on a variety of projects and were back at Capitol in December 1968 recording "Come to Me" with, of all people, Murry Wilson (he had, the previous year, produced his own solo album, *The Many Moods of Murry Wilson* on Capitol).[31] A few weeks after those sessions, and four-and-a-half years after their last studio collaborations, Brian resumed work with the Honeys and recorded covers of "Tonight You Belong to Me" and "Goodnight My Love," both released by Capitol on March 24, 1969. As with previous Honeys singles, they sank into chart oblivion.

In the first quarter of 1969, Brian recorded "Loop De Loop," "All I Wanna Do," and "Break Away," of which the latter would become the next Beach Boys single. Brian also helped on Bruce's "Deirdre," and likely saved the song from what promised to be a mundane exercise of Moon-in-June pining. Brian was given second credit on the song, but as Bruce stated "I gave him 50% of the song ... but it should have been 5%. He came up with two lines, that was it."[32] One listen to the song demonstrates that Brian's input was minimal but effective.

Murry, under the pseudonym Reggie Dunbar, collaborated with Brian to compose "Break Away," an upbeat song along the lines of "Do It Again" with classic production values and strong hooks. The single did not reach the top

50 and was another disappointing stateside showing for the band. In what had become standard practice, it was a top-10 hit in Britain. While a great post-*SMiLE* single, it was never an album track at the time of its release and did not acquire wider exposure until the mid-1970s when it was included on *Spirit of America* and later compilation albums. From 1968 to 1970, Brian continued to produce an array of musical styles with an emotional range that demonstrated his efforts to expand his own compositional palate. While the band worked on *20/20*, Brian led the Beach Boys in a session for which only a fragment was captured. Brian had long been an admirer of Burt Bacharach and had, in the unwinding of *SMiLE*, considered having the Beach Boys record "My Little Red Book," which had been a modest hit for Manfred Mann in 1965 and in 1966 for Arthur Lee's band, Love. In May 1968, Brian led the band through vocal sessions for Bacharach's "Walk On By," the iconic song Dionne Warwick fixed into the firmament of pop music history in 1964. Brian takes the lead on this simple demo and the Beach Boys's vocal harmonies provide the rhythm track after which Dennis takes over. He forgets the words and carries on with a wordless lead, which brings the song to an end before they can arrive at the second verse. Another cover, "Ol' Man River," like the Bacharach excerpt, was released as a bonus track on the 1990 two-fer of *Friends/20/20*.[33] Brian's vocal arrangement turned the song into an effective and tender lullaby.

Brian and the Beach Boys found themselves without the services of Capitol Records, who purportedly had expressed interest in re-signing the band, but were rejected by the Beach Boys who felt they could find better offers elsewhere. Given the poor promotion they had received as far back as *Pet Sounds*, it is not surprising they chose to look elsewhere, but they may have overestimated their appeal to other labels. Through much of 1969 they were without a label and their ongoing legal issues with Capitol would result in the company deleting their back catalog, which removed a consistent source of revenue from the band. While this resulted in belt-tightening, they undertook a very successful European tour where they performed behind the Iron Curtain, in both East Berlin and the former Czechoslovakia. Fred Vail who, in 1963 and 1964, had booked them for their Sacramento, CA, concerts was brought into the organization to assist Nick Grillo with the band's daily business duties. This is of note because in the spring of 1970, Brian produced 15 tracks with Vail under the working title, *Cows in the Pasture*. This was a country music album with sessions contracted by Diane Rovell and recorded over 12 days at Wally Heider. Vail completed vocal tracks for a third of the album, but we can only guess at its contents as it was neither completed nor released. It serves to show the range of projects to which Brian would commit himself, even if he was likely to lose interest before completion. While the group was on its European tour in the summer of 1969, Nick Grillo was in discussions with Deutsche Grammophon, who expressed an interest in the band as their popularity in Europe and England remained quite strong even while it was on the decline at home. It is interesting to think of Beach Boys signed to the same label that produced so many legendary classical recordings with conductors such as Herbert von Karajan and Karl Bohm, but in an abrupt about-face, the label lost interest in the group.[34] In late 1969, the Beach Boys signed with Warner Brothers, under whom they would revive their Brother Records imprint on the Reprise Records label. Warners president, Mo Ostin, expressed an interest in the group, but it soon became clear that business with Warners would not be as it was at Capitol. Some Warners executives were less than enthusiastic about signing the group, but it was Van Dyke Parks who convinced Ostin that Brian could (and would) make music of the sort that could make the band popular once again.

Warner Bros. Records had developed a reputation as a label that was artist-focused, though they were a relatively young concern compared to Capitol, RCA, Decca, and Columbia. In spite of this, they had an enviable roster of artists and an impressive A&R team that included Lenny Waronker, Russ Titelman, Ted Templeman, and John Cale, formerly of the Velvet Underground.[35] Brian had previously worked with Titelman and Van Dyke Parks, who also was on the Warners's roster, but label executives expected more of the Beach Boys than the group could deliver, and wanted something different than what the group had to offer. They also wanted *SMiLE* and tried to leverage its release through a signing advance, which never came to fruition.[36] With Capitol, the band submitted albums that were released without question; but at Warners the label repeatedly rejected albums, which forced the band back to the studio to produce something that would meet with the label's approval. As a result, many of their albums from the 1970s featured tracks that might have been recorded some years prior, or were rejected from an earlier collection. An album released in any given year was not necessarily an accurate reflection of Brian's, or the band's, creative agenda at that time. The semi-mythical catalog of never-released Beach Boys albums is a tangled history of a band in the midst of a creative renaissance while they tried to reclaim their identity. They created a significant amount of music throughout this period, and in the 18 months between the respective releases of *20/20* and *Sunflower*, Warners rejected the band's first collection before *Sunflower* was accepted. They had an album worth of material to fulfill their final commitments with Capitol, on which the label passed, so they arrived at Warners with enough good music to fill two albums.[37] Every member of the band was creating music, Brian included, and various tracks recorded from mid-1968 into early 1970 would be configured and reconfigured until their label was satisfied.

The Beach Boys would mine works from *SMiLE* for both *Sunflower* and *Surf's Up*, as they did with *20/20*, to bolster the quality of those albums, but this only served to pique Warners's interest in the already famous "lost" album, which was of more interest to the label than were the band's efforts to promote a "new" model of the Beach Boys.

After the April 1969 sessions that produced "Break Away," Brian was seldom in the studio until August when he produced "Old Man Sunshine" and an album of poetry from Stephen Kalinich who had come to the attention of all three Wilsons and Brother Records employee (and cousin to the Wilsons), Steve Korthof. Dennis Wilson collaborated with Kalinich on "Little Bird" and "Be Still" from *Friends*, and was signed to Brother Records as part of a to-be-determined group, not as a solo artist. Brian elected to produce a spoken-word album of Kalinich's poetry under the title of *A World of Peace Must Come*, and though completed in 1969, it was not released until 2008. This album is often viewed as a footnote in Brian's catalog, but as with many of his non-Beach Boys projects, he was dedicated to this work and not concerned with making a commercial, hit record. His output with the Beach Boys had fallen precipitously throughout 1969, though the band was in the midst of preparing songs for their Warners debut. Brian was only involved in a handful of Beach Boys's songs at this juncture, and was more invested in his collaboration with Kalinich. Where humor had played a large role in the creation of *SMiLE*, with Kalinich he wanted to make a statement on humanity and world peace because he truly believed in the messages expressed in Kalinich's poetry. There is some confusion as to when sessions for this album were scheduled, but it is known that Brian held a session at Wally Heider's studio on August 22 where he directed members of the Wrecking Crew on "America, I Love You." According to Kalinich, Brian directed this session by giving verbal directions to the musicians and providing space for them to improvise their parts through the use of words that described air, wind, and other natural sounds, and under Brian's direction, the players created a calm soundscape for the track. The more "arranged" works on the album would not have been out of place on *Smiley Smile*. Brian and Stephen shopped this album for a deal, but the fact that it was not released may be a result of Brian's insistence that the album "not" be a commercial, profit-generating record, but a record that would encourage people to bring peace and balance to the world. Both artists insisted the album would be an emotional and spiritual experience above all else. What is unique about this work are the parallel themes of patriotism and love. Kalinich believes this is one of the first examples where a popular artist boldly and unabashedly expressed, in a measured balance of patriotism and protest, their love of country in tandem with a rejection of their country's insistent dedication to war and violence.

According to AFM contracts, two untitled, three-hour sessions for this album were held on October 28 and November 3 and were produced under Brian Wilson Productions, for which Diane Rovell was the contractor.[38] The session on the October 28 occurred the same day the Beach Boys recorded Brian's stately "Add Some Music to Your Day." At the end of August, Brian worked on "Soulful Old Man Sunshine," a jazzy, upbeat tune that first appeared in 1998 on *Endless Harmony*. Coauthor Rick Henn had been a member of the Sunrays, the Beach Boys-clone band Murry Wilson managed after Brian fired him from the Beach Boys. In spite of this unusual connection through Murry, there was no ill will between Wilson and Henn. They composed this song at Brian's home and Henn led a session at Sunset Sound at the end of August. In the liner notes to *Endless Harmony*, Henn claims Brian did not come into the studio which left him to arrange the song and manage the session, though vocals were recorded at Brian's home studio in November. Another work recorded in late autumn 1969 is Brian's "Where Is She." It was never considered for either of the first two Warners albums and was not released until 2013 when it was included on *Made in California*.

The first album submitted to Warners, originally titled *Add Some Music*, was rejected for the lack of a strong single. A second submission replaced six of the tracks and provided a new title, *Sunflower*. Brian worked on four of the new tracks that made the final cut of *Sunflower*, the majestic "Add Some Music to Your Day," plus "At My Window," "Our Sweet Love," and "This Whole World," in addition to "Cool, Cool Water," "All I Wanna Do," and "Deirdre." Brian also produced five tracks that would be released later in the decade. In addition to the stunning *Til' I Die*, included on the band's second Warners album, *Surf's Up*, Brian recorded "Games Two Can Play," which was released on 1993's *Good Vibrations* boxed set. Another "a-day-in-the-life-of" song, this is an upbeat number where Brian name-checks Joe South's 1969, Grammy-nominated hit, "Games People Play." It has a rollicking, roller-rink style organ accompaniment, and while a tad sloppy, it is a fun song. Another song that would wait a decade for a proper release is "When Girls Get Together." This song is a head scratcher for most fans and critics, though I find the piece endearing, if only for its uniquely un-Beach Boys sound.[39] Recorded a day after what is believed to have been Brian's last session for the Kalinich album, this is a lazy, drawling tune that could have fit either on *SMiLE* or *Smiley Smile*. "Back Home," a collaboration with his original Inglewood roommate, Bob Norberg, was also recorded at this time. It would remain unreleased until 1976 when it was rerecorded and added to *15 Big Ones*.[40]

Though Brian and Murry were successful in their collaboration on "Break Away," their relationship was saddled with the same issues Brian had struggled to resolve since he fired Murry in 1964. Throughout the decade, Murry cheated Mike Love from a number of song credits and harassed Brian to sign over to him complete control of Sea of Tunes (the publishing company Murry set up for Brian in 1962). As *SMiLE* failed and the band's fortunes began to decline, he continued to pressure Brian for control of the company. While the Beach Boys continued to record new music, they released little of it and what was released did not sell. Murry, sensing an irreversible decline in the band's popularity and a permanent drop in records sales and royalties, decided in November 1969 to turn $700,000 of quick cash with the sale of Brian's catalog to Irving Almo Music, the publishing arm of A&M Records. He did so without Brian's full consent, and set into motion the lifelong business conflicts between Brian and Mike. The publishing rights sold to Irving Almo would begin to earn millions of dollars with the band's resurgence in popularity in the mid-1970s, but not for Brian or the Beach Boys.

"Carnival," another of Brian's works from this period is typically omitted from his works list and has never officially been released. Based on the waltz, "Sobre las Olas" by Mexican composer Juventino Rosas (1868–1894), it is one of the most famous waltzes ever published in Mexico and is familiar to many on first hearing.[41] Brian's rendition, barely a minute in length, was included on the track list for a second Warners album but has never appeared on any official release.[42]

There were high expectations at Warners when it came time to release their first Beach Boys single, "Add Some Music" b/w "Susie Cincinnati." This majestic and spacious song with a powerful group vocal led by Mike, demonstrated that Brian was still in the spiritual zone that informed such works as "God Only Knows." This beautifully produced track, with Al Jardine's storming rocker on the B-side, was an unexpected failure and a disappointment for both Warners and the band. The record made no impact overseas, where the Beach Boys popularity had been consistently strong. It performed well in selected domestic markets where it cracked the top 30, but the Warners sales team encouraged preorders for the single that simply were too high.[43] Without national radio coverage, the song died in the charts and in response, Warners rejected the first configuration of their label debut.[44] A second Warners single, released on June 29 was Dennis's "Slip on Through" backed with Brian's "This Whole World," which sold no better than its predecessor. "This Whole World" is Brian's excellent and all-embracing song that taps into the era of peace and harmony.[45] The melody and accompaniment seemingly come from two distant points in Brian's color scheme, as the melody gently floats from one cadence to the next, while the accompaniment and background vocals drive ahead in an irresistible groove. This glorious work is under two minutes in length and ends all too quickly.

While Warners demanded that the Beach Boys produce stronger material for what would become *Sunflower*, Brian was at work on a rich collection of songs. In addition to the aforementioned "Carnival," there was the "I Just Got My Pay," a slightly humorous ditty that was an update on materials he first introduced in 1964 with "All Dressed Up for School." "Good Time" is a Jardine coauthored work, and an odd track that remained unreleased until *Love You*, though Brian did produce a version of "Good Time" for the American Spring album in 1972, where the awkwardly sexist tone is played down when delivered from a woman's perspective.

"At My Window" existed under other working titles, and while it is mostly Al, there are just enough odd phrases that point to Brian having been involved in this work. "Our Sweet Love," composed by Brian, Carl, and Al is a lovely and overlooked work. While Brian had no hand in its composition, the exquisitely beautiful "Forever," composed by Dennis, features Brian's absolutely stunning falsetto backing vocal.

"Cool, Cool Water" was back under Brian's hands in January 1970 as a vocal chant that emerged from the May 1967 track, "I Love to Say Da Da." When Brian returned to this for *Sunflower*, he combined the chant from " . . . Da Da" with the core of his original version of "Cool, Cool Water" to create an entirely new work. On the 1993 *Good Vibrations* boxed set we had the first official release of "I Love to Say Dada," and the original vocal fragment of " . . . Water," and can hear the relationship of these two works. The song, as it appears on *Sunflower*, is a lighthearted, finger-snapping vocal callisthenic. Its inclusion on the album was the work of Warners A&R manager, Lenny Waronker, who referred to this as representative of the "kind" of work he liked to hear from Brian.

One of Brian's most ethereal works, "All I Wanna Do," is an overlooked masterpiece that originally was included on the "Last Capitol Album." It was first demoed during sessions for *Friends* and recorded at Gold Star in March 1969, before it appeared on *Sunflower*. From arrangement to production, this song is absolute magic with its echo-washed organ and guitar, which float under Mike's ghostly lead vocal. Like so much of *Sunflower*, Beach Boys engineer Stephen Desper deserves acknowledgement for capturing Brian's songs so masterfully and giving the album an aural sheen that had been missing on Beach Boys albums since *Pet Sounds*. Brian's songs from this period convey a range of emotions and techniques, what Lambert describes as Brian's " . . . crafting songs of great stature and musical ingenuity . . . a songwriter secure in his abilities and confident in his instincts . . . ."

Sunflower was the strongest album the band had delivered since *Pet Sounds* and demonstrated, more than any Beach Boys album before or since, that the six-members could work democratically and deliver songs of real depth. While Brian contributed some extraordinary works, Dennis, Al, and Carl showed that they too could offer works that, if not equal to Brian's impressive catalog, were anything but ordinary. While the album garnered strong reviews, no one purchased it as it only managed to reach number 151 on Billboard (the only album to fare worse was *Stacks-O-Tracks*).

Brian's activities as a Beach Boy were varied and unexpected. He could give unpredictable interviews to the press that only served to expose and exacerbate the band's many financial, social, and personal issues. In the midst of his non-participation in making music on a semi-regular basis, Brian managed a West Hollywood health food store, the Radiant Radish, where at times he could be found working the register. While the store was an extension of his part-time interest in health food and clean living, it ran at a deficit and went out of business. Brian poked fun at the unhealthy state of his own life when he wrote "H.E.L.P. Is on the Way," in which he name checked the Radiant Radish.[46] Many photographs of Brian taken at this time show a sad, hollow-eyed young man, still handsome but with a ghostly, haunted expression. In the past, when the Beach Boys were on tour, Brian would be at work in the studio. Now, when the band was on the road, Brian was busy doing nothing in particular. When Warners signed the band, it appeared the group had a renewed energy and direction, with each member contributing their best work to the effort. But with the commercial failure of *Sunflower* they had to regroup, and as the recipient of yet another creative disappointment, Brian showed little interest in contributing to the band's next project.

Soon after the release of *Sunflower*, a master was compiled for a second Warners album. The group had come to Warners with a great deal of new material already recorded, and the second proposed album carried a few songs that were rejected from the first album, tracks from the proposed final album for Capitol, and some new works. While this collection of tracks has passed into Beach Boys lore with the title *Landlocked*, no album of that title was submitted to/ rejected by Warners. It simply was a working collection of songs under consideration while they crafted their next work.[47]

Longtime associate Fred Vail found it more difficult to secure bookings for the band, and Nick Grillo had come under pressure to address their shrinking financial reserves. Brian's brief interest in the band's business matters had evaporated in 1967 with the departure of David Anderle and the stillbirth of Brother Records, and he distanced himself further from the group. On July 29, 1970, Brian, Mike, and Bruce, were interviewed on Los Angeles public radio station KPFK by Jack Rieley, who quickly ingratiated himself to the band, in part through his presentation of bogus credentials and big ideas.[48] This did not matter and no one bothered to ask for references as the band was desperate for any change to reverse their retreating fortunes. After placing himself in the role Fred Vail had served for so long, he also took over the band's financial matters and replaced Nick Grillo. Rieley ultimately damaged the band's finances, but he provided them with a creative agenda that enabled them to acquire new audiences and reclaim their status as one of the country's leading bands. For all the positive changes he helped the band to affect, his most egregious misstep was contributing to the band's creative mix as he wrote lyrics for nearly a dozen songs and appeared as a lead vocalist on a pair of tracks.[49]

The Beach Boys played the Big Sur Music Festival in Monterey, CA on October 3. This concert gave the Beach Boys a chance to redeem themselves in the fall of 1970 and where, thanks to festival board member Van Dyke Parks, the Beach Boys (sans Brian) would begin their commercial rehabilitation. The band's fortunes had fallen steadily over the preceding three years, and with the deletion of their albums from Capitol's catalog, the band was largely forgotten among popular music audiences. With the exception of "California Girls," the band's set at the Big Sur festival featured music from *Pet Sounds* onward, for which they received an enthusiastic response. One month later they played eight sold-out shows over four nights (Brian joined them for the first three shows) at Hollywood's Whisky a Go-Go.[50] While this was a significant improvement for the band, associate band member Daryl Dragon recalled that Brian and Mike continued to have their difficulties with each other which, in Dragon's view, tempered the overall experience of the shows. In their quest to sustain this upward trajectory, Jack Rieley convinced the band to drop the short, oldies-focused sets and replace them with longer shows focused on their post-*Pet Sounds* repertory. He also encouraged them to align themselves with environmental and political causes and got them to start writing music along these topics. The whimsical Americana that was featured so prominently on *Sunflower* and on unreleased tracks such as "Loop de Loop" and "Old Man Sunshine," would be replaced with songs that spoke to young, socially conscious audiences.

Aboard a Tidal Wave

While the Beach Boys's fortunes as a concert attraction were on a slow ascent, they still needed a hit record. Rieley made Carl the de facto musical director for the band, as he had assumed most of the production duties since 1967 when it was clear that Brian would not assume this responsibility. The album released in August 1971, *Surf's Up*, would turn out to be the band's best-selling record since *Wild Honey*.[51] The album remains a fan favorite and was a thematic departure from *Sunflower*. Over the preceding three years, Dennis had emerged as the next talented Wilson songwriter but his works are missing from this album, the result of a disagreement with Carl in selecting tracks for the album. Brian was represented on this album by two odd works and two masterpieces.

"Take a Load off Your Feet" was a Jardine/Wilson/Winfrey song that was originally offered on their first offering at Warners. It is a pleasant song with a clever arrangement but has little else to recommend it. "A Day in the Life of a Tree" was Brian's second offering on the album for which Jack Rieley was listed as coauthor and delivered a warbling lead vocal. The group whose many hits were, in part, defined by their extraordinary vocals, now had an untrained, unmusical, and undisciplined voice featured on their album. While the lyrics have inspired ongoing discussions as to their meaning, Rieley's vocal is seen by some either as a big put-on from Brian, or as a write-off for a song in which he had lost interest. Beyond the many contradictory stories about the origins of this song, the harmonium and organ driven track is beautiful. Van Dyke Parks was enlisted as a background singer and the final chorus features one of Brian's classic vocal rounds. It is more *Smiley Smile* than anything else, and is gorgeous in its awkward simplicity. This was followed by "Til' I Die," one of Brian's most stunning songs and what perhaps is his last Beach Boys masterpiece. The song was initially recorded a year earlier and was rejected for *Sunflower*, ostensibly because others in the band considered the song too much of a downer. A source close to Wilson believes this is the last instance where Brian was fully engaged in the creation and execution of one of his songs for a Beach Boys record. It is all Brian, from composition to production, as it was in the pre-*SMiLE* era. An earlier biographer has described the song as "a window into Brian's heart and soul . . . and it was the last time a Beach Boys album would include a Brian Wilson song that so openly expressed his emotions." Curnutt describes Brian's music as "sorrow within sunshine," and "Til I' Die" captures this sentiment perhaps better than any other of his compositions.

The decision to include "Surf's Up" on the album was controversial, but Carl and Rieley pushed Brian into exhuming this song with a hope to deliver that still elusive hit. Brian had been crushed by the rejection that accompanied *SMiLE*, yet the band had already resurrected two of its songs for *20/20*. He created a severely truncated "Heroes and Villains" for *Smiley Smile*, and now they wanted the song whose lyrics (as with "Heroes . . . ") had created unresolved conflicts among all involved. The initial rejection of this song had precipitated Van Dyke Parks's departure from *SMiLE*, and it was the piece that loomed larger than any other connected to the unfinished masterpiece. In order to complete "Surf's Up," Carl would have to construct a new master track from Brian's original tracking sessions. Stephen Desper engineered the *Surf's Up* album and has confirmed that Carl added vocal and keyboard tracks to Brian's original instrumental "first movement," originally recorded November 4, 1966, and used Brian's piano and double-tracked vocal recording from the December 15, 1966, session at Columbia Studios, to which he added a bass part and some vocal sweetening. In regard to the coda, Desper claims that Brian sang the "child is father to the man" coda in one take, and maintains that Van Dyke Parks sang backing vocals on the record. "Surf's Up" was the album's final, stellar track and would be the last *SMiLE* excerpt released on a Beach Boys album until the release of *The SMiLE Sessions* in 2011.

Brian's emotional issues had become of concern to many within the family, but the tenor of the era was not conducive towards the discussion, to speak nothing of treatment, of mental illness. Brian was a creative person and an artist, so his behaviors, however odd, were always tolerated or laughed at as the actions of a funny, if slightly strange, prankster. His personal troubles should never have been our business, but as an icon and public figure who was never cut out for either role, he created a body of work that was seen to possess both value and meaning, and as a result, his family, his management, his friends, and his public, all had an opinion as to how Brian could once more become the person he once had been.

Brian is a courageous man because at some point he had to choose between being an artist or simply surviving. As rejection upon rejection continued to define his creative life, his greatest accomplishment would be his survival. People could see he was crying for help, but no one knew whether his behaviors were to be taken seriously. When he dug a grave in his backyard, how were they supposed to address this? While his collaborators had been removed from his creative activities, his friends served as his anchor. Van Dyke Parks, Tandyn Almer, and Danny Hutton were three friends who were not there to get "something" from Brian (as so many others wanted), but were there because they genuinely liked him. The cute 16-year-old teenager who married Brian had grown into a beautiful woman in her early twenties with two toddlers and a husband whose significant emotional issues were beyond her ability to handle, let alone reach. Brian moved into the pool house and lived a life quite separate from the relative normalcy Marilyn hoped to provide for their daughters.

Surf's Up was released in August 1971, but despite its positive reviews, the Beach Boys appeared to be a band in breakdown mode. Dennis's songs were absent from *Surf's Up*, so he embarked on a solo project with Daryl Dragon.[52] Brian embarked on a project with Marilyn and Diane Rovell's new group, Spring. Minus Ginger Blake, the Honeys were reborn as Spring, and Brian, along with David Sandler and Stephen Desper, produced their debut album.[53]

So Tough a Spring

Spring released their self-titled debut album in July 1972 on United Artists Records. Recorded from October 1971 to May 1972, the album featured a healthy studio contingent backing the rich voices of Diane and Marilyn Rovell. This eclectic collection featured country (Tennessee Waltz), R&B (Mama Said), power pop (songs by Carole King, Leon Russell, and Tommy Roe), and some Wilson originals (from both Brian and Dennis). All-in-all, it was strong collection of early 1970s pop, and this radio-friendly record should have kept company with artists such as the Carpenters, Cat Stevens, Carole King, Linda Ronstadt, and the like.

They revisited Brian and Mike's song first recorded in 1964 by Sharon Marie, "Thinking' Bout You Baby" in a version that tops the original and is comparable to its later cousin, "Darlin'," that the Beach Boys had recorded four years earlier. There is a beautiful cover of Dennis's "Forever," Brian and Al's "Good Time," Brian's "This Whole World," and a new song Brian composed with David Sandler, the dreamy "Sweet Mountain."[54] The album was rounded out with the Leon Russell and Bonnie Bramlett ballad, "Superstar" (the Carpenters's hit recording was released in August 1971), a pair of songs by Carole King, Tommy Roe's "Everybody," the Shirelles's hit, "Mama Said," and a track for which there is little information, "Awake." Composed by Floyd Tucker, it appears on the infamous "Bedroom Tapes" but little information exists as to the song or its author.

The duo had changed their name from Spring to American Spring as another group owned rights to the name. It may have been the inconsistent marketing or the album's weak reception, but regardless, it was their only release on UA. Brian took Diane and Marilyn to Otho, IA, where he produced four sides with the hope to find them another label.[55] They recorded "Shyin' Away," Dennis Wilson's "Fallin' in Love," "It's Like Heaven," and "Had to Phone Ya."[56] The first two tracks were released in 1973 on Columbia Records, and made no mark on the charts.

At the end of 1971, the Beach Boys began work on a new album, *Carl & the Passions—"So Tough."* While work continued into the new year, there were three significant changes in the Beach Boys's camp. Brian's withdrawal from group activities had intensified throughout the year to a point where he is a phantom presence on this album. In addition, Bruce Johnston left, or was removed, from the band. The stories on this narrative have never been in agreement, and Bruce appears only on the backing vocals for "Marcella."[57] The other change involved the addition of two new members to the band, their first since Johnston replaced Brian on the road in 1965. Blondie Chaplin and Ricky Fataar, formerly of the band the Flame, joined the group on guitar (Blondie) and drums (Ricky). Dennis Wilson had severely injured his hand and thanks to the fast thinking of his then-wife, Barbara, a doctor was able to repair the damage so that he could eventually play the drums again. But he would not be drumming with the Beach Boys for the foreseeable future, so Ricky's addition was timely and fortuitous. The two South African musicians brought a new edge to the group, both musically and visually. Blondie's guitar playing enabled the band to play with a harder edge than had been previously possible.[58]

In his 1991 autobiography, Brian, or more directly, Eugene Landy, dismissed *Carl and the Passions—"So Tough."* This album has minimal input from Brian, and while his contributions are buried within the record's eight tracks they have been watered-down through the album's many contributors. He provides backing vocals on some of his songs and not much else. If you listen to the album and do not think of it as the Beach Boys, it is a good, early 1970s rock album, and not a disjointed and unfocused release by the band Brian Wilson had willed into existence barely a decade earlier. The group was short on steam and inspiration, so two songs were taken from Dennis's then-in-process solo album, and two were offered by Blondie and Ricky. Stephen Desper was no longer working with the band, and the album lacked the clean lines that Desper was so skilled in creating from the band's diverse source materials.

"You Need a Mess of Help to Stand Alone" was a Wilson-Rieley song originally titled "Beatrice from Baltimore." Rieley's desire to bring more "relevant" themes and lyrics to the group led to a rewrite of the lyrics so that this solid rocking number had a "message" attached to it. "He Come Down" is a Jardine/Wilson/Love song and is the closest the Beach Boys come to creating an old-timey revival spiritual. With Al and Mike's TM leanings and Brian's spiritual views on music, the song manages to work on a very crowded agenda. The Hammond Organ and backbeat finger snaps give the song an authentic, if at times slightly contrived, feel. The final a cappella choral gesture was either borrowed from or arranged by Brian. Side one closes with Brian's last contribution to the album, "Marcella," which worked with themes from the as yet-unreleased "I Just Got My Pay," which itself was borrowed from the earlier track, "All Dressed Up for School." Composed with Tandyn

Almer, the original lyrics about a masseuse whom Brian was known to visit were changed by Jack Rieley to provide a more innocent boy-girl tale. Though Brian was not listed as an author, "All This Is That" is Brian channeled by Carl, Al, and Mike as the rhythmic figures and floating vocals are similar to some of Brian's more ethereal works.

The release of *Carl and the Passions—"So Tough"* is notable for the packaging Warners selected for the album. The band had acquired licenses for their Capitol recordings from *Pet Sounds* through *20/20* that allowed the band to reissue them on Brother/Reprise.[59] Packaged with the new album was a reissue of *Pet Sounds* in a two-fer configuration. Record labels hit upon a marketing plan in the recession-logged 1970s to reissue their artists' back catalog in 2-for-the-price-of-1 sets. MCA Records had been successful in repackaging the Who's early catalog in this manner, so Warners, still looking for that magic hit from the Beach Boys, decided to try something similar with the hope that fans would want to buy a new Beach Boys record if it came with an album that had been unavailable for two years. Warners fortunately elected to release a clean monophonic mix of *Pet Sounds* that allowed fans to reengage with the album as Brian had originally intended.

On Jack Rieley's suggestion, the Beach Boys decamped to Baambrugge, Holland, to record their next album. This was a massive and expensive undertaking as it required the relocation of the band, their families, and the various entourages employed by each member of the group, in addition to moving an entire recording studio because they could not find an available space for the length of time they would require. Brian had minimal involvement in the making of *Holland*, and his increasing emotional and (still undiagnosed) psychological conditions worsened throughout this period. Getting Brian to Holland was enough of a challenge, but it was over 1972–1974 that Brian cast himself further adrift amidst the food, the drugs, and his withdrawal from reality. The band had announced that *SMiLE* would be forthcoming, so as anticipation began to swell among fans and the press, it simply increased tenfold the pressure on Brian to once more provide something he no longer had within himself. The move to Holland turned out to be a disaster for Brian. Marilyn and the girls had gone over with everyone else, while Brian required three attempts to get to the Netherlands. The entire agenda upended Brian's internal landscape and "shattered his will to create."[60] In the end, it was one of Brian's songs that salvaged the album once they had returned stateside, and it was the rejection of his imaginative internal travelogue that simply added to his list of failures. "Mount Vernon and Fairway (A Fairy Tale)" was roundly rejected by the band when Brian presented it in Holland. This sent him back into a depression and he offered nothing else to the group. After some consideration, Carl and Rieley assisted Brian with the completion of the track that would not be on the album, but included with the album as a bonus 7″ single. This work is one of Brian's most confusing creations, and as a contemporary review remarked, "it evaporates time as nothing Brian Wilson has ever attempted before." Leaf argues that Brian "retreated into something of a fairy-tale world out of a sense of self-preservation." The story is touching but its delivery is ruined by Rieley's pedestrian narration. Brian had been engrossed in Randy Newman's *Sail Away* and was inspired to write a dreamy vision that was both fantasy and reality through the story of a prince whose life is transformed by the music that comes to him through a magical transistor radio. The title refers to the intersection where the Love family lived in the Baldwin Hills neighborhood of Los Angeles, where Brian and Mike first learned to sing together. The story is wonderfully surreal with Brian represented by each of the story's characters, the Prince, the Pied Piper, and the radio. As a fairy tale, it can engender a number of colorful interpretations.

Brian was listed as coauthor (with Carl and Rieley) on "Funky Pretty," a pleasant track that evolved when Brian happened to be present and active for one day in the studio. The eighth-note accompaniment figure on the piano is a standard gesture of Brian's and it was around this progression that the band constructed a song that served as the record's closing track.

The sojourn to the Netherlands was costly and the band returned not with a finished product, but with backing tracks that would be completed in Los Angeles. As with earlier efforts, Warners rejected the album for the lack of a single. Van Dyke Parks helped salvage the day and played for David Berson a cassette with a song he wrote with Brian and which he felt could be a possible hit. "Sail On, Sailor" was a song Brian wrote on-demand for Van Dyke in 1971, and was encouraging enough that the label directed the band to complete the work. What began as a Wilson-Parks song ended up in committee and the final version credited them along with three coauthors. Blondie Chaplin delivered a commanding vocal on what became the album's lead-off track. The single did not make the splash Warners hoped for, but did slightly better when rereleased in 1975. The song is a fan favorite and is the most widely recognized work from *Holland*.

Warners released *Holland* in the first week of 1973. The album received decent reviews in the states and, after *Surf's Up*, was the Beach Boys's most popular work on Warners. The graphics for this album were, excluding *Pet Sounds* and *Surf's Up*, the best cover artwork the band had received across their 19 albums. The back cover presented individual pictures of each band member instead of a group shot and listed each of their songs alongside their pictures. The unposed image of an unshaven, unkempt, and scowling Brian is the telling image of a man about to descend into a personal hell and who would be unrecognizable when, two years later, he would be forced to reengage with the world.

Brian produced little music in 1973 except for the American Spring single of "Shyin' Away." Murry Wilson died on June 4 and his death left three emotionally damaged sons in his wake. Brian did not attend the funeral and, accompanied by Diane Rovell, chose instead to visit New York to promote "Shyin' Away," and appeared on Pete Fornatale's show at WNEW. To hear the interview 40 years later is disconcerting. Diane tries to keep him on topic but he rambles on in a rapid, nervous patter and jumps from topic to topic. He said that American Spring has been his band for the past two years, and goes on to say they were going to appear on the Ed Sullivan Show. The Sullivan show had ceased production in June 1971, and while everyone in the studio breaks into a nervous laugh, Diane defuses the situation by saying Brian has a great sense of humor. Brian did not think of himself as a Beach Boy, but it was clear that he was far away from any reality the band had once represented for him.

Dr. Landy Loves You (1974–1987)

5

Following Murry Wilson's death in June 1973, Brian accelerated into his "shut-down" years. While he retreated into his home, the country was mired in the Vietnam War, was burdened with double-digit inflation and rising unemployment, and was shackled by a gas crisis that emerged as a result of an OPEC-initiated oil embargo. Then-president Richard Nixon, extended an unpopular and unsuccessful war, struggled to silence the counterculture movement, and, with members of his cabinet, was disgraced by the Watergate scandal. Amidst this backdrop, Americans were drawn to their not-so-distant cultural memories and a romanticized innocence of the 1950s and 1960s. On August 1, 1973, Universal Pictures released George Lucas's *American Graffiti*, a low-budget film about teenagers living in central California in late-summer 1962.[1] The film was set over the course of one weekend and every scene was constructed around more than three dozen songs from the 1950s and early 1960s. It helped to spark a renewed interest in "oldies," rock and roll that was less than 20 years old, but was a distant generation removed from the music of 1973. Lucas used a pair of 1963-era Beach Boys songs in the movie and scored "All Summer Long" under the final credits. The film and its successful MCA Records soundtrack clicked with the executives at Capitol who, in June of 1974, released *Endless Summer*, a two-disc set that contained 20 of the band's greatest songs from the pre-*Pet Sounds* era. It went to the top spot on Billboard and helped to make the Beach Boys a hot commodity for the second decade of their career.[2] The month following its release, they began to play their first stadium shows as an opening act for Crosby, Stills, Nash, & Young, yet Brian was nowhere to be seen. An attraction to this period led to a proliferation of 1950s and 1960s era nostalgia on record, in movies, and on television. In April 1975, Capitol released *Spirit of America*, a follow-up to *Endless Summer* that reached the number eight spot on Billboard. In November 1973 Warners released a live album, *The Beach Boys in Concert*, which comprised of one-half post-*Pet Sounds* tracks and one-half oldies. It too went gold and reached number 26 on Billboard. Choreographer Twyla Tharp created two ballets to the Beach Boys music, *Deuce Coupe* in 1973, and three years later, *Deuce Coupe II*. The Beach Boys were suddenly "hip" again, but Brian Wilson was submerged into the most painful and difficult decade of his life.

Woke Up . . . Got Out of Bed

Murry Wilson's death sent Brian into a psychological and emotional spiral from which it appeared he might not reemerge. Brian made the occasional visit to recording studios in 1974 but seldom completed anything. Marilyn had removed the home studio prior to the Holland excursion, and with that gone, Brian's interest in recording also vanished. Stephen Desper has been quoted as saying that the choice to place a recording studio in Brian's home in 1967 was the Beach Boys's attempt to "... bring the mountain to Mohammed."[3] Brian was a troubled, depressed, self-destructive man, whose rare and embarrassing appearances in public fueled the legends that would follow him for years. In a rare and relatively coherent interview with Jim Pewter on Los Angeles's KRTH-101 in August 1974, it appeared Brian had to come to terms with the renewed popularity of his work. The Beach Boys, while very successful as a live band, were engaged in a myriad business issues that had escalated upon their return from Holland. They fired Jack Rieley as their manager and hired Steve Love, Mike's younger brother, to replace him. In December 1973, Blondie Chaplin left the band, and in the final days of 1974, Warners released a new Beach Boys single, "Child of Winter." Composed by Brian and Stephen Kalinich, it was released too late in the season to have any impact, and with a label that was fast losing interest in the band, the record had little chance for any success. This utterly charming song was a full Wilson family affair. Arranged by Brian, it was performed by Dennis, Carl, and Mike, in addition to Brian's daughters, Carnie and Wendy. Brian sang the part of the Grinch in a voice that was not dissimilar to the voice he used for the Pied Piper in "Mount Vernon and Fairway." A few weeks before he cut "Child of Winter," Brian recorded another song coauthored with Kalinich, "California Feelin'."[4] This song remained unreleased until Brian rerecorded it in 2002 with his own band and presented it on a hits collection he curated for Capitol, *Summer Classics Selected by Brian Wilson*. Brian's original demo was released in 2013 on the *Made in California* boxed set.

While absent from the Beach Boys, Brian would appear as a supporting player on other artists' records. He sang backing vocals on Jackie DeShannon's "Boat to Sail" from *New Arrangement* and on Johnny Rivers's recording of "Help Me, Rhonda," from *New Lovers and Old Friends*. Brian was under increasingly strict rules at home as the family sought extreme measures in an effort to stem his increasing drug usage. Without the knowledge of Marilyn or the band, he maneuvered an arrangement with Equinox Music, an RCA-funded imprint run by Bruce Johnston and Terry Melcher, to play and coproduce up to 26 sides for the studio unit, California Music. Brian managed to coproduce a new cover of "Why Do Fools Fall in Love" and play the organ on "Jamaica Farewell," neither of which had any impact on the charts. The band was furious when they found out about this deal because Brian managed, once again, to create work outside of the Beach Boys, who struggled to redefine themselves in the 1970s. Brian also teamed up with old colleague Lou Adler to sing background vocals on "Just 14," an Adler-produced track for Tim Curry, who was on the verge of cult-stardom with *The Rocky Horror Picture Show*. Brian was content to give his time and his talents to anyone except the Beach Boys.

Through rounds of financial bullying (a reminder of his contract with Warners, the risk of litigation if he did not produce new work, and the threat of exclusion in revenue sharing from the band's now-lucrative touring fees) Brian could no longer try to extract himself from a band whose members he no longer liked, nor could he simply disappear without a significant loss of income. He was coerced into bathing regularly, wearing clothes (instead of his ubiquitous pajamas and robe), and engaging with the band and with other people.

Marilyn had come to accept she had lost control of the situation and called in a professional. Eugene Landy was a psychologist who specialized in the treatment of figures in the entertainment field. He was loud, outrageous, egomaniacal, and unorthodox in his methods. His professional (and personal) ethics were questionable at best, and his résumé was filled with achievements that were difficult, if not impossible to verify. His methods involved 24-hour, round-the-clock observation and therapy. He put Brian on a strict diet, and got him out of bed and exercising. Though Brian continued to make music for himself, and on rare occasions, as a backing singer for other artists, Landy got him to the piano to write songs, and by January 1976 Brian was back in the studio and running sessions. It is believed the initial plan called for him to record an album of cover songs followed by an album of original songs. What the Beach Boys wanted was not exactly what either Warners or Brian wanted, but Warner Brothers was about to get what they had waited six years to receive, a Beach Boys album that read—Produced by Brian Wilson.

The Beach Boys needed Brian to rejuvenate their career. They made some fine albums from *20/20* to *Holland*, and while generally well-regarded, they did not ship units. Brian's presence would attract publicity that would lead to album sales. Steve Love dreamed up the abysmal marketing angle of "Brian's Back," and Mike Love wrote an equally banal song to tell fans that after all the crazy stories and years of creative silence, Brian was once again making records with the Beach Boys. Steve Love hastened Brian's decline by placing him into the center of a media frenzy that would turn him into a hollow caricature of himself. Brian was an unhappy man who needed love and affection more than he needed an adoring public.[5] Some in the family naively thought Brian would be fine if had some hits and could get out in front of concert audiences again. He was the subject of countless articles and a guest on numerous talk shows. David Felton's November 1976 article in *Rolling Stone*, "The Beach Boys: The Healing of Brother Bri," presented a picture of Brian, Marilyn, the band, plus extended family and friends that was not at all flattering. In many ways it was an extension of Tom Nolan's two-part essay on the band from 1971, and it was through these articles that Brian's "legacy" would be enshrined and we could both marvel and wince at the exploits of a man now engulfed in attentions he never wanted.

Brian Is Not Back

While all efforts were directed towards moving Brian out of bed, into the shower, dressed, and into the studio, the Beach Boys in early 1976 were at work on what would become their highest charting record in a decade, *15 Big Ones*. Blondie Chaplin and Ricky Fataar were no longer in the band and once again the Beach Boys were the original five-man unit that first auditioned for Hite and Dorinda Morgan in 1961. In spite of eight years of low album sales, the Beach Boys regained their concert appeal and developed an identity that did not include Brian. They had moved from college auditoriums to large theatres and stadium shows, and though the band filled their sets with Brian's songs, they no longer existed as an extension of their cofounder, so as Brian returned to lead sessions for their new album, conflicting agendas divided the band into separate factions. Beginning in the late 1960s, Brian had withdrawn from activities that caused him emotional pain, much of which came from being with the Beach Boys. His reengagement with the band was intended to improve the group's profile and their opportunity to secure a better record deal, but they mistakenly believed their next album would be their last for Warners.[6] The band was divided into "Partiers," with Carl and Dennis on one side, and the "Meditators," Mike and Al, on the other. Both sides fought for control of Brian but what no one understood was that by controlling Brian, they would undo all the work they had, since 1970, invested into rebuilding the group.

From January 1976 to the middle of 1977, Brian produced some of his most creative and interesting (if not necessarily commercial) music since he abandoned *SMiLE*. In *Pet Sounds* and *SMiLE*, his obsessive quest for perfection resulted in some of the most extraordinary music of the decade, and over 18 months in the middle of the 1970s, his impressive productivity resulted in a body of work what was diverse in its variety of styles and forms. Once Brian was up and at work, the band and Marilyn fired Eugene Landy at the end of

1976. The Beach Boys organization had paid for part of Brian's treatment with an understanding that Brian would be able to work with (for) them again. Brian was out of bed and working, and in their hubris they believed they could keep him on track. What everyone ignored was that Landy had enabled Brian to face his psychological and emotional problems, and writing songs was part of Brian's therapy and not part of a larger marketing agenda. Landy made Brian face all the things that made him uncomfortable such as being in the studio with the Beach Boys, performing in concert, and giving interviews. The family saw Brian's return as a business decision and completely ignored the fact that all of this work had been to help him face the psychic scars that had debilitated him for so many years and had prevented him from creating music. Landy also holds blame here for placing his own self-interests over the needs and confidentiality of his patient, as the publicity he acquired in treating one of the most famous auteurs of the period could only enhance his professional profile. The doctor displayed questionable ethics in discussing Brian's diagnosis with the press. The public airing of Brian's many issues was embarrassing to him, though no one seemed to care because it made good press. Brian was the pawn in a public relations pitch, and no one seemed to take note that it might be wrong.

Brian was paraded back on stage and in front of the cameras as anticipation around *15 Big Ones* began to gather steam, and after July 2 he began to appear with the Beach Boys in concert. When the album was released, the cover presented a new facade for the band. Gone were the woodsy, folksy, and arty covers of *Holland* and *Surf's Up*. The cover artwork sported a new Dean Torrence-designed logo (a variant of which is used by the band to this day) that featured five interlocking rings with individual pictures of the band and Brian in the center of a graphic that resembled the official Olympic logo.[7] The entire project was a compromise on all sides. The process behind the making of the album was therapy more than anything else. Brian's return to the studio brought old tensions to the surface because during his absence they had learned to function quite well without him, and the pressure to succeed was too great. Brian and Mike's ever-present issues would reemerge. Mike and Al wanted to push the album out as quickly as possible, while Carl and Dennis thought they would record an album of oldies and pair that with an album of original songs. The conflicts caused Brian to lose interest in the work, so he decided the album was finished to put a stop to the pressure to deliver what others wanted. Even with Landy as an intermediary, it would appear no one in the band displayed any sensitivity to Brian's needs. The album contained mostly oldies with a smattering of new tracks, but none of that mattered when the album actually made it to number eight on Billboard and went gold. The cover songs, which often receive the harshest criticism in reviews of the album, are among Brian's strongest work on the record as he brings real passion and love to those works. While it sold well, the record was subject to a great deal of scrutiny because it was "Produced by Brian Wilson." In spite of the enthusiasm that greeted its release, criticism was not spared in discussions about the arrangements, the less than stellar performances, Brian's newly rough-hewn vocal timbre, and the choice of songs. Ultimately, the album has not aged well.

The production values on this album do not share the level of detail or precision he exhibited in the mid-1960s, though the expansion of his timbral canvas is effective. The album's opening track is a stiff and orderly cover of Chuck Berry's "Rock and Roll Music." Mike delivers a lead that sounds like a petulant teenager, and it lacks swing, though the mix used for the single was somewhat less restrained.[8] "It's O.K." is a Wilson-Love composition with a rich and raucous arrangement. The backing track for this dates back two years to a session when members of Roy Wood's band, Wizzard, were in the studio with Brian, and Ricky Fataar was still on drums for the Beach Boys.[9] "Had to Phone Ya" is a Wilson/Love/Rovell track, and one that Brian had recorded three years earlier in Iowa with American Spring. "Chapel of Love" (The Dixie Cups, 1964) features a wonderfully idiosyncratic arrangement, and while it lacks the lightness found in the original, it is wonderfully effective. "Talk to Me" (Little Willie John, 1958) is mashed with "Tallahassee Lassie" (Freddy "Boom Boom" Cannon, 1959). "That Same Song" is another Wilson-Love composition and a partner to "He Comes Down" from *Carl and the Passions—"So Tough."* They performed it on their NBC special later that year and did a far more convincing job while accompanied by the Los Angeles-based Alexander Hamilton Double Rock Baptist Choir, and it is here Brian succeeds in making truly spiritual music. Side one closes with "TM Song," a quirky song that, along with "Transcendental Meditation" from *Friends*, is utterly forgettable.

Side two opens with "Palisades Park," Freddy "Boom Boom" Cannon's most enduring hit from 1962, and one that previously served as a template for two of Brian's songs, "County Fair" and "Amusement Parks USA." The Wrecking Crew provides the backing track and delivers a solid, in the pocket, performance. "Susie Cincinnati" was the B-side of the Beach Boys's first Warners single in 1970, and the B-side of the unpublicized 1974 single "Child of Winter." A 1956 hit for the Six Teens, "A Casual Look" gives the band an opportunity to flex their doo-wop chops, but feels half-finished. Brian's arrangement of Fats Domino's 1956 smash, "Blueberry Hill," is one of his best on the album. The track suffers only for Mike's mannered lead vocal. This is followed by a previously mothballed Wilson-Norberg song, "Back Home." This country-lite song is not terribly memorable as Brian had attempted it twice before, once in 1963 and again in 1970, before settling upon this version in 1976. The song is mildly autobiographical when Brian sings of going back to Oh-High-O, since his great-grandparents hailed from farm stock in Meigs County, Ohio. The Five Satins's 1956 masterpiece, "In the Still of the Night" is a near copy of the original and shows Brian's arrangement chops can hold an original template and expand it enough to create a song that works on many levels and shows his sincere love for the work.

The album closes with a cover of the Phil Spector/Righteous Brothers 1965 hit, "Just Once in My Life." Spector has always loomed large in Brian's life and for so many years he felt he needed to be as good as Spector, but he never considered the fact that his own production and arranging skills had moved far beyond Phil's extraordinary aesthetic. Brian managed to create a track that, while it does not top the original, is as tasteful an homage as one could imagine and features some of Brian's most emotional vocals on the album.

Session dates for the album show that Brian preferred to record oldies, the majority of which did not make the album. It is clear Brian was comfortable producing cover songs, but if only the organization (Brother Records, Inc., and the Wilson family) would have let him follow this path for as long as he needed, he may have come around to creating his own music, on his own terms, and on his own schedule. The band, the label, and his family kept pushing him to make new music. In hindsight, this scenario has a parallel story to Wilson's great-uncle Johnny Wilson. Johnny's brother Charlie, in speaking about his older brother, said "Maybe if he'd gone slow .... But no one let him go slow ... full of ideas and dreams bigger than all the rest of us." Since Brian had returned to the studio, they had begun to reject and criticize his work, and no one would allow him to move slowly. In Newsweek of July 19, 1976, a brief article titled, not surprisingly, "Brian's Back" paints an uncomfortable picture of the group. Janet Maslin described "mirthless oldies" and "obsessively lighthearted new songs" and clearly is not impressed in any way. Various members of the band shared their misgivings as to his basic competency, and Carl shared his opinion that it was a mistake to put Brian in charge of the album. Writing songs began as an exercise, and that was how Landy approached it in order to get Brian back into work routines. The band took his songs and once released proceeded to vent their dissatisfaction with the entire record. One of the original Wrecking Crew members who played on *15 Big Ones* shared "Everyone's demanding stuff out of him, and he's trying to satisfy everyone."[10]

The following year, Dennis Wilson recorded his first solo album, *Pacific Ocean Blue*, which made it clear that the Beach Boys had consciously chosen to underutilize the "other" high-functioning songwriter within the group. As the first Beach Boy to go solo, Dennis accomplished something that Brian had not dared to consider, but probably should have back in 1967. The middle Wilson brother demonstrated to all that he was capable of writing strong and moving material, but stretching back to *Sunflower*, his songs were often passed over, so he struck out to make his own record. Once *Pacific Ocean Blue* was released, he began work on a second solo album, the unreleased *Bambu*. His personal issues would soon engulf him as his drinking and drug use would explode to where he could no longer function as an adult, let alone as a Beach Boy.

Brian had become, once again, the commodity upon which the band pinned their futures, and in their selfishness and narrow-mindedness they would balk at Brian's next two offerings, *Love You* and *Adult/Child*. Brian continued to perform on occasion with the Beach Boys and in the fall of 1976 began work on tracks that would become *Love You*. Steve Love was anxious to maintain momentum from the success of *15 Big Ones*, and continued to force Brian on-stage to "parade him like a 'trained monkey.' " If Brian was on tour, then Landy and his henchmen would be there to watch Brian's every move. It was also decided that Brian and the band would be the subject of a prime-time television special to be directed by Lorne Michaels, the mastermind behind *Saturday Night Live*.[11] Brian's still-fragile emotional and psychological condition would be exposed and fetishized as part of the Brian Wilson mythology. Eugene Landy, as his doctor, should have refused to allow his "patient" to be used in this way, but the business machinations between the Beach Boys, Eugene Landy, and Stephen Love were interconnected, so if any press was good press, then turning Brian's private life into "... marvelous and perverse entertainment" was completely acceptable.[12] Michaels worked with Brother Records to produce a show that would include live concert footage and profiles for each band member, with the primary focus on Brian. There was an interview from his bed, footage from his 34th birthday party attended by Paul and Linda McCartney where everyone seemed to enjoy themselves except for the guest of honor who all but disappeared into the background. The highlight of the show is the now famous "Failure to Surf" skit where Brian is arrested by two uniformed cops, played by *Saturday Night* regulars Dan Aykroyd and John Belushi, who drive him to the beach and force him to go surfing. Brian had never surfed, so a 250-plus pound man in a terry bathrobe carrying a surfboard into the ocean and fumbling to "catch a wave" was as much absurdist humor as it was an abusive stunt where Brian is the central buffoon in his own show. Brian would also make a solo appearance on *Saturday Night Live* on November 27, 1976.[13] Brian's awkward solo performance would further sear into viewers' collective memory, the image of an overweight, awkward, former genius, as if Michaels was out to prove that the sixties were in fact dead. Singing "Good Vibrations" from a piano situated in a sandbox would drive home the truth that Brian was a damaged artist, and by showing that he was "back" it allowed us to feel okay with an invasion of both his recovery and his privacy because it was packaged as a public trial and humiliation. Taped a few days prior to his appearance on *Saturday Night Live*, Brian appeared on the Mike Douglas show in an interview that was equal turns touching and disturbing, as he waxes on about his drug use, the function of money as a pathway to happiness, after which he gamely performs "Back Home." Bruce Johnston, who was not with the group at this juncture, would acknowledge "I think he's doing something he doesn't want to."[14] Though the music to come would be stronger, it would continue to chip away at Brian until he was an even larger shell of someone who once was.

Brian Loves Iowa

Through the fall of 1976 into the winter of 1977, Brian organized enough material for two albums that would best have been suited as solo albums, but the contract with Warners and pressures from the family dictated this substantial body of new work would become Beach Boys product. One of Brian's lesser known contributions from this period is the song "Cruise to Harlem," coauthored with America's Gerry Beckley and sung by teen idol David Cassidy. While this is an odd connection, the Cassidy album was released on RCA, and the partnership with Beckley came about through the Johnston/Melcher/Equinox/RCA connection. Andrew Doe references a 13-track collection from this period known only, and unofficially, as *New Album*. Little is known about this album except for the proposed track listing. It included songs recorded in sessions for *15 Big Ones*, the *Last Capitol Album/Sunflower*-era, a track from the mid-1960s, and a couple of newer songs. There was no release date, and no proposed title, so its existence cannot be verified. This bears mention because from early-1977 until 1980, Brian's work with the Beach Boys has been conflated into a couple of convenient, though imprecise narratives. With the exception of three tracks, the *New Album* materials would end up on *M.I.U. Album*, *Keepin' the Summer Alive*, the *Good Vibrations* boxed set from 1993, and *Made in California* from 2013.

Love You, originally titled *Brian Loves You*, was changed to *The Beach Boys Love You*, and is the result of Brian's extraordinarily productive sessions in the fall of 1976. Though Landy was fired at the end of that calendar year, Brian sustained work on the album into the new year, and its highly personal tone makes the collection one of his more memorable works. A collection that became known as *Adult/Child* was recorded on the heels of *Love You* in the winter and spring of 1977, was prepared for submission that summer, and was unanimously rejected by the band. The music on both albums was certainly not Beach Boys music, but it was Brian Wilson in his truest and most creative state in over half-a-decade. While Carl and Dennis hated *15 Big Ones*, and Mike and Al embraced the public's positive response to the album, the band's response to the *Love You* and *Adult/Child* was one of confusion and incredulity. The rejection of his music by a band that rejected his work for the better part of a decade was the final straw for Brian and he would, until *That's Why God Made the Radio*, choose the path of least, or no, resistance when working with the Beach Boys. His disinterest in the band enabled him to make mediocre records. As Brian became a prisoner between the "meditators" and the "partiers," his music continued to be devalued by the very people who wanted his creative soul. By 1978, Brian's only option was to shut down and do whatever they wanted. He may have wished he was not a Beach Boy, but it was made very clear that no other option was available to him, though food, alcohol, and drugs could temper his desperate situation. The only problem was that audiences expected Brian Wilson to be "Brian Wilson," and when his songs on Beach Boys albums did not meet a certain standard, he would be further criticized and written-off.

Love You remains one of the most divisive albums in Brian's catalog. For all purposes, this is a Brian Wilson solo album with only brief contributions by other members of the band who added their parts after the bulk of the work was finished. Earl Mankey engineered much of the album and has said that approximately 80 percent of what is heard on *Love You* was Brian handling all vocal and instrumental tracks. For all the criticism Brian received throughout the decade, he still was able to play all instrumental parts and sing all lead and backing vocals. This was not the sign of a drug casualty or burned out has-been as the press would portray him in the upcoming years. The rest of the band contributed their vocals to the album in place of Brian's tracks, which left him with only two solos. The graphics for the album were unusual not so much for the design, but for the effusive love and appreciation the band expressed for Brian, as if to thank him for his participation in their group effort.

Band dynamics aside, the music on *Love You* is extraordinary in its sheer originality and its rejection of contemporary trends in popular music. In some ways it was the *Smiley Smile* of 1977, and was the most unexpected album of the year. Neither did Brian pander to the oldies/nostalgia set nor did he try to harvest his ideas with the same tools and directives he had used a dozen years earlier. Brian also avoided grandiose theatrical spectacles, which makes *Love You* all that more startling since it compares to nothing else that was released in 1977. The songs are at turns funny, raucous, romantic, light-hearted, intimate, at times flat, but are utterly honest. Brian makes extensive use of the Mini-Moog and mines early rock and roll tropes to inform the majority of the songs, so the album remains as surprising and refreshing today as it did upon its original release. The album earned its share of strong reviews. Lester Bangs of *Creem* called it "their best album ever." Other reviewers called out its "... ragged harmonies ... juvenile lyrics ... and quirky tunes." England's *Melody Maker* provided a fairly true prediction, "This album can appear insubstantial on early acquaintance, but further attention yields many riches."

The opening track, "Let Us Go On This Way," is a raucous, full-bodied song that uses Lambert's "Celestial Choir" at the end of each verse on "God, please, let us go on this way." "Roller Skating Child" is another solid rocker where he borrows early rock tropes with the lyrics "well oh my, oh gosh, oh gee, she really sets chills inside of me." "Mona" is a classic Brill Building-style song delivered with gusto by Dennis, who by this time vied with Brian for the most ravaged voice in the Beach Boys. It lacks a bridge, which gives the song an imbalanced deportment, but does not detract from the pure fun of the work. This was followed by "Johnny Carson," a song about the one-time king of late night television. While there is a slightly familiar groove similar to "The Monster Mash," it comes off as a very tongue-in-cheek appreciation for a talk show host. "Good Time" is the one weak link on the album as Brian produced a much more effective version for American Spring back in 1972. The song had its origin in the early iterations of *Sunflower*, and was rejected at that time. It was out of place on *Love You*, as its half-decade old arrangement does not compare to anything else on the album. "Honkin' Down the Highway" like the album opener is a driving rocker with a great bridge, where Brian provides a driving bed of keyboard ostinati under Al's confident lead. Side one closes with "Ding Dang," a work coauthored with Roger McGuinn in 1973.

"The Night Was So Young" is one of the album's ballads. Brian and Carl deliver a wonderful lead vocal, as Brian's falsetto soars over Carl's lines. "I'll Bet He's Nice" must have some connection to the multiple and tangled relationships that were part of Brian's unconventional world in the mid-1970s, but without reading too deeply into it, the shared vocals by Dennis, Brian, and Carl are stunning in their raw emotion. The gravitas of the song is rescued by the distracting colors of the Mini-Moog, but without them, the song's lightheartedness would be lost in the painful tone of the lyrics. Whether Brian was talking about Marilyn, her sister Diane, or one of the other women in his life at this time, the song that follows asks us to imagine an innocent and simpler time. "Let's Put Our Hearts Together" is a lovely duet sung by Brian and Marilyn where her velvety alto contrasts against Brian's nasal lead vocal. Dennis could deliver powerful and honest vocals, but on "I Wanna Pick You Up," he sounds like a leering uncle. One redeeming feature of the song it its tag, which is pure magic with Brian's Four Freshman-esque arrangement. "Airplane" starts with much promise and the vocal work on the song is stellar, but then it all somehow dies out before a seemingly unrelated shuffle tag is added as a coda. "Love Is a Woman" closes the album and while Brian's pastiche of a 1950s doo-wop could have worked real magic, it falls short both vocally and instrumentally. The song was not helped by Brian's performance of the song on *Saturday Night Live*, where his sincere but frozen demeanor left most listeners anxiously waiting for it to finish.

As Brian continued to be the center of media coverage about the Beach Boys, and continued to produce work under the supervision of Eugene Landy, the band had grown weary of Brian's increasing profile and of Landy's extraordinary bills. Their frustration was justified as the band had persisted on the road for over six years, playing concerts to audiences large and small. They would reclaim an enthusiastic fan base while Brian lived in his bed, but they also created the monster of "Brian's Back" as a hook to acquire media attention. Stephen Love had become wary of Landy when the doctor suggested that he be paid with a percentage of Brian's earnings in lieu of a flat, hourly rate.[15] The cost of Brian's "treatment" had escalated from $10,000 to $20,000 per month, and that was enough for Steve to rally Marilyn and Brian and call for his dismissal.[16] Landy and his minions were gone by the end of 1976.

Had Eugene Landy been retained through 1977 and 1978 to "treat" Brian, it would surely have resulted in financial impropriety and an abuse of professional ethics, as would occur in 1988–1990, but the alternative that was put into place in early 1977 would result in even greater damage to Brian, and by 1983 he would be months, if not weeks, from death. Stephen Love hired his brother, former professional basketball player, Stan Love, and his friend, former athlete and Playgirl centerfold, Rushton "Rocky" Pamplin to "watch" Brian, to keep him off drugs, keep him exercising, and keep him writing songs. The "trained monkey" act had to go on, and surely, with two muscled meats looking over his shoulder, Brian would not get out of hand.

Crossroads

In early 1977 Brian looked well, was active, writing songs, in shape, and expressed an intention to rejoin the Beach Boys on tour. Warners had little interest in promoting an album from a band that was on its way out the door. Steve Love struck a lucrative deal with Walter Yetnikoff and Columbia (CBS) Records for sums of money they had never earned from a label. Their records would appear on James William Guercio's successful Caribou label through CBS. Yetnikoff was interested in the Beach Boys but was equally, if not more, interested in taking any artist from Mo Ostin's stable at Warner Brothers. As label head, he made it his duty to acquire for CBS anyone who was comfortable on a rival label, and Warners was the label he loved to raid whenever the opportunity presented itself. Once CBS announced their new signing, Warners was disinclined to promote *Love You*, which doomed it to the lower reaches of the charts. Amidst the posturing and negotiations, someone had miscounted as it turned out the Beach Boys owed one more album to Warners. They would be going nowhere for the time being, and the next two years would usher in a period of irreversible declines that would conclude with the death of Dennis Wilson at the end of 1983.

Brian sustained his creative streak into early 1977 and began sessions for an album that would come to be known as *Adult/Child*. Brian hired Dick Reynolds, the arranger he used on the 1964 Christmas Album, to provide arrangements for some of the songs on which he was working. *Adult/Child* was never released, though unlike other of the "reputed" albums, it was a complete collection submitted to the Beach Boys and to Warners where it was quickly rejected.[17] This unique collection of songs made for great listening and was a window into Brian's imagination, but it would never see an official release. Had Warners not been fed up after seven inconsistent years with the group, the label could have developed an effective marketing agenda because the album featured some of Brian's most unique musical choices and his enthusiasm can be heard on every one of its tracks. The Dick Reynolds-arranged works are wonderfully offset with Brian's newer songs, but it arrived too late in the band's tenure at the label to give Warners any incentive to promote such a collection. In an era when artists as diverse as Randy Newman, Leon Redbone, and Tom Waits could amass an impressive fan base, an album of this variety from a legendary 1960s songwriter had the potential to be a hit, however atypical it was under the Beach Boys banner. The album contained two tracks from the *Last Capitol Album/Sunflower-era*, "H.E.L.P Is on the Way," and "Games Two Can Play," which were carried over from the half-idea that was *New Album*. To this Brian added Dick Reynolds arrangements of Wilson originals, "Life Is for the Living," "It's Over Now," and "Still I Dream of It." A heartfelt cover of Derose and Parish's "Deep Purple" completed the Reynolds-arranged tracks. Also carried over was "Hey Little Tomboy," a cover of "On Broadway," an arrangement of Brian's longtime favorite riff, "Shortenin' Bread," plus some newer recordings, "Everybody Wants to Live," "Lines," and "I'm Trying to Say."

Adult/Child was submitted to Warners in the fall of 1977 and rejected as being uncommercial. The album has never been released, but as a bootleg it developed a small but dedicated following who love the stylistic diversity of the album. In the end, the album died and while one track would be carried over to their next "official" long player, four songs would not be released until the *Good Vibrations* boxed set and six of the tracks have never been released, though "Shortenin' Bread" was rerecorded for *L.A. (Light Album)*. Brian's singing on the album was stronger than on either of the two previous records, but the styles he adopted were criticized by some in the group. Two of the songs have a Sinatra-esque feel, in part due to their arrangements, but also because the melodies were in a more traditional mid-century ballad style, while in "Life Is for the Living," Brian sounds as if he is a Las Vegas lounge singer.[18] The tracks show Brian's admiration for mid-century American song, his love for vocal rounds, and his inconsistent interest in healthy living. Until the 2012 release of *That's Why God Made the Radio*, this was Brian's last fully engaged effort to lead an album under the Beach Boys name.

Once *Adult/Child* was assembled, the band traveled to London to play a CBS Convention on July 30, 1977. The label had a lot riding on the group, so their appearance at the label's international convention was a must and Brian had to appear. There is a photograph of Brian at the event, seated at a piano with a resigned and downcast look on his face that tells the full story. Just as with Warners, the CBS contract stipulated that Brian be a major contributor on each album. While he had been the primary artist on both *Love You* and the soon-to-be-stillborn *Adult/Child*, the band's lack of support for either project would guarantee that Brian would have no initiative or desire to lead anything more for the group. With a contract that was agreed upon by his cousin and manager, Stephen Love, Brian was trapped, or "contractually obligated," into the group with no other path available to him. Ironically, Elvis Costello was arrested four days earlier for busking outside the CBS Convention on July 26, 1977. This stunt was a set up directed by his manager, Jake Riviera, with the goal to land Costello a North American contract with CBS.[19]

By mid-1977, Brian was in the last throes of an 18-month creative spurt. In September, the band played Central Park and the following day there ensued the legendary fight on the tarmac at Newark International Airport, at which point the band nearly broke up. Brian retreated while the "partiers" and "meditators" factions became even more estranged. They would, in the upcoming months, travel separately in the air and on the ground, and in concert they would enter the stage from opposite wings and engage with each other only when necessary. They would argue over every business detail, from who would be their manager to which of their friends would be in the backing band, and most importantly, what was to become of the Beach Boys's musical direction? Brian was unwilling (or simply not interested) to do what either faction wanted, so why would he take charge of the band since both sides had been critical of his latest efforts.

Brian produced two sessions for American Spring in 1977. One, in the summer as he finished work on *Adult/Child*, and the second, on November 16 in Fairfield, IA, where three-fifths of the band were recording enough songs for two complete albums. Rocky Pamplin, one of Brian's new "minders" and with whom Marilyn Wilson was having an affair, was included in the American Spring sessions and believed that Brian was going to help him launch a singing career. Many of these tracks did not see a release until 1986 when they were included on a nine-track Honeys album, *It's Like Heaven*. Brian is credited for producing/arranging five of the albums' tracks while other parties handled the remaining four. Rocky Pamplin is not credited on this album and any contributions he made were omitted from the final mix. One unique track Brian produced in the fall of 1977 was the American Spring/Honeys recording of "Don't Be Cruel." Elvis Presley had died that August, so it is likely that Brian wanted to record the song as a tribute to him.

Surfing in Iowa

Mike and Al had decided that the band should travel to the Maharishi International University in Fairfield, IA, to record their next album. Dennis and Carl refused to go, and Brian preferred to avoid conflict. This would, for the next five years, be his path to survival in the intractable situation in which he found himself within the Beach Boys. The sequence of events at this juncture of the Beach Boys history (November 1977–February 1978) is a challenge to place because existing narratives elect to separate a number of events that transpired simultaneously. Research undertaken independently by Elliott and Doe provides a clearer narrative as to what occurred in both Iowa and California throughout this period. It has been long accepted that the Beach Boys recorded a holiday album that was rejected by Reprise. The reality is that the Beach Boys worked on two individual projects, one being a holiday album and the other a collection of non-holiday songs. Once the holiday album was rejected, they changed lyrics on three of the tracks to non-holiday themes and compiled an album with tracks prepared in their other project.

Two projects the Mike-Al-Brian configuration of the Beach Boys began in Iowa were *Merry Christmas from the Beach Boys* and *California Feeling*. The holiday album was rejected by Warners, and *California Feeling* would evolve into *Winds of Change*, before a final boilerplate was renamed *M.I.U. Album*.[20] "California Feelin' " was a song Brian wrote with Stephen Kalinich in 1974, but he was adamant that it not be included on the new album. The *M.I.U. Album* listed Brian as the Executive Producer and credited him as coauthor on a number of songs. The title of Executive Producer was honorary since Al Jardine and Ron Altbach handled the production duties.

The scrapped holiday album is often referred to in less than glowing terms. A number of the tracks were made available on the 1998 collection, *Ultimate Christmas*, and I believe it had the potential to be an enjoyable, if slightly unorthodox collection, and given the limitations of seasonal marketing it is understandable why the label rejected it. It is believed a track list would have included the 1974 holiday single, "Child of Winter," and a new work coauthored with Diane Rovell, "Winter Symphony." "Loop de Loop" was transformed into "Santa's Got an Airplane" Brian also offered "(I Saw Santa) Rockin' Around the Christmas Tree" which was first recorded a year or two prior. There were a few outtakes from *15 Big Ones* given new holiday lyrics in addition to tracks from Mike, Al, and Dennis. It is documented that another track from 1969, "H.E.L.P. Is on the Way," was transformed into "Santa's on His Way." *M.I.U. Album* was released in October 1978, nearly a year after the sessions in Fairfield. Of the album's 12 tracks, Brian is the composer or coauthor on eight. If this was intended to show that he was with the team once more, a single listen would prove otherwise, and the effort taken to make Brian appear engaged and involved could not hide the fact that the album was thin, unimaginative, and a dud.

The three Beach Boys albums that bridge the late-1970s into the Ronald Reagan decade, *M.I.U. Album—L.A. (Light Album)—Keepin' the Summer Alive*, are generally overlooked works. None of the three are memorable and though a good song would occasionally show through the cracks, the albums show the Beach Boys as a mediocre, middle-of-the-road rock band of late-1970s. Brian was at the lowest point of his entire tenure with the group, and he showed no motivation or interest to engage with the group. Just one year before *M.I.U. Album*, Brian completed two unorthodox but wonderfully original albums, with only intermittent help from the Beach Boys, but as they moved from Warners to CBS, it was expected they would present a unified front. Brian was the dog-and-pony show placed at the center of the band to demonstrate that the Beach Boys were of the period and were making music once again. The band began to see a decline in concert grosses and faced a cash crunch that necessitated layoffs in both the touring band and with Brother Records. They were in no place to repay CBS their multi-million-dollar advance, so there was no option but to go forward. Brian's name appears on the credits for many of the songs on the Caribou/Columbia albums, but his role in bringing these to record, if not less engaged, was executed with even less interest than were his contributions to the group's albums from 1971–1973.

In Name Only

The opening track on *M.I.U. Album*, "She's Got Rhythm" showed promise with its opening phrase. Brian's falsetto leads the track, and while not as elegant as it was a decade earlier, it was proof that he had not ruined his voice. But before the first verse is finished you realize that the Beach Boys have mastered the sound of an inoffensive middle-of-the-road rock group in the vein of Orleans or Starland Vocal Band, and aside from Brian's lead, there is nothing remotely original about the song. With all the songs the band could have carried over from one proposed album to another, it is incomprehensible as to why they chose to hold onto "Hey, Little Tomboy." While Brian may have sought to write a cute song about a little girl who grows up ("The Little Girl I Once Knew" was nowhere as questionable, and was an excellent song), when delivered by a nearly 40-year-old Mike Love, it sounds creepy.[21] Side one closes with "Wontcha Come Out Tonight," a song that almost sounds like Brian except for its music-minus-one arrangement. Side two opens with Carl's lead vocal on "Sweet Sunday Kinda Love." The arrangement has certain of Brian's touches, such as the eighth-note piano ostinato and the backing vocals, which are not dissimilar to what he was writing in the 1970s. It is a memorable track only in comparison to the remainder of the album. "Belles of Paris" was originally one of the holiday tunes, "Bells of Christmas," which was a far superior record to its *M.I.U.* counterpart. The feel of the original is washed in fuzzy, holiday warmth, but as "Belles of Paris" it is an embarrassingly cheap song delivered by Mike in the best high school French he can muster about the lovely belles of Paris. Even the arrangement managed to be dumbed down from its original holiday version.[22] "Pitter Patter" tries to sound authentic, but again, the arrangement is lifeless. This song could have worked on *Love You* in one of Brian's idiosyncratic settings, but it is empty shell on *M.I.U.* While Dennis did not travel to Iowa, work on the album resumed in Los Angeles, where he provided vocals on "My Diane." This is the album's closest effort to a "real" Beach Boys song because Dennis's soulful and whisky-soaked voice conveys real emotion, even if his pitch and phrasing are unsteady. Brian initially tracked this song in 1976 for the *New Album* collection, and his relationship with Diane Rovell clearly inspired this song. The arrangement barely avoids being stuck in the mud, but it has enough of Brian's touches, from the coda to the subtle change in instrumentation in the second verse, to be passable. The coda could have been one of those "Celestial Choir" moments, but someone felt the need to extend the track with a drawn-out repeat of the chorus. Brian's last credit is attached to "Match Point of Our Love," one of the most banal and ordinary songs in the Beach

Boys catalog.[23] I assume the body of the song belongs to Mike and the choruses were Brian's, except that Brian's attempt as lead vocalist is embarrassingly uninspired. The bland disco-lite drum track prepares us for a grand misstep that would come on the next album.

Mike Love was the front man for Celebration, an entity put together by Beach Boys touring member and *M.I.U.* coproducer, Ron Altbach, who was responsible for the soundtrack to a middling teen-flick, *Almost Summer*. The basic tracks for the album were recorded in Iowa during *M.I.U.* sessions and were provided by their touring band, who also did much of the playing on *M.I.U.* For the 11-track soundtrack album, Brian coauthored the title track, "Almost Summer" with Mike and Al. Altbach's production is not dissimilar, but is more palatable than the work he did on *M.I.U.* Surprisingly, the title track carries some of Brian's imprint, in both the chord progressions and rhythm track, and is not an unpleasant exercise. Mike adds the requisite "oldies" tag on the choruses, borrowed from "Surfin' U.S.A," to cheapen the whole effect. In some perverse turn of events, the soundtrack album reached the lower twenties on the charts, higher than *M.I.U.* would ever see. Celebration did perform live and in one show at the University of Southern California, Mike, Brian, and Jan & Dean appeared as guests. This proxy collective recorded a self-titled second album, and though Mike was not a "Featured" artist on their sophomore effort, he does provide vocals for three songs, the first of which is the most generic, late-1970s take on the *Smiley Smile* riff "Gettin' Hungry." There is a track that has yet to appear on any other official release, "How About a Little Bit," composed by Brian, Mike, and Diane Rovell. The subject is pure Mike, but likely was inspired by the Brian/Diane relationship. It is a decent, if generic, song in Altbach's production, so why did it not appear on a Beach Boys album?

Before *M.I.U. Album* was finished, the Beach Boys, with Brian, had to fulfill a tour of Australia and New Zealand as part of their contract with CBS. Again, all five Beach Boys were involved, as required by the label, while in reality the group was falling to pieces. Were it not for the band's collective greed and their insatiable appetite for money, they might have chucked it in at this juncture, but there was no going back for any of them. This tour was legendary for its many disasters, not least of which was Carl's newly acquired appetite for drugs in the aftermath of his collapsed marriage to Annie Hinsche. Dennis, while he remained inconsistent, unreliable, and unprofessional, was there in body, and Brian, under the eye of his handlers, Stan and Rocky, was slipping back to old habits and finding ways to get around their mock tough-love, bullying presence. Upon their return, Brian was nominally involved in random recording sessions while Dennis attempted to push forward on his *Bambu* project. Brian's life had unraveled so badly after his separation from Marilyn that he embarked on a glutinous routine of food, nicotine, alcohol, and drugs. He was pressured to write new material, but it was supposed to be the material they wanted, not what he wanted. There were periods of hospitalization, but he could easily talk a good story and check himself out of the hospital. He disappeared one day only to be discovered some days later in San Diego, playing in bars and sleeping on the street. No ID, no wallet, no keys, nothing. After another hospitalization, he was talked into coming to Florida to start work on a new album. The band commenced in Miami to begin work, with Brian in the production chair, at Criteria Studios. When CBS president Walter Yetnikoff paid a visit to "hear" the new work and delivered his now legendary response, "Gentlemen, I think I've been fucked," it was clear that something had to change.

Yetnikoff signed the Beach Boys on an $8.5 million package that guaranteed close to $1 million per album and a $2 million signing bonus, in addition to highly lucrative touring and publicity support. There was no back catalog in the deal, but they could not sell enough units to make it worth CBS's investment.[24] It soon became clear that by throwing money at the Beach Boys, nothing of note would come to pass. When it became clear that Brian would be unable to produce anything for the band, Bruce Johnston was called in to help. The band came back to Los Angeles and Bruce was able to get all five members to pull together a record that, for all of its indifferent material, was far superior to their previous effort. Dennis, as per usual, provided the most emotional and honest work on the album. Mike, Carl, and Al's contributions were good, and Brian was tagged in a most unexpected manner. The album's opening track, "Good Timin'," originated in 1974 sessions at Caribou Studios and was resurrected for this album. Bruce was able to salvage enough of it to make a strong lead-off song that sounded more like the Beach Boys than anything they had recorded in years. It is neither complex nor memorable, but the vocals are unmistakably the Beach Boys. The album's final track was Brian's riff on "Shortenin' Bread," and while there was a Brian-led recording of the work from the mid-1970s intended for *Adult/Child*, it was rerecorded for *L.A. (Light Album)* and credited as "arranged by" Brian Wilson. The great misfire on this album and one that still resonates among fans is the disco rendition of Brian's "Here Comes the Night," an otherwise acceptable rocker from *Wild Honey*. While "dance" music remained wildly popular, the suburban sounds of white-bread disco had outlived its shelf-life by 1978. Someone in the tone-deaf offices of CBS should have known better to stop to this, but Bruce and Curt Becher (née Boettcher) concocted a disco take on "Here Comes the Night." Brian was not involved, and cannot be held responsible for this piece. Unfortunately, this one track tarnished whatever quality work was created for *L.A. (Light Album)*, and the reputation of the entire record suffered as a result of this foray.

Though Brian had minimal involvement with *L.A. (Light Album)*, this was the last time the five original Beach Boys would work together on an entire project. While *L.A. (Light Album)* was a relative success when compared to their previous effort, their follow-up was an abject failure. Dennis had refused to take part in the sessions for *Keepin' the Summer Alive* that was released in

March 1980. A combination of his personal issues compounded with his alcohol and narcotic addictions inspired his unwillingness to participate on the album. He had pushed, for the better part of a decade, to move the band in a forward direction and to not be anchored to the nostalgia/oldies circuit. When it was clear the band would not evolve, his nonparticipation was his protest against a group that continued to re-tread the same thin creative soil.

Another attempt was made to bring Brian back into the production chair via a "Time Machine" approach where they would put Brian into a familiar space that might renew his interest in making work. He was brought back to Western with members of the Wrecking Crew, with a hope that familiar faces and a familiar location would inspire him to take charge once again. Chuck Britz came out of retirement and dug out the original analog equipment Brian used in the 1960s and set it up in place of the modern, 72-track gear. While Brian had a few good days in the studio, he quickly lost interest, so it was up to the group to cobble together a new album. The band pressured Brian to produce what they wanted, but Stephen Desper, who came back to engineer some of these sessions, believes Brian's opinions were only tolerated by the group, because "they felt their musical judgment was superior to his."[25] Given the deep psychological issues with which Wilson has struggled, it is absurd to think how the band believed that good intentions and reminders of the good old days would somehow resolve his problems. Many felt that these sessions would perhaps be Brian's last for it appeared that Brian was not long for the world.

For an album with only 10 songs, it is amazing that the band tracked close to three-dozen tracks in sessions for *Keeping' the Summer Alive*, but still managed to come up short for material. Sessions stretched from late July into December, and while Mike tried to coax Brian into writing with him, numerous tracks were recorded then discarded, and in the end, they pulled no less than three songs from past projects. Brian's name was attached to six of the album's tracks, and again, his name and body were there, but he was nowhere in sight. Bruce Johnston was once more back in the production chair, and while the album is disappointing, it is hard to imagine how any label would pay $1 million per album for this quality of work.

Brian's "Oh, Darlin" is one of the most unfortunate works ever placed on a Beach Boys album. The song is decent, but the arrangement is plodding and unimaginative, and Brian's disinterest is obvious in every measure of the song. The next track, "Some of Your Love" is a solid rocker whose origins went back a few years under the title, "Mike, Come Back to L.A." The enthusiasm heard in this song was carried over from its initial tracking sessions, for it has more energy than the remaining tracks on the album. Side two opened with "Goin' On," the second of three Beach Boys "feel good" songs to appear on their trio of CBS albums.[26] This is followed with "Sunshine," an utterly vapid attempt to merge calypso colors into a Beach Boys song.[27] This track would have been better served had it been passed over. "When Girls Get Together" was pulled from nearly a decade earlier, and while it is generally dismissed, I find this slice of the *Sunflower*-era Beach Boys wonderfully charming and atypical for Brian and the band. It is not helped by the fact that it is miscast on this album. Brian's last contribution, "Santa Ana Winds," is an inoffensive song originally recorded for *L.A. (Light Album)*. It was resuscitated for this album with a new arrangement that features strong group vocals that prevent the song from falling victim to utter blandness.

The Almost Final Descent

In any film of the Beach Boys from 1980, you will see a person who resembles Brian Wilson hammering out chords on the piano, and if he sings, his voice can barely hold a connection to the extraordinary music he had composed. The first three years of the decade would prove to be difficult for Brian, as well as his brother Dennis, who would be suspended or fired from the band on multiple occasions, or would be a source of embarrassment or trouble whenever he did appear with the band.

The Beach Boys appeared on an episode of *Fridays* that aired on June 20, 1980. Recorded in April of that year, they performed "Keeping' the Summer Alive," "Good Vibrations," and "Goin' On." The band takes a single line downstage with Bruce, Al, Mike, Carl, and Brian, who is seated behind a grand piano. The camera avoids Brian for the most part, but when it does pan on him, he appears detached and disengaged with a vacant expression, playing block chords, in contrast to the rest of the band who attempt to give a full performance. The day following the broadcast, they appeared at the Knebworth Festival in England at the conclusion of their eight-show European tour.[28] Brian is a little more engaged with the group on this show and sings on a handful of songs, but there is sadness to his very presence, and try as he can, even Dennis cannot pull him out of his vacant, far-away space.[29] While the show was broadcast in an unedited state, warts and all, the video and album used vocal and instrumental tracks that were sweetened post-concert in the studio.

December was a particularly bad month for the band, and Dennis's behavior simply added fuel to a flame that was about to engulf the band. Three days before John Lennon was murdered in front of his apartment building in New York City, the group appeared live, via satellite, on *Good Morning America* on December 5, 1980. Though it was the early morning in Los Angeles, Dennis, at one end of the couch, is clearly stoned and incapable of sitting up or looking at the camera while he fidgets back and forth or leans against Carl's shoulder. Al and Mike sit there stiffly while Brian sits between the two factions with a frozen expression on his face. Already fatter and more unkempt than earlier in the year, he does not say much until he has to respond to a question directed at him. Dennis refuses to answer any questions for the first part of the interview but in a moment of inspiration he grabs onto Carl's lapel microphone and starts to speak in a comparatively coherent and sincere manner. Always the peacemaker, Carl attempts to reiterate Dennis's answer then Brian goes into his best monotone to talk about a variety of topics and says "Be My Baby" is the record he listens to the most. The interview is a shambles while the host, Joan Lunden, manages to hold it all together. Mike and Al can barely contain their anger, but they are able to conclude the interview when their manager and former Elvis associate, Jerry Schilling, comes out to move things along. In the process he inadvertently acknowledges that the band has all manner of problems as a result of familial dynamics and their long history as a performing band. Later that month, Brian was present, though Dennis was not, when the band received their star on the Hollywood Walk of Fame. What was clear was that the Beach Boys had devolved into a band who could stir up their enthusiastic audience night after night, no matter how badly they played and no matter who of the original five were on the stage. They seldom, if ever, rehearsed and sounded like a ragged mess, but it seemed audiences did not care.

Things did not improve for Brian in 1981. Carl decided to pursue a solo tour in support of his new album, so for the first time since Carl was detained by the FBI in 1967, the band would perform without their "dependable" Wilson. The trio that recorded *M.I.U. Album* was now the core band, with Bruce and on increasingly rare occasions, with Dennis. They performed at Ronald Reagan's inaugural event, and appeared on the mall in Washington D.C. on July 4, in what was another underwhelming concert, but it was a show they played the following day in Long Beach at the Queen Mary that was the nadir of their career, and is one they had the misfortune of having broadcast live coast-to-coast. The show, hosted by Wolfman Jack and Los Angeles DJ Charlie Tuna, began with footage of the previous day's show in Washington. They clearly were exhausted from the cross-country flight, so much so that even Mike, the consummate showman, is off his game and can barely hold key. Brian looks disheveled, unwashed, and vacant, and Dennis is clearly under the influence of some or other substances, and wears the same clothes from the day prior on the mall.

The year carried on with Carl and Mike going out on solo tours between intermittent Beach Boys shows. If they could not humiliate themselves any further, in a splendid display of poor taste, they decided to break the United Nations anti-apartheid sanctions by performing for nine nights in Sun City, South Africa. Doing these shows meant that they would not play their traditional end of year show in Los Angeles, but no one seemed to care.

Carl returned to full-time work with the group by mid-1982, and while Brian made occasional forays into the studio, nothing evolved beyond initial sketches of work. He and Dennis continued to consume quantities of narcotics, and Brian had ballooned well beyond 300 pounds. Behind the scenes, there were discussions among the band (minus Dennis), Marilyn, and the band's management, in an effort to decide "what to do" with Brian. None of their previous attempts to help Brian had worked because their actions were ultimately in support of putting Brian back to work and not back in life.

The Beach Boys and Eugene Landy came to an agreement that would allow Landy to treat Brian with no interference from the band. An elaborate ruse was maneuvered to separate Brian from his latest live-in companion, a nurse he met during his last psychiatric stint and who was not about to let her meal ticket go without a fight. Brian was a filthy and broken mess, but Landy was able to get him checked into the hospital for tests in early 1983, after which he was whisked away to a private compound in Hawaii. As before, the treatment worked, and any resumption of work with the Beach Boys would require Landy or one of his crew to be present. Eugene Landy was paid to be Brian's voting proxy within Brother Records, Inc., which would create a new wealth of complications for Brian.

Brian played a few shows with the band in Hawaii in February 1983, where he continued to reside under Landy's care, but did not return to part-time work with the band until that summer. Dennis played his last show with the band in September 1983, and once again was suspended from the group. Unlike Brian, Dennis would never seriously commit to treatment for his many addictions. He continued to spiral away and on December 28, 1983, drowned in the harbor at Marina Del Rey when he dived off of a friends' boat to look for belongings he dumped into the harbor when he lost his boat, Harmony.

Brian - 1/Dennis - 0

Much has been written about Dennis's role in forming the Beach Boys and developing a myth that Brian channeled through the band into extraordinary success and fame. He was the brother with whom Brian felt the deepest personal connection, and his death could have sent Brian into another decline, but to Eugene Landy's credit, he shepherded Brian through that crisis. The band resolved to continue on and record the final album of their CBS agreement. Bruce Johnston, as always, sought to help the band however he could and recommended Steve Levine, a hot young producer he met when working in London in the 1970s.

Levine was the producer behind the massive success of the Culture Club, and while he may have seemed an odd choice to pair with the band, he was, like Brian, a perfectionist but with a complete mastery of the recording studio of the 1980s. This allowed a newly trim and healthy Brian to resume work with the band. It also allowed the band to work unhindered by the various distractions and conflicts that Dennis always brought to the group, and allowed them to create a work they dedicated to him as they attempted to ignite the second-half of their career.

Levine contributed an essay on "Getcha Back" in Dillion's *Fifty Sides of the Beach Boys*. In one session, after delivering a weak vocal track, Brian was roundly congratulated by the rest of the band. As it had been throughout the 1970s and early 1980s, Brian was encouraged, regardless of the quality of the work, just to keep him at work in the studio. Brian asked Levine for his opinion to which he replied "...It's shit. You need some singing lessons..." In anticipation of his firing, Levine showed up the following day to collect his materials, but received a call from the band's manager, Tom Hulett, who thanked him and informed Levine that Brian would not be in that day as he was receiving singing lessons. While Landy, who had begun to impose his "creative" agenda into Brian's work, did not appreciate Levine's critique, Brian appreciated it, improved his voice and was supportive of Levine's work while the rest of the band became exasperated over the producers' dedicated efforts. The result of Brian's renewed vocal discipline is heard on "Getcha Back" where his falsetto is clear, smooth, and provides the unmistakable hook for the song.

The Beach Boys, released in June 1985, came five long years after the band's last album of new material. *The Beach Boys* was the best work of their three albums on Caribou/CBS, but the label had already lost interest in them and the record only managed to make it to 52 on Billboard, though the single of "Getcha Back" broke into the top 30. While the record did not sound exactly like the Beach Boys, it showed that they could make good music in a contemporary style. Brian was coauthor on four tracks, plus "Male Ego," the B-side for "Getcha Back." Brian is not on his full creative game, but like *15 Big Ones* and *Love You*, his work on *The Beach Boys* shows him attempting to regain his footing as both a songwriter and musician. For the first time in years, you could clearly hear his unmistakable tenor, unlike the previous two albums where you would struggle to hear him buried within the mix. Levine's production style tamps down some of Brian's signature rhythmic gestures, but his harmonic and melodic choices are present throughout his songs.

"Crack at Your Love" is a thoroughly pleasant mid-tempo song. "California Calling" lists Al as the primary author, and from its introduction you can hear Al's perpetually upbeat, retro sensibility of the good old days, while Brian's touches are most apparent in the vocal and instrumental arrangement. "I'm So Lonely" has a feel-good air to it, while its lyrics tell an honest and sober story. "It's Just a Matter of Time" has Mike and Brian re-creating their 1950s shuffle/doo-wop sound. "Male Ego" is more than a bit of tongue-firmly-in-cheek.

Either the record did not sound like the Beach Boys, or no one really cared to hear America's Band embedded in layers of 1980s sheen. Regardless of the public's apprehension, Timothy White stated the album was "nearly as strong as *Sunflower*..." as if to acknowledge that it had been 15 years since the entire band contributed to a record that sounded like a group effort rather than a collection of solo artists or haphazardly patched semi-pieces. Levine supported White's assessment in saying "Everyone contributed in every single way the best they could." For a band with no prior experience in working with samplers and digital workstations, the learning curve was high and everyone in the group went the full distance to invest themselves into the work.

Over the next two years, Brian began to refer to the "doctor" as his executive producer. In that role, Landy encouraged Brian to reconnect with his first partner, Gary Usher, and start writing songs. While this continued to move Brian towards being an active composer and artist, Landy worked to remove Usher after a year-and-a-half of their resumed partnership. Brian's "Executive Producer" would control every aspect of his client's life, and once he secured Brian's contract with Sire Records, he would dictate his expectations and screen each and every contributor who came into Wilsons' orbit. In spite of this, Brian's 1988 solo album would demonstrate that he had not lost any of the magic. The path to true freedom from Landy, from his personal demons, and from his band would take additional time.

Landy's Return/Landy's Exit (1988–1998)

6

Brian Wilson's performance of "On Broadway" on January 22, 1987, at Jerry Lieber and Mike Stoller's induction into the Rock and Roll Hall of Fame, showed Brian was not reliant upon the studio or the Beach Boys to prove his skills were fully intact. His performance led Seymour Stein, president of Sire Records, to offer Brian a two-album solo recording deal that opened the third stage in Brian's career. *Brian Wilson*, released in July 1988, was the solo album for which fans had waited for over 20 years. Kamron Hinatsu's photographs for the album cover showed Brian as a trim, clean, and pensive man of 46 years, when only five years earlier, he was an obese and unrecognizable wreck of a man who appeared to be on a death march. Still under the care of Dr. Eugene Landy in 1988, the Wilson-Landy relationship was viewed with suspicion by many, but no one could deny that Brian had not looked this healthy, or "together," since *Pet Sounds*. *Brian Wilson* hit the market in the same month that the Beach Boys released "Kokomo," their first number-one single in 22 years. That song was composed by John Phillips and Scott McKenzie, with a clever hook provided by Mike Love and frequent Beach Boys collaborator Terry Melcher.

Second Chances

While the touring concern of the Beach Boys made their millions on Brian's songs, Brian Wilson was for many synonymous with the Beach Boys. Still, his name could not move copies of his debut solo effort that managed to spend 12 weeks on the Billboard charts and peaked at number 54. The album was warmly received by fans and was the first step in Brian's middle-age and mid-career renaissance. Seven years would pass before he would make that crucial second step, but at the time of its release, *Brian Wilson* shocked, surprised, and pleased legions of fans, while reviews ran from the ecstatic to the cynically dismissive. When we consider Brian's last appearance on record, three years earlier, was on *The Beach Boys*, *Brian Wilson* is all the more extraordinary. Steve Levine, the producer of the band's 1985 album gave the Beach Boys a clean, contemporary sound, but for all his talents he could not make a Brian Wilson song "sound" like a Brian Wilson song. The strength of that album is in its clean, radio-friendly sheen, but Brian's contributions on that album sound like cover tunes performed by a top-notch studio band. For all of the overproduction imposed by Eugene Landy, *Brian Wilson* managed to transcend his doctor's aesthetic limitations and sound like Brian Wilson was there in body, mind, and sprit.

Brian's music has always reflected the era in which it was composed. *Brian Wilson* follows this pattern, and woven through it are many of the aural hallmarks of the late 1980s that includes the liberal use of synthesizers, the Fairlight CMI, and the big, echo-filled, "gated" drum sound that engineer Hugh Padgham first introduced on Peter Gabriel's "Intruder" in 1980.[1] Much of the criticism leveled at *Brian Wilson* is rightly focused on Landy's suffocating influence, but when we consider that five producers were credited on the album, it is remarkable there was any focus to this record. Thanks to skill and patience of Russ Titelman and Andy Paley, the album was spared Landy's odious sensibilities.

In 1986, Brian reconnected with his first collaborator, Gary Usher, after a break of 20 years. Their rekindled partnership was prematurely ended thanks to Landy's full-time "care" of Wilson and his agenda to keep Brian away from anyone he (Landy) could not manage.[2] The first of two Wilson-Usher songs to be released was "Let's Go to Heaven in My Car," Brian's first single for Sire Records.[3] With its innocent, elder-adolescent lyrics, it is not unlike "Little Honda." The core of the song would be recycled for "Water Builds Up" on Brian's unreleased second solo album, *Sweet Insanity.* The B-side of this debut single, "Too Much Sugar," is a flashback to songs from Brian's health kick of the late 1960s.

Russ Titelman, Brian's collaborator on 1965's "Guess I'm Dumb" and "Sherry, She Needs Me," was, at Stein's request, brought onto the project as a coproducer. He described events around the sessions as "... less like making a record, more like a Marx Brothers movie," stating "Landy has no qualifications to make creative decisions."[4] Still, the album has many extraordinary moments, a minimum of filler, and is filled with numerous guest artists. It is clear, across much of the album, that Brian was fully engaged with these songs and not since *Beach Boys Today!* or *Pet Sounds* had his narratives been so personal. Many of his songs since *Friends* utilized his "a-day-in-the-life-of" approach found in "Passing By," "At My Window," "Had to Phone Ya," and others. While there were exceptions such as "The Night Was So Young" and his contributions on *Surf's Up*, Brian's acquiescence to the artistic preferences of other parties often resulted in works with substantially different themes and narratives from what we had come to expect from him. The album's opening track, "Love and Mercy" is a stunning song and one that Brian continues to use as an encore in concert. Titelman has called it "an anthem about forgiveness and compassion."[5] In this, Brian managed to express heartfelt emotions with a scent of the sweet melancholy that infuses so many of his songs.[6] With the opening phrase, "I was sittin' in a crummy movie with my hands on my chin. All the violence that occurs seems like we never win.," it was clear that Brian's songwriting and singing was stronger than it had been since the mid-1970s, and such emotion had not been heard in his work since "Til' I Die." One less than kind reviewer said that when you "... filter out the gated reverb and the glutinous DX7 .... ("Love and Mercy") wouldn't sound out of place on *Wild Honey*." I disagree, and while neither the structure nor the final production bear the hallmarks of Brian's more complex works, the song conveys Brian's deeply spiritual emotions and it continues to elicit an emotional response as a concert encore nearly three decades later.

The next track, "Walkin' the Line," was coauthored with the Dream Academy's Nick Laird-Clowes, but in the 2000 reissue of the album, Brian originally credited Usher as the song originated in their working sessions. There is a Wilson-Usher-produced demo of the song from 1986 that in some ways is superior to the finished version. This is followed with "Melt Away," another stunning track that follows the introspective thread Brian shared two decades earlier in "I Just Wasn't Made for These Times." The wonderfully resonant percussion frame harkens back to his earlier work, and the vocal round on the coda is simply magical. "Baby Let Your Hair Grow Long" follows up with the girl Brian first told us about in "Caroline, No." Though not as memorable, it is a solid song that goes for one verse too many. "Little Children" was written in the 1970s when he was the troubled family man to Marilyn, Wendy, and Carnie, but he somehow transforms a song from that challenging period into one of the album's sunnier songs. In the very real absence of the Beach Boys, Brian recorded all the vocal parts in "One for the Boys," a moving lullaby and wordless chant built on a simple, three-note sequence. Side one closes with "There's So Many," a tender love song Brian first demoed in the late 1970s that suffers only for its synth-heavy arrangement.

Side two begins with one of Brian's collaborations with Andy Paley, "Night Time," a solid rocker with an arrangement that does not go too far off track. Paley, with Titelman, had the most positive influence upon the sessions for *Brian Wilson*, and they can be credited for supporting Brian's creative agenda. Paley described Landy as "a force to be reckoned with," and expressed the difficulties he and Titelman encountered both from Landy and his various lieutenants who kept a round-the-clock presence in Brian's personal and professional lives, saying, "Anything good we got out of those sessions was done totally on stolen time."[7] In Dillon, Titelman said that Landy kept Brian off-guard all the time and kept interrupting the creative flow. He described it as "so chaotic and unpleasant that it became rather untenable." The next song, "Let It Shine," has the least Brian Wilson input as it was basically a Jeff Lynne song to which Brian added the vocal round in the introduction. I believe the next song, "Meet Me in My Dreams Tonight," is one of the most underrated works in Brian's solo repertoire. This song was reportedly saddled with Landy's lyrics as he forbade the engineers from mixing the original Wilson-Paley lyrics, but through some maneuvering and tactics of distraction, Brian's overseer was removed from the room and they were able to mix a version with the original lyrics. The song has an opening not terribly unlike "California Girls," where the notes fall from above into a downy soft rhythm bed, but instead of jumping into a "country shuffle," Brian's up-tempo "a-day-in-the-life-of" love song marches ahead with a Spector-ish arrangement and rich background vocals. His use of the organ to lead the accompaniment, with the repetitive block-chord, quarter-note figure, drives the song without it ever feeling rushed. The hand claps are another effective touch in this gem, and the brief, but dreamy bridge is a wonderful swirling detour before the song's final verse. When Brian sings "Cause I just can't wait to see your face, in the usual time and the usual place," he delivers it with the same naïve, passionate, and romantic excitement he displayed in earlier songs such as "I Do" and "We'll Run Away."

The final song on the album is another Paley collaboration, "Rio Grande," and like *Sunflower's* "Cool, Cool Water," was created at the request of Lenny Waronker. Waronker was an executive at Warners when the Beach Boys signed to the label in 1970 and had been unsuccessful in prying *SMiLE* for a Warners release. Though not as strong as "Heroes and Villains" or "Cool, Cool Water," it has many lovely moments. The song's introduction is reminiscent of the cantina section from the extended "Heroes and Villains," but it is the fourth section, the "Take Me Home ..." theme that fits so nicely into one of Brian's reassuring grooves. The album was a stunning comeback and, with the exception of "Night Time" and "Let It Shine," showed that Brian was still able to create an album of wonderful music. Rolling Stone named Brian as their comeback artist of the year, but his name could not move units and the album stalled without ever reaching the top 20. The expanded reissue released in 2000 removed the Eugene Landy/Alexandra Morgan credits from Brian's songs, though Landy's credit as "Executive Producer" remained intact.[8] The B-sides of "He Couldn't Get His Poor Old Body to Move" (a Lindsey Buckingham coauthored and coproduced B-side for the single of "Love and Mercy"), the aforementioned "Too Much Sugar," and "Being with the One You Love" (B-side for the single of "Melt Away") were included in the reissue.

One month after the release of *Brian Wilson*, he contributed a cover of "Goodnight Irene" for a Woody Guthrie tribute album on Columbia,

Folkways: A Vision Shared—A Tribute to Woody Guthrie. The following year he contributed "In My Car" to an odds-and-ends collection, *Still Crusin'*—a record that marked the Beach Boys's temporary return to Capitol Records.[9] "In My Car" was part of a deal the Beach Boys had with General Motors to promote the Chevrolet Corvette. The song, from Brian's solo sessions, is busy, over arranged, and constructed with classic rock tropes, a bit of "Shortenin' Bread," and a kitchen sink of brief extras. Carl Wilson is heard briefly on the vocal to give the impression it is a Beach Boys song.[10] One composition that has flown under the radar and has never been released on any album is "I Sleep Alone," a forgettable Wilson-Landy work captured in a December 1988 performance at the National Academy of Songwriters.[11]

The Beach Boys were the marquee draw in *Endless Summer*, a summer replacement television show. While it featured live footage of the Beach Boys, there were guest musical artists and "campfire" segments with the Beach Boys that were used to close the show. These vignettes featured all of the Beach Boys sitting around a campfire, playing songs a' la *Beach Boys Party!* These shows are interesting because they show Brian making music in the period between the *Brian Wilson* and the unreleased *Sweet Insanity*. Brian was still under the control of Landy and his minders, but he is trim and healthy and these shows present him in as "normal" a setting as was possible. While the show ran for 11 episodes in the summer of 1989, the final four episodes were reedits of previously aired shows. That same year, Brian sang on records for Paul Shaffer and Linda Ronstadt. Jimmy Webb's "Adios" was featured on Ronstadt's *Cry Like a Rainstorm, Howl Like the Wind*, an eclectic album that featured multiple songs by Webb in addition to works from Karla Bonoff, Nick Lowe, and Paul Carrack. On "Adios," Brian provides an exquisite arrangement and backing vocal, with Aaron Neville, on Webb's song. Peter Asher, Ronstadt's producer, was able to keep Landy's production and opinions outside of the studio. The song was a top 10 adult contemporary (AC) hit for Ronstadt, and is one of the purest examples of Brian's work from this period as the production is not burdened by his "handlers." Brian also appeared on the track, "Metal Beach" from Paul Shaffer's album, *Coast to Coast*.[12]

The most difficult and trying of Brian's works is his second solo album, *Sweet Insanity*, which was produced by Brian and Landy without the involvement of either Lenny Waronker or Russ Titelman. Landy's brutish production aesthetics may have been kept in check by Titelman and Paley on *Brian Wilson*, but they were allowed free rein on *Sweet Insanity* that led to it being rejected twice by Sire.[13] One has to listen closely to find Brian's magic as every song is slathered with pedestrian synthesizer textures mixed into a flat sound palette one might expect of television-quality audio of the period. Brian produced three solid rock songs, the stadium anthem variety rockers, "Someone to Love," "The Spirit of Rock and Roll," and "Hotter," but many of the songs feature the most juvenile and simplistic lyrics ever used in his work, and show the overbearing presence of Landy and his writer/girlfriend, Alexandra Morgan.[14] Andy Paley described the record as being entirely Landy, as he directed Brian in what he should do on every song. Five of the stronger songs that escaped Landy's crushing thumbprint would end up in reworked versions on Brian's 2004 solo album, *Gettin' in over My Head* (*GIOMH*).[15] There are good songs on *Sweet Insanity*, but listeners may be hard pressed for patience to sift through the materials.

The opening track, "Intro," is a truncated version of the longer "Concert Tonight," from the first version of *Sweet Insanity*, and is a bumpy vocal round with a final cadence that sounds as if it might have come from one of Pete Townshend "commercial" jingles on *The Who Sell Out* (1967). The second track, "Someone to Love," has a couple of identifiable Wilson hooks and as one of Wilson's three barnstorming rockers on the album, it is a full-throttle song, not unlike "The Girl from New York City" or "Let Us Go on This Way." "Water Builds Up" is a remake of an earlier Wilson-Usher track that first appeared as "Let's Go to Heaven in My Car," and what starts off promisingly enough falls into an unfortunate arrangement that buries all of the song's strengths. "Don't Let Her Know She's an Angel" would be reworked for *GIOMH* in an arrangement that is slightly, but not significantly improved. Had Brian revisited this work on 1998's *Imagination*, Joe Thomas might have brought a more effective AC arrangement to bear on what is an otherwise sweet and touching song. "Do You Have Any Regrets" is one of the strongest works on the album. Brian takes the song at an overenthusiastic tempo with latin/calypso rhythm that prevents the listener from taking in one of his best songs from the period. Darian Sahanaja, of the Wondermints, recorded a stunning version of this piece for his 1997 single (*Love You's* "I Wanna Pick You Up" was the B-side). Sahanaja claims he tried to channel Brian of the 1965, *Summer Days (and Summer Nights!!)* era, and he succeeded in every way. Within two years of Darian's homage, he and the remaining members of the Wondermints would become Brian's collaborators and enable him to create the wealth of recordings he has produced over the past two decades. This is followed with "Brian," an embarrassing slice of autobiographical therapy-in-song that is "Landy-as-Wilson." In his 1991 autobiography, Brian (or more correctly, the voice writing as Brian) holds this song in high regard and uses Stein and Waronker's rejection of its lyrics to demonstrate that no one truly understood him. The melody and harmonies are pure Wilson, the lyrics are Landy-Morgan speak, and the arrangement is another example of the latter's mastery of the 1980s television movie-of-the-week soundtrack genre.

The second side opens with "The Spirit of Rock and Roll."[16] This otherwise solid rocker features a guest vocal by Bob Dylan, and would have been a solid Beach Boys track. Next is "Rainbow Eyes," a charming song he would revise with an updated arrangement on *GIOMH*. It has a slightly unusual tenor but the melody is lovely and could have been developed into something far stronger. "Love Ya" is a classic 1950s style rocker in the vein of "Stay," has one of the less egregious arrangements on the album, and would not have been out of place on *15 Big Ones.* This is followed with "Make a Wish," another track to end up greatly improved on *GIOMH.* It has a strong chorus and overall is a good song, but is ruined by the arrangement. Brian's vocal delivery in this song veers towards speak singing, and is a warm-up for the unfortunate closing track, "Smart Girls." In his autobiography, Brian used this song to take another shot at the Warners executives who rejected the album and claimed that Alexandra Morgan wrote this song as a pro-woman rap song. He also claimed it was not an attempt to create an authentic rap song, but rather, a send-up. Ironic? It is a mash-up that blends samples from his classic Beach Boys songs and is a perplexing and embarrassing end to an album that had, at moments, shown some promise. Another notable element in Brian's performance on *Sweet Insanity* was his, at times, awkward vocal delivery. His singing on *Brian Wilson* had been well-produced and he deftly layered multiple harmony lines under his lead vocals, but on *Sweet Insanity,* his voice is less confident and controlled, and likely was a reflection of his precipitous physical decline due to the overmedication Landy continued to heap onto Wilson.

There were two "bonus" tracks on the Brains & Genius cassette, "Country Feelin' " and "Hotter." The former is an inoffensive tune in the vein of "Farmer's Daughter," and the latter has great potential but is a missed opportunity. "Hotter" is the third of Brian's solid rockers from this period, but is burdened with overtly sexist lyrics. The track does not begin with much promise, but builds to an extended chorus in a classic Wilson groove.

Please Raise Your Right Hand

Brian produced little from 1990 to 1994 as he was occupied with a variety of creative and legal activities that included the preparation of his ghost-authored autobiography, *Wouldn't It Be Nice: My Own Story,* the recording of *Sweet Insanity,* legal actions initiated by the California Board of Medical Quality Assurance against Eugene Landy, Brian's lawsuit against Irving Music, and multiple lawsuits between Brian and Mike Love. In regard to Landy, the board required him to surrender his license to practice psychology, though before the release of *Brian Wilson,* both Brian and Landy publically claimed that Landy had ceased his work as Brian's therapist and the two were now business and creative partners and cofounders of the company "Brains and Genius." Landy maneuvered complex financial arrangements into Brian's life that covered a range of scenarios that could be used to protect Landy from future litigation. To insure this, Landy arranged it so that Brian's family was blocked from direct contact with him. The almost 400-page autobiography, *Wouldn't It Be Nice: My Own Story,* was a skillfully constructed narrative authored with the assistance of journalist, Todd Gold. It supported the Landy-Wilson relationship, painted the Beach Boys and others as villains who made Brian's life intolerable, defended the quality of the unreleased *Sweet Insanity*, and conveyed the narrative of a hero who had regained his "sanity and artistry" thanks to therapy. The book offered little information that was new and while it lifted scenarios from earlier biographies, it served as a testament to the benefits of therapy. The narrative enabled "Brian" (or whoever was speaking on Brian's behalf) to call out the Beach Boys and other family members for a variety of transgressions.[17] The battle for Brian's personal and professional independence would last for over two years, and it was only in the first part of 1991 that Landy agreed to separate himself from Brian for 90 days.[18] The disclosure of Landy's financial machinations in regard to his star client finally brought this battle to a positive resolution. For over eight years he billed Brian $35,000 a month for professional services and arranged a deal in 1984 (when Brian was in the first stages of recovery) that gave him 25 percent of Brian's earnings for writing and production duties. Brian also paid him $300,000 annually as an advisor, all on top of the $150,000 that the Beach Boys (Brother Records, Inc.) paid him for serving as Brian's representative at corporate meetings. It was discovered Landy had named himself the primary beneficiary in Brian's will, which positioned him to inherit up to 70 percent of Brian's fortune. In an expose that aired on ABC's *Primetime Live* in October of 1991, Brian, in conversation with Diane Sawyer, defended his relationship with Landy and denied the various accusations that were leveled at his former doctor. Ultimately, Brian was freed from all aspects of Dr. Eugene Landy's control in February 1992. All financial and personal arrangements would be dissolved, a restraining order was put into place, and the state appointed a conservator to help Brian reclaim his life and his work.

A lawsuit for $100 million ($50 million in royalties with an equal amount for punitive damages) was filed in 1989 on behalf of Brian against Irving Music, the publishing division of A&M Records, who had purchased Sea of Tunes publishing from Murry Wilson in 1969 for $700,000.[19] It was contended that Brian's signature on the 1969 agreement was a forgery, and as Brian suffered from paranoid psychosis, he was incompetent to sign the document. The lawsuit claimed Murry accomplished this through forged documents and a relentless barrage of threatening and guilt-inducing phone calls to Brian for over two years prior to the sale. Brian filed a lawsuit the following year against the law firm that represented Murry Wilson and handled the sale of Sea of Tunes, claiming misrepresentation, malpractice, and breach of contract.[20] The autobiography and the settlement with Irving Music led to a new series of suits filed by Mike Love. Mike initially received a $1.5 million settlement and claimed he had been slandered in Brian's autobiography, but he also sued Brian for a portion of the Irving Music settlement. Love received nearly half of Brian's settlement in addition to amended coauthorship credits on 39 songs Brian composed between 1962 and 1966.[21]

After Landy's court-ordered removal, there remained a great deal to be undone in Brian's life.[22] In spite of his illegal, unethical, dishonest, and generally unforgiveable acts, it cannot be denied that Eugene Landy saved Brian Wilson from a premature death, though in the process of saving him, he nearly killed him. Brian's second period with Eugene Landy came at a time when he was at the nadir of his then-young life in 1983, and in a far worse condition than when Landy had first treated him in 1975. He was over 340 pounds, smoked packs of cigarettes per day, consumed extraordinary amounts of food and narcotics, the latter often acquired with the assistance of Dennis, who died later that year. The reasonably stocky and depressed man who appeared in concert with the Beach Boys as of 1977 had, by 1983, ballooned to an unwashed and unrecognizable mass. Landy's intensive methods of treatment had worked, and by 1985, Brian had shed the weight, was running, working out, taking care of himself, was free of drugs, and had begun to play music once again. Landy also blocked all family members from contacting Brian. His first period with Wilson in 1975–1976 had been derailed by the family and the group, and he was not going to allow that scenario to be repeated.[23] Any interaction with the Beach Boys could only occur under the supervision of either Landy or his paid assistants.

When Landy was hired to treat Brian for the second time, he demanded there would be no outside interference from either the band or his family. Within two years, Brian was well enough to contribute a few songs to the band's 1985 album, and then came the Lieber & Stoller induction that was followed by his solo debut. In spite of these achievements, a few years would be required for Brian to extricate himself from Eugene Landy's 24/7 care, and it was in February 1992 that Brian was legally free of his former psychologist/business partner, and would take the second step of his creative renaissance.

Thirty Years of Marketing

Capitol began their compact disc reissue campaign of 1960s-era Beach Boys albums in "two-fer" sets, but there was little new music from Brian in the early 1990s. The Beach Boys released in fall 1992, their first album with no active input or participation from Brian, *Summer in Paradise.* This album holds the distinction for having the lowest sales of any Beach Boys album, and is considered by many as an embarrassment in their catalog. If 1983 was the lowest point in Brian's life, 1990–1991 had to be the lowest point in the Beach Boys's tenure as a performing unit. Mike and Al, the two meditators of the group, were no longer on parallel planes as Mike sought to remove Al from the band. That crisis was averted, but the new album had minimal participation from either Carl or Al, and it functions as a Mike Love solo effort. It was one of the first albums recorded wholly on the Pro Tools software, but this did nothing to excuse the abysmal quality of the music contained within.[24]

Capitol released the career-spanning, five-disc set, *Good Vibrations: Thirty Years of the Beach Boys* in July 1993. This generously packaged set contained a booklet with numerous photographs and liner notes by David Leaf. A wealth of unreleased tracks was scattered over the five discs, but the real draw for serious fans were the 30-plus minutes of material from *SMiLE*. The longer "cantina' version of "Heroes and Villains" had been released in 1990 on the *Smiley Smile/Wild Honey* two-fer, but the new boxed set offered a number of unreleased variations on that song's idée fixe, plus original versions of "Wonderful," "Wind Chimes," "Vegetables," "Do You Like Worms," and Brian's piano demo of "Surf's Up" were also included. Also featured were a number of unreleased tracks that are believed to have been from proposed, though unreleased albums that included *Last Capitol Album* through *Landlocked*, in addition to two of the Dick Reynolds-arranged songs from the aborted *Adult/Child* album. In spite of its riches, not all reviews for this set were glowing. Exhaustion from the legacy of *SMiLE* had dissipated interest for many fans and critics, and while most listeners welcomed this compilation, not everyone was so effusive in their analysis.

The following year, Brian and daughter Carnie, partnered with Rob Wasserman on *Trios* where Carnie sang the beautiful, Don Was-produced song, "Fantasy is Reality/Bells of Madness."[25] Carnie's richly hued alto glides effortlessly over a classic Wilson harmonic progression. Brian's background vocals combined with Wasserman's emotive playing transform this simple song into an extremely heartfelt work.

Old Friends, New Friends, New Faces, a New Life

At mid-decade, Brian was involved in projects that included the composition of new songs, a soundtrack album, cover songs of artists whom he has long admired, and he worked with prior collaborators on new projects. In spite of this, Brian's work with Andy Paley was a mystery for many fans. What was composed and recorded? Why was nothing released in the early 1990s? Brian's work with Paley began in 1987, and not only served as a collaborative partnership with scheduled working sessions, similar to his methods when working with Usher, Christian, Asher, and Parks, but it also allowed Brian to create work that could become solo material, songs for the Beach Boys, or for other, unrelated projects.

The gradual rebirth of Brian's career between 1994 and 1998 would be accompanied by a significant new chapter in his life when, on February 19, 1995, he married Melinda Ledbetter, whom he had dated nearly a decade earlier when Landy believed it would be good for Brian to "date" someone. Landy then excluded her from Brian's life in the late 1980s, but a serendipitous reconnection led to their dating and a partnership that has lasted over 20 years. Brian resumed work with Andy Paley, and the two began work on a number of songs and generated a buzz among fans who believed a new Brian Wilson album could be just around the corner. As the reality in Brian's world is never straightforward, the Paley sessions did not result in a new album, though selected of the tracks would be released over the next decade on various Wilson's albums. Another collaborator with whom Brian worked was Detroit-based musician and producer Don Was, who produced the documentary, *Brian Wilson: I Just Wasn't Made for These Times.* Brian also reconnected with Van Dyke Parks and together they created *Orange Crate Art*, an album that served as an important step in the evolution of Brian's career as a performing artist. Carnie and Wendy Wilson, two-thirds of the late-1980s pop trio, *Wilson Philips*, were also reunited with their father and together they worked on songs for *The Wilsons.* Brian lent his voice to four of the album's 12 tracks that included a touching cover of "Til' I Die." A new collaborator, Joe Thomas, entered Brian's creative and personal world at mid-decade, and assisted on a pair of albums released in 1996 and 1998. Brian made an unexpected appearance on backing vocals for Belinda Carlisle's "California," from her 1997 album *A Woman and a Man.* The Wondermints partnered with Brian and enabled him to revisit and engage with his legacy, to complete *SMiLE* and undertake a number of new projects. They also have served as the core of his touring band, and their multi-instrumental and vocal skills have enabled Brian's elaborate and complex compositions to be performed in concert with a level of ensemble and precision the Beach Boys could never have achieved.

The mid-to-late-1990s were an extraordinarily rich period for Brian, and when we listen to the range and variety of music he created, it is clear he had so much to share. While fans may have been genuinely excited to hear the music Brian was creating, record labels were not jumping at the opportunity to sign him based solely on rumors of highly productive sessions with Andy Paley. Brian's life post-*SMiLE*, the inconsistent success of his work on Beach Boys albums from the Warners and Columbia years, Sire's rejection of *Sweet Insanity*, the cautious trail left in the wake of Landy's departure, and his various legal issues did not endear him to an industry who had already written him off. It was easier to believe he was finally finished, but the reality of Brian's life and career is often contrary from public or industry perception.

The first song Brian released in 1995 was the Andy Paley-produced "Sweets for My Sweet" for *Til the Night Is Gone: A Tribute to Doc Pomus.* The Wilson-Paley performance was the penultimate track on this compilation that sadly went out of print soon after its release. Two months later, Brian's recording of Harry Nilsson's "This Could Be the Night" was featured on the tribute album, *For the Love of Harry—Everybody Sings Nilsson.* Brian chose to perform a Nilsson-Spector tune originally recorded in 1966 by the Modern Folk Quartet, but held from an official release by Spector. Nilsson had written this song in 1965 as his own homage to Wilson's then ascendant influence in popular music. Though the MFQ version would only appear as the theme song in the Spector-produced *The Big TNT Show*, Brian had hoped to record it in 1972 with American Spring. As with the Doc Pomus tribute record, Nilsson's song was performed by Brian and Andy Paley (who served once again as producer), with contributions from Andy's brother, Jonathan, and harmonica player, Tommy Morgan.

MCA released a CD-single for the German and Swedish market in July 1995 to accompany the soundtrack to the forthcoming Don Was-directed documentary. The single featured "Til' I Die "and "Do It Again," tracks drawn from the yet-to-be-released soundtrack, with the addition of a third song, a gentle and dreamy lullaby titled "This Song Wants to Sleep with You Tonight." This Wilson-Paley song was not featured in the documentary, and was the first of the post-1992 Wilson-Paley compositions to be released. It was not available in North America (except as an import), and has yet to be included on any other collection. This song, along with "I Sleep Alone" from 1989, is one of the rarer items in Brian's catalog from this period.

Later that year, MCA Records released a soundtrack for *Brian Wilson: I Just Wasn't Made for These Times.* The documentary was an honest and respectful presentation of Brian that featured archival film footage, new interviews with family members and peers, and unplugged-in-the-studio segments that featured Brian singing 11 of his songs. Though the majority of songs were familiar Beach Boys works, and Brian performed a range of pieces from "The Warmth of the Sun" to "Love and Mercy," in refreshing and effective performances. The interviews with Carnie, Wendy, and Marilyn are touching without being needlessly sentimental, but we could not know this would be one of the last times that Brian and Carl would sing together.[26] Another Wilson-Paley performance appeared on the compilation, *Pulp Surfin.*[27] The Paley authored "In My Moondreams" is a wonderfully evocative instrumental that references the sonic landscapes originally created by Joe Meek on the Tornados's "Telstar" (1962). The wordless backing vocals and the reedy, echo-saturated aural canvas pay a respectful tribute to the pioneering producer whose work has never acquired the full recognition due its creator. Paley and Wilson delivered a taut, yet dreamy performance, but this is another work that has all but vanished from Brian's catalogue. Brian's work on the documentary provided him with an opportunity to strengthen his vocal skills, which had been affected by the years of overmedication that followed years of abuse that Brian heaped onto his own body. The disciplined and consistent work he had undertaken with both Paley and Was prepared him for his next project, *Orange Crate Art.*

The publicity around the release of *Orange Crate Art* led fans to believe the album was an equal Brian Wilson-Van Dyke Parks collaboration and a reunion of the creators behind *SMiLE.* In truth it was a Van Dyke Parks solo album, with music and lyrics by Parks, sung entirely by Brian Wilson.[28] This album is an underrated gem, if only that it featured some of Brian's best vocal work in over two decades. The record is a wistful paean to a California, when the Golden State was a distant dream in the imagination of thousands of people from across the nation, and this loosely constructed cycle of songs are both whimsical and twisting at turns. Brian deftly handles both lead and backing vocals and does a more than admirable job handling Van Dyke's unique turns of phrase. A California that, for Brian, Van Dyke, and millions of longtime residents, is both a state of mind and a place of being would be revisited by Brian on his 2008 solo album, *That Lucky Old Sun.*

Back Where He Belongs

Once Wilson returned to making records in 1988, the question of *SMiLE* would come up in interview after interview. Brian would move away from the topic or claim its release was not a realistic proposition. In the wake of the *Good Vibrations* boxed set, the Don Was-directed documentary and soundtrack, and *Orange Crate Art*, there was a renewed interest in *SMiLE.* This time it was accompanied with encouragement from Don Was, who tried to convince Brian to release an interactive, multi-CD set that would allow fans to "finish" the album with their own preferred sequencing. Was had been turned on to *SMiLE* through many bootlegged recordings of the work and approached this not only as a producer but also as a recent convert who made his own attempts to "finish" the album from various pirated sources.[29] This expansive, though artistically dangerous proposition eventually faded away in the wake of renewed activities. Brian had expressed an interest in working with the Beach Boys again, with Don Was signed on to produce the sessions. Over the preceding decade, the Beach Boys had managed just fine, as an oldies stage act, without their one-time leader who was at the center of all media attention whenever he appeared with the band. While the then decade-old Steve Levine-produced album was their last studio work of any consequence, they had remained a strong concert draw, so a renewal of activities between Brian and the band was accompanied with cautious optimism. Recently resolved legal issues notwithstanding, Brian and Mike were at work again as they attempted, but did not complete, revisions of a song from the Wilson-Paley sessions into a track for the television series, *Baywatch.*[30] As nothing is ever too strange for the Beach Boys, they made an appearance on *Baywatch* (with Brian) in October 1995. While an unfortunate exercise on many fronts, it offered Mike Love an opportunity to air a pair of songs from the forgettable *Summer in Paradise.* In an episode entitled "Surf's Up," Brian, Carl, and the band mime "Summer of Love" (with John Stamos behind the drums) just after the opening credits.[31] In the following scene, Mike and Bruce have speaking parts in a scene where they offer to present a benefit show as part of the episode's thinly devised storyline. For the last half of the show, the Beach Boys perform at an outdoor venue where they sing "Fun, Fun, Fun," "Summer in Paradise," and "Don't Worry Baby." For this scene, Brian and Carl are nowhere to be seen, but David Marks is there, along with Al's son, Matt Jardine, who sings "Don't Worry Baby."

The group went to work with Brian and Don Was in late 1995, and it seemed something might come of this effort. Five Wilson-Paley songs were tracked, background vocals were recorded behind Brian's lead on "Still a Mystery," and backing vocals were recorded for "Soul Searchin'," with Carl on lead vocals. Carl came back a month after the sessions for "Soul Searchin' " and in an abrupt change of face said he did not want to go forward with the project, nor did he care for the new work because he felt it did not have commercial potential. Even Mike Love acknowledged that he had "... no idea why that didn't come together ..."[32] Brian, in a December 1995 interview, was forthright as to the reasons why he and the Beach Boys were in such disagreement over current projects. He expressed his anger and irritation with Carl for his decision to pull the Beach Boys from his latest work and in the same interview expresses his displeasure and irritation with Andy Paley. As an associate has articulated, "Brian changes his opinions all the time," so his feelings are temporary and of the moment. This is another reminder that Brian's views are fluid, and anything he says is drawn from a single moment within the millions of moments that pass through his reality. Don Was accepted some of the blame for not having pushed the sessions when they had momentum, but he also believes that Carl's recent cancer diagnosis may have contributed to his abrupt cancellation of the project.

Late 1995 into 1996 was an active period for Brian, who maintained his collaborations with Andy Paley, Don Was, and the Beach Boys, and would engage with newcomers to the Beach Boys's creative circle, such as Joe Thomas, a variety of country and western artists, and Irishman Sean O'Hagan of the Irish avant-pop band, the High Llamas. Each of these parties has different recollections on exactly who connected with whom, and each recalls different responses and outcomes in regard to Brian's level of enthusiasm and participation (or nonparticipation) on a given project. Brian had been productive in his work with Andy Paley as he developed new and healthy work routines, but Brian's wedding to Melinda in early 1995 appears to have brought a calm and grounded balance to Brian's life that, when we consider everything he has endured throughout his very public life, was the best that anyone could hope for him. Melinda's presence has provided a layer of protection for Brian as he, once again, became the commodity from whom the Beach Boys and the music industry always wanted their pound of flesh. Melinda's presence may (or may not, depending on whom you ask) have been just what Brian needed to prevent him from another decline, similar to what he experienced between 1978 and 1982. A third decline likely would have been irreversible, so Melinda's patient and caring support enabled Brian to consider new creative opportunities as he began to reengage with the field on his terms.

The Beach Boys attempted to pair Brian with Sean O'Hagan of the UK pop group, the High Llamas, as a move to "help" Brian become more current. O'Hagan shared his side of this tale in his essay on "Let's Go Away for Awhile."[33] The irony of this arrangement was quite rich as the Beach Boys had struggled to find relevance in their post-Brian existence with mixed success. They had comparative success in the Rieley-managed years and indifference to failure in the era that followed the marketing ploy of "Brian's Back," but when faced with the opportunity of a collaboration with Brian, they would find a way to derail the project because someone in the Beach Boys camp would believe they could help Brian. This partnership did not come to pass, but Brian's next collaboration with the Beach Boys was even less expected than was the Boys's 1987 work with the Fat Boys on "Wipe Out."[34]

In October 1995, Brian and the Beach Boys began work on the album *Stars and Stripes, Vol. 1*, an album produced for the Nashville subsidiary of Chicagoland's River North Records.[35] Joe Thomas, a former professional wrestler-turned producer, studio head, and songwriter, was Brian's partner on this album. This unusual album in the Beach Boys canon involved country artists providing lead vocals on Beach Boys songs with the Beach Boys providing backing vocals. Whether this was an attempt to bring country artists to a pop market or to bring the Beach Boys to a country listenership, it accomplished neither, though it sold better than *Summer in Paradise*. With the exception of three songs, "Long Tall Texan," "I Can Hear Music," and "Sloop John B," the album featured nine of Brian's songs that have appeared on any number of "Greatest Hits" collections. A video that chronicled the making of the album, *Nashville Sounds*, showed the Beach Boys at work in the studio with these artists. The songs sound like the Beach Boys, and the backing vocals were the Beach Boys, but take away the occasional fiddle or slide guitar and there is nothing particularly "country" in these tracks. A majority of the album used a wealth of young country stars but the real gems of this project involved two legendary artists, Willie Nelson and Tammy Wynette, and it is their contributions that make this an effort worthy of attention.

Willie Nelson has been around longer than Brian and has had his full share of living. He is a towering figure in the field, and his music and legacy span multiple generations and cultures. Nelson sings "The Warmth of the Sun" in an effective and moving performance. He takes one of Brian and Mike's most heartfelt songs and brings it to life with his sincere interpretation. As a legendary storyteller, Willie delivers the song with poetic grace.

Tammy Wynette's contribution to the project was held back from Vol. 1 for a proposed Vol. 2, which never came to fruition. Her session in June 1996 was the last for the project and would also be her last recording session, as she passed away in April 1998 at the age of 55. The footage of Brian and Tammy in the studio is touching, and the interaction of these two icons, whose lives have filled volumes of column space and album sides, is the gem of the entire project. She and Brian sang "In My Room," in a performance of extraordinary beauty. The arrangement is also one of the more tasteful of the whole project and makes one wish the entire album could have been infused with this level of emotion and subtlety.

The album was released in August of 1996 but did not succeed on the scale that had been hoped for both by either the Beach Boys or River North. Eleven years had passed since the five core members of the Beach Boys had released an album of any interest, but *Stars and Stripes, Vol. 1*, would be the last Beach Boys project to involve both Brian and Carl Wilson. The brothers' relationship had weathered so much, and Carl's refusal to sing Brian's new works in the recently aborted Don Was sessions had strained their relationship one final time. There would be a number of "lasts" for Brian around this project. It was the last time he and Carl would work in the studio together, and it would be the last time Brian would work in the studio with the Beach Boys until the sessions for *That's Why God Made the Radio.* A performance at Chicago's Navy Pier in September 1996 would be the last time Brian performed with the band for over 15 years.[36] Carl lost his battle with lung cancer and died in February 1998 at the age of 51, two months after the Wilsons's mother, Audree, passed away in December 1997.

Transitions

While the Beach Boys continued to perform on the road, Carl's illness required that he remove himself from concerts, and he played his final shows with the band in August 1997, and was replaced on stage by the original substitute Beach Boy, David Marks. In July, Brian was in the studio with Carnie and Wendy, for their upcoming album, and in his home studio in St. Charles, IL, he was at work on tracks for his next solo album, while Capitol Records released the four-CD boxed set, *The Pet Sound Sessions.*

Carnie and Wendy Wilson, as two-thirds of the pop dynamo Wilson Phillips, sold over 10-million copies of their debut album in 1990, and their single "Hold On" was a smash around the globe. Reduced to a duo when Chynna Phillips released a solo album in 1995, the sisters secured a deal with Mercury Records and released a self-titled album with their father providing backing vocals on four tracks. Carnie, Wendy, and Brian were each listed as executive producers, and six producers were credited across the entire album. As a result, the album has a 1990s pop sheen that is not entirely memorable. Still, Carnie and Wendy's talents are not lost in the production and they gamely attempt Brian's masterpiece, "Til' I Die" (with their father on backing vocals) in a setting that concludes with more optimism than does Brian's original. There is a new Wilson-Asher composition, "Everything I Need," which is perhaps the strongest song on the album. Joe Thomas was present for the handful of tracks on which Brian was involved, so his connection with Brian continued beyond *Stars and Stripes, Vol. 1*, and into Brian's next project.

Working for a Poison Dwarf

Since the expiration of his contract at Sire/Warners, Brian had been without a record deal despite the fact that he was in one of his most active periods since the late 1970s. The work with Paley had yielded no contract, the Don Was documentary was released through MCA, and River North, an upstart label with muscle and industry support, released *Stars and Stripes, Vol. 1.* In the November 29, 1997, issue of Billboard, an entry at the bottom of page 12 announced that Brian had signed to Irving Azoff's Revolution Records. When his next album, *Imagination*, was released in June 1998, it appeared on Azoff's Giant Records, of which Revolution Records was a subsidiary. When Brian's music was released on Warners, and later on Sire, he was working with labels who believed in nurturing artists. By signing with Giant, Brian would be in a relationship not dissimilar to the Beach Boys's relationship with Columbia from 1979 to 1985, where the label invested money in the artist and expected high yield results.

If Brian was going to record for Azoff, who previously acquired the nickname "The Poison Dwarf," it was expected that he would deliver hits, not art. Joe Thomas was retained to produce the album and the effort to transform Brian into an AC artist was underway. Thomas's aesthetic tendencies resulted in productions that "... tended to slide down the glossiest lanes in the middle of the road."[37] When *Imagination* was released, it received mixed reviews and in its two weeks on the charts, it only reached number 88. Fans were perplexed because the Paley sessions, rumored for so long, had produced no record save for the handful of cover tunes recorded earlier in the decade for various tribute albums. Brian may have been effective in the Don Was documentary, and his voice was strong on Parks's album, but the perplexing *Stars and Stripes, Vol. 1*, was followed by *Imagination*, and had many people asking why Brian would acquiesce to a production that was aimed straight into an AC marketplace, the artistic pablum of popular music market.

Media coverage on Brian was far from kind and some attempted to find a "reason" for this perceived lapse in taste. The British music monthly, *Uncut*, produced a story on Brian that seemed to further the opinions and agendas of vocal, though unnamed, sources. Wilson's unique personality became the subject of yet another expose to prove that something was wrong with him. Since his legal emancipation from Eugene Landy, Brian had produced music on his terms to watch it be rejected by record labels and by the Beach Boys. Rejection has been a constant for the majority of Brian's life, except for the years from 1962 to 1966. As he began to break free from constraints with the orchestral sweep of *Pet Sounds*, and the modular construction and multicolored brilliance of *SMiLE*, he faced rejections with greater frequency. Now signed to the subsidiary of a major label, perhaps Brian wanted to produce songs that the masses would enjoy, as they had 25 years earlier; and how better to do it than by collaborating with a producer whose skills landed squarely into the highly profitable AC market.

While many listeners chose to hold their nose at this album, it was obvious that Brian was invested in this project to the extent it was possible. If you focused on the vocal arrangements Brian recorded for *Imagination*, it was clear he was still an extraordinary arranger who could create luscious, complex vocal arrangements and perform each of the parts.[38] What of the songs on *Imagination*? The album was relatively short, just under 40 minutes in length at a time when many artists would strive towards 60–70 minutes as afforded by the compact disc. Also featured were three of Brian's songs from his classic period remade in a contemporary style, "Keep an Eye on Summer" (from his first mature album, *Shut Down, Vol. 2*), and two songs from the period around the *Summer Days (and Summer Nights!!)* album, "Let Him Run Wild" and "She Says That She Needs Me." Because Brian chose to remake three works from his youth, which suffer in comparison to their original versions, they are the weakest links on the album. In "Keep an Eye . . ." Thomas took a perfectly charming, sweet, and breezy doo-wop song, one of Brian's later, Four Freshmen-esque songs, and turned it into a 30-year high school reunion slow dance that, thanks to its watered-down production, could have been used in a television commercial to promote products marketed towards middle-aged men. In "Let Him Run Wild," Brian transposes the song into a more "appropriate" (non-falsetto) range and with Thomas's karaoke-lite arrangement and the loss of Brian's brilliant timbral splashes (the tack piano and vibraphone line with the echo-washed guitar punctuation heard in the original) the song is transformed into an average-of-average cover song. Brian was sensitive about his "high" voice and with the help of alcohol and cigarettes had developed a more "manly" voice in the 1970s.[39] While the lower key may have been a better fit for Brian's vocal range, it also dispenses with any memory of his younger voice that conveyed a yearning romanticism in the song's original iteration.[40] "She Says That She Needs Me," originally titled "Sherry, She Needs Me," was one of Brian's 1965 collaborations with Russ Titelman (the other was the Glen Campbell single, "Guess I'm Dumb"). Brian recorded the song in 1965 without a vocal track, but returned to it in 1976 and added a vocal part. That version was unusual since the backing track was the Brian of 1965, married to the darker vocal timbres of Brian's mid-1970s voice.[41] Wilson and Titelman came back to the song in sessions for *Brian Wilson*, but it was scrapped from the album by Landy. When it finally appeared 22 years later, there were new lyrics by Carole Bayer Sager and a slightly different title. Given its history, the song sounds surprisingly contemporary for 1998 and is the best of the remakes on *Imagination*.

Joe Thomas would work with Brian on both the Beach Boys's 50th anniversary album, a live album that documented the accompanying tour and Brian's 2015 solo album, *No Pier Pressure*. In each instance, songs from each of the studio albums can be traced to the sessions around *Imagination*, which disproves the argument that Brian was dealing with writer's block in the late 1990s. What exactly in Thomas's arrangements on this album are criticized as being so objectionable? His penchant for arranging pristine colors in an antiseptic aural canvas was contrary to Brian's approach of blending colors. Thomas prefers to isolate individual instruments in clearly defined aural layers, which leaves nothing in the way of a blend, or mix, of colors. He also has a penchant for using pairs of woodwinds, usually clarinets, as a tool to color entrances and exits of phrases. Another disconcerting item was that none of Brian's previous collaborators were found on this record. Andy Paley appeared only on a credit for his one coauthored song, "Where Has Love Been." The musicians were from Thomas's crew and some fans objected to the pedigree of the utility players who served as Brian's band.[42] He also was paired with artists from Azoff's managerial artist roster, notably J. D. Souther (an associate of the Eagles) on "Where Has Love Been" and Jimmy Buffett on "South America." Buffet, who is only four years younger than Wilson has parlayed his entire career on a margarita and a cheeseburger, and might appear as an unconventional pairing, but it was one that would prove to be very helpful and supportive to Brian in the year that followed *Imagination*. Buffet's laid-back image and the cool party vibe of his concert audiences provided an ideal (and safe) entrée for Brian to safely reengage with live performances. The winds on this album were performed by Paul Mertens, a multitalented winds and reeds man (who continues to work with Brian) who was invaluable in the reconstruction of *SMiLE*.

The opening track, "Your Imagination" is an unexpectedly cheery-sounding song for Brian, but with his signature, descending bass line and richly stacked vocals, the song is much more than it might seem on first listen. Though the phrases are shorter, the harmonic progression bears more than a passing similarity to "Love and Mercy." The lyrics reflect Brian's past battles but also celebrate his newfound happiness with Melinda and their children. "South America" has the Jimmy Buffett hallmarks and beach-bum grooves upon which he has built a successful and lucrative career, but Brian's chorus and bridge prevent the song from capitulation into beach bum ennui. "Where Has Love Been," the one Paley contribution to the album, has additional material from J. D. Souther. You can hear Brian channeling his skill, circa-1965, in capturing light and dark, but it is the arrangement that leaves us wishing for what might have been. "Dream Angel" is one of the most optimistic songs in Brian's catalog. This upbeat lullaby for his newly adopted daughter is touching and the song has one of the least oppressive arrangements of any on the album save for the guitar solo in the middle eight. This is followed by "Cry," one of two songs wholly composed by Brian, and the one that shows he could compose an effective AC, radio-friendly love song. "Lay Down Burden" is a song Brian claims to have written as a duet for himself and Carl, but never had the chance to record it as a result of Carl's passing. The vocals are richly arranged and I believe the chorus is one of the most moving moments on the entire album. Brian dedicated this song to Carl at his debut Ann Arbor concert in 1999 in one of the more emotional moments from an evening that ran very high on emotions for artist, band, and audience. The brothers' personal difficulties were widely known, and now that all the other Wilsons had passed, Brian had so much to say as the last man standing.

The final two tracks on the album are oddly dissimilar. The first, "Sunshine" is Brian's cod-calypso tune, and provides little until the bridge, where it expands into a long, beautiful coda. "Happy Days" is a two-part, light/dark exercise that begins with a children's toy piano but devolves into a disjointed, dark passage that builds into a beautiful organ-led chorale. This final touch offers a classic, Wilson esque color we had not heard previously on the album. An instrumental bridge carries the song into an upbeat second-half that lets us know that Brian is in the midst of a newfound life filled with many happy days.

Fans were not prepared for what was next to come.

Interlude (1999–2004)

Following the release of *Imagination* in summer 1998, it was not entirely clear what step Brian would next take when he and his family relocated to St. Charles, IL, the home base of his most recent collaborator, Joe Thomas. While certain members of the press constructed a scenario to explain the development of Brian's recent middle-of-the-road and metal-lite leanings, fans were not content to simply let Brian Wilson do what he wanted. Melinda Wilson and Joe Thomas began to plan a short tour after Brian had worked up the nerve to play a single theater show in St. Charles in May 1998, a few weeks prior to the album's release. Filmed for a promotional video intended to accompany the album, he was backed with a band that included many of the musicians who played on the *Imagination* sessions in addition to Beach Boy, Bruce Johnston, 1981 three-time Grammy winner, Christopher Cross, and Timothy B. Schmidt of the latter-day Eagles. Much of Brian's footage was filmed after the event as stage nerves prevented him from delivering his best performance.

Melinda encouraged Brian to perform in concert and stated "I was pushing him to tour because he never really got to realize the impact that his music had on people. I just felt he needed to go out and see how much people loved him, because he didn't know."[1] It could be said the Beach Boys used the same argument when they pushed Brian on stage in 1976, but the difference in 1998 is that it was a celebration of Brian, not of the Beach Boys. Melinda had demonstrated her dedication to Brian long before this, and her encouragement was for him, not his former band. Through the summer of 1998, Brian made an appearance on *The Late Show* and guest appearances at select

Jimmy Buffett concerts where they performed "South America." Capitol Records released the *Endless Harmony* soundtrack to accompany the newly released VH-1 documentary of the same name. The soundtrack included live tracks and new stereo mixes of selected songs, previously unreleased gems, such as "Soulful Old Man Sunshine," "Loop de Loop," "Sail Plane Song," and other rarities that included Brian and Van Dyke's 1966 KHJ-AM radio performance of "Heroes and Villains." In fall 1998 he appeared on The Nashville Network and at Farm Aid. Brian's decision to perform for country audiences may have been unexpected, but *Stars and Stripes, Vol. 1*, was released two years prior, and Willie Nelson, one of the founders of Farm Aid, had sung on that collection, so this was a return favor to Nelson. Brian appeared at more Jimmy Buffett shows in California where, in addition to "South America," he performed a few Beach Boys-era songs. After a few more informal guest appearances, it was announced Brian would perform a solo show in Ann Arbor, MI, in March 1999.

A new band would be required, so Melinda reached out to the Wondermints, the band who had so impressed Brian in 1995. Darian Sahanaja, Nick Walusko, and Mike D'Amico were joined by Probyn Gregory, along with long-time Beach Boys sideman, Jeff Foskett on guitar and vocals. Chicagoland musicians, Scott Bennett, Paul Mertens, Bob Lizik, Todd Sucherman, and vocalist, Taylor Mills completed the band. In addition to the show in Ann Arbor, MI, on March 9, they played shows in Illinois, Wisconsin, and Minnesota, picked up again in June for concerts in Massachusetts, Pennsylvania, New York, Connecticut, and Washington D.C., and the following month flew to Japan to perform in Osaka and Tokyo. In the fall of 1999, they toured the West Coast, and greeted the new millennium on December 31 with a show at the Redondo Beach Performing Arts Center located in the former Aviation High School campus at the corner of Aviation Blvd. and Manhattan Beach Blvd., six-and-a-half miles from the Wilson family's original Hawthorne home at 3701 W. 119 St. Brian had disproved the critics again, and was back with a band of multi-instrumentalist virtuosi who honored and respected his legacy and could recreate his most complex and elaborate records in concert. They played a pair of shows at Hollywood's legendary Roxy Theater in April of 2000 that was recorded for an album released that June, *Live at the Roxy Theater*.[2] He performed songs that spanned his entire career and included a few surprises. He presented two previously unreleased songs, "The First Time" and "This Isn't Love," the latter coauthored with Tony Asher. He also performed "Be My Baby" and a snippet of the Barenaked Ladies' "Brian Wilson." At a show on July 7 at the State Theater in Easton, PA, Brian and his band gave the first live performance of the complete *Pet Sounds* album.

In March of 2001, there was an all-star tribute to Brian at Radio City Music Hall. This aired on television in July with a DVD released in November. The gem in an evening of honors filled with performances by artists from across the field was Brian's performance of "Heroes and Villains." The central work of *SMiLE* had not been performed by Brian for decades as it represented everything connected to his perceived failure as an artist. His rejection by the Beach Boys and by the industry was tied to this song, so his performance of the work was a surprise to all.[3] On May 22, Capitol released another rarities anthology, *Hawthorne, CA: Birthplace of a Musical Legacy*. This collection included more odds and ends, interview excerpts, radio spots, backing tracks, new stereo mixes, and other session highlights. Throughout the summer, Brian was the opening act on Paul Simon's tour and headlined shows in Japan that fall.

He opened his British tour with a performance at the Queen's Jubilee concert and throughout 2002 he performed in Europe, Japan, Australia, and England. There were more releases, the first being *Pet Sounds Live* on Sanctuary Records, drawn from performances at London's Royal Festival Hall in January of that year. Capitol released another anthology, *Classics Selected by Brian Wilson* (released July 2, 2002), a 20-song collection that included a new recording of "California Feelin'." The Wilson-Kalinich song was originally recorded with the Beach Boys but would not be released until the 2013 *Made in California* boxed set. The following year was slower as there were no lengthy, continent-hopping tours, just a few domestic shows in the early summer. Beginning in late 2002 and continuing for over a year, Brian worked in the studio on songs for *Gettin' in Over My Head* (*GIOMH*). Released June 22, 2004, this album featured works from his rejected second solo-LP, *Sweet Insanity*, selected Wilson-Paley songs from the early 1990s, and miscellaneous works.

In the winter of 2004, Brian and his band returned to Europe to premiere *Brian Wilson Presents SMiLE* at London's Royal Festival Hall. After 36 years, Brian conquered the long shadow of his own legacy and participated in the reconstruction of his legendary masterpiece. In the Showtime-produced documentary, *Beautiful Dreamer*, fans observed the reconstruction process for *SMiLE* that documented Brian's initial reluctance and inevitable enthusiasm in bringing this work to life.

Brian's life has so often been presented in the media as a tragic drama. Countless interviews and articles about him till the same plot of land in the hope of offering (or discovering) one new kernel of truth. In reality they simply magnify his story to reinforce the fact that his life and career have been on public display for five decades. The integrity and intentions of his wife, children, family, collaborators, and friends is always questioned, and even within the construct of celebrity culture, there is an unforgiving level of intrusiveness upon Brian that has few parallels in the field. Like many popular music groups, the Beach Boys's story has been "told" by multiple voices, from multiple perspectives, and with multiple agendas. Steven Gaines's admirable, tell-all biography first published in 1986, *Heroes and Villains: The True Story of the Beach Boys*, was, in 1990 (the same year Capitol began their reissue of the band's catalog on compact disc), developed into the distressingly convoluted ABC miniseries, *Summer Dreams.* This fictional and cheaply dramatized narrative purported to tell the band's story, except for the fact that everything was so poorly represented, from the narrative arc of the band's history, to the overly dramatized caricatures who represented the members of the band, especially Brian. The miniseries was laughably bad and nothing could excuse this tawdry exercise for home consumption. It was an easily forgettable show even when it found a life on cable television.[4] A decade later, Mike Love took the opportunity to set the group's history straight (from his perspective) in a two-part series on ABC, *The Beach Boys: An American Family.* John Stamos, the Beach Boys's proxy for Dennis Wilson, was a producer, while the Beach Boys and their archivist, Alan Boyd, had a hand in the production of this miniseries. In any "authorized" narrative, the subject can tell the story from their perspective, and Mike Love, who stood as the last remaining Beach Boy, was given an opportunity to present the band's history from his viewpoint.[5] This is easy to understand since virtually every shred of information about the band from the moment of their inception has been focused on Brian. Mike, who had been awarded millions of dollars over the previous decade, in connection to Brian's autobiography and his songwriting royalties, must have felt some level of satisfaction at having been vindicated on so many fronts. Still, with a tidy stream of new income and the willing participation of the Brother Records organization, he grabbed the opportunity to distort not only the band's history, but Brian's story, and he colored the contributions and influences of nonfamily members who had any role in the band's work. He elevated his own participation in the creation of the band's extraordinary repository of hits and framed himself as the "normal" but equally talented creative partner in the band.

An American Family landed at the halfway mark between the release of *The Pet Sounds Sessions* boxed set and *Brian Wilson Presents SMiLE,* the two masterpieces Brian reclaimed in the form of *Pet Sounds Live* and the reconstruction of the long assumed to be unsalvageable *SMiLE.* No matter what other parties may attempt to do, whether it is television, movies, or interviews, Brian's work will continue to be shared, discovered, and enjoyed by millions of fans because in the end, his music is all that matters. What Anderle described as Brian's "innocence" or what Marks identified as "naïve and honest" are qualities that have enabled Brian to survive and continue to evolve in ways that few of his generation have achieved. In the first years of the new century, Brian was able to dispense with past ghosts and reclaim his story, his legacy, and his art. As the last surviving Wilson, and now as an established solo artist, it seemed that nothing was impossible for him.

In the spring of 2004, Brian and his band recorded *SMiLE.* This was possible thanks to the dedication and effort of everyone in his band, especially guitarist Jeffrey Foskett and Darian Sahanaja, whom Brian credits as his "Musical Secretary." They, along with Brian and the assistance of recording engineer Mark Linett, were able to reconstruct Brian's work from the archived tapes. The band learned the work from the original recordings (as seen in *Beautiful Dreamer*), and had to gently cajole Brian into joining, and remaining with, the project. Melinda's loving and steady presence could reach Brian to calm his paranoia and the negative memories that for so long defined not only his career but a significant portion of his life. He had survived the rejection and bullying back in 1967, and once he could see that everyone who surrounded him in 2003 was there for him, it was then safe to come back to the work that decades earlier had damaged his creative and personal spirit.

Van Dyke Parks had, since 1967, forged a rich and diverse career as a composer, performer, and producer, but was always remembered as the guy who worked with Brian Wilson on *SMiLE*. For Brian to fully reengage with *SMiLE*, it would be necessary to reconnect with his original collaborator. Van Dyke had, throughout his career, worked to distance himself from *SMiLE*, and as Brian's star had begun to ascend once more with events such as *Pet Sounds Live* and the Radio City Music Hall tribute, Parks did not try to ingratiate himself into Brian's spotlight. As the *SMiLE* reconstruction began to unfold, it was clear Brian could not properly complete the work without Van Dyke's assistance. When Parks left the project in the spring of 1967, there remained sections for which lyrics had not been completed. Van Dyke and Brian completed the missing gaps and tied up remaining loose ends. In the end, *Brian Wilson Presents SMiLE* was the Holy Grail for millions of fans, and a healing process for Brian and Van Dyke.

Life after SMiLE (2004–2016)

7

Cat out of the Bag

Brian Wilson Presents SMiLE (BWPS). What remained now that Brian's greatest mystery was resolved? Since its 2004 release, Brian has experienced the second most prolific period of his career. With the pressure of his legacy now retired, he would make new music, record albums of cover tunes, sing backing vocals on records for a number of new and longstanding artists, tour with guitar legend Jeff Beck, record songs for kids' programs, and work with the Beach Boys for what would appear to be last time. He would oversee the release of *The SMiLE Sessions*, an album that answered questions of authenticity (as it relates to *BWPS*), would continue to make new music, and would take *Pet Sounds* on a 50th-anniversary concert tour around the globe.

Prior to the release of *BWPS,* Brian released *Gettin' in over My Head (GIOMH)*. With the live premiere of *SMiLE* in London in the winter of 2004, and the discussions that surrounded *BWPS's* imminent release, *GIOMH* was lost in the mix. Brian worked on this record for over a year-and-a-half, and though it is an unconventional collection, the combination of varying periods and influences worked against the album. It featured guest artists that included Eric Clapton, Paul McCartney, and Elton John. There was one final collaboration with the late Carl Wilson on "Soul Searchin'." A number of long-overlooked Andy Paley songs from the *Sweet Insanity* era and the years immediately following Brian's emancipation from Landy were also included. While the album should have been a celebration of Brian's creative renaissance, it silently fell flat. Anticipation for the release of *BWPS* drowned any interest in *GIOMH,* but its few shortcomings are a result of the album's piecemeal construction rather than the quality of the music. The Peter Blake-designed cover and slipcase led one to believe this could be Brian's grand slam, but without a steady collaborator, the production was scattered, and no collection of guest artists or designers could bring the work to its full potential. Still, the album is enjoyable on its own merits.

David Leaf's liner notes provide context for Brian's first studio album since *Imagination*. Two songs "You've Touched Me" and "A Friend Like You" were composed with old friend Stephen Kalinich (the latter song provided Paul McCartney a guest turn on the album). It is a sweet work and touching homage to their unique friendship. Elton John made a guest appearance on the album opener, "How Could We Still Be Dancin.' " The song had a great bridge, but the production did not support Elton's wonderfully overwhelming vocal presence. While "Soul Searchin' " features Carl Wilson's 1995 vocal track, Brian's vocal and the instrumental track were entirely new. "You've Touched Me" can be read as a sweet letter to Melinda. Eric Clapton gives an electric performance on "City Blues," one of the few songs we have from Brian and Dennis's overindulgent "hamburger and cocaine" sessions from the early 1980s. The album's title track was cowritten by Andy Paley and has a calm, floating vibe, similar to other works they created in the mid-1990s. Another Paley coauthored work, "Desert Drive" is a perfectly acceptable rocker written in a style Brian might have used earlier in his career.

The first of four *Sweet Insanity*-era tracks is "Make a Wish" and has a catchy chorus and wonderfully messy arrangement. "Rainbow Eyes" erased Eugene Landy's influences but one wishes Brian had dedicated more time to bring these songs to their full potential. "Saturday Morning in the City," another of Brian's works with Paley, has a whimsical, humorous quality. "Fairy Tale" is one of the album's strongest compositions and is utterly charming. The final two tracks came from *Sweet Insanity*. "Don't Let Her Know She's an Angel" is a perfectly good song with effective vocal work, and "The Waltz," filled with odd turns and unexpected twists, was finished off with Van Dyke Parks.

Brian undertook projects where he provided background vocals on other artists' records, including those led by members of his band. In 2004 he sang on Scott Bennett & The Dotted Line's "No Wrong Notes in Heaven." Bennett worked with Brian from *Imagination* until 2015 and would become a central collaborator on *That Lucky Old Sun*. Brian recorded a holiday album in 2005 for Arista Records, *What I Really Want for Christmas*. The album barely scraped into the top 200 on Billboard, a pity since it was an enjoyable holiday record with good arrangements and performances, but it seemed no one was interested in hearing Brian sing holiday songs. He included new recordings of "The Man with All the Toys" and "Little Saint Nick," which originally appeared on *The Beach Boys' Christmas Album*, in addition to a collaboration with Bernie Taupin on the title track, a collaboration with Jimmy Webb on "Christmasey," plus a number of holiday standards. The three bonus tracks originally were available on Wilson's Web site in the early

2000s. They have a different feel than the rest of the album, and provide a pleasant conclusion to the record.

In addition to the holiday album, Brian was a background vocalist on Neil Diamond's "Delirious Love" from the Rick Rubin-produced album, *12 Songs*. Sadly, the song was a bonus track on a special edition of the CD and has been unavailable on later issues of the album. Brian also released a CD single, "Walking Down the Path of Life," as a benefit for victims of Hurricane Katrina. The song was joined to an "unplugged" recording of "Love and Mercy," and released through Oglio Entertainment. It is a beautiful revival-style song and is one of Brian's more spiritually informed works (with more than a passing similarity to "That Same Song"). It was recorded with Scott Bennett, Nelson Bragg, and Taylor Mills, who share the lead vocal with Brian.

In May 2006, Hallmark, the greeting card company, released a live album by the Beach Boys titled *Songs from Here and Back*. It contained nine live tracks recorded in 1974 and 1989, plus three studio recordings, one each from Brian, Mike, and Al. Brian's contribution was "Spirit of Rock & Roll." He also appeared on Carnie Wilson's album, *A Mothers Gift (Lullabies from the Heart)*, where they sang "You Are So Beautiful," the show-stopping song Dennis sang at the end of many Beach Boys shows.

For the soundtrack of the 2007 movie *Arctic Tale*, Brian provided "Live Let Live." The Van Dyke Parks coauthored song would return the following year on Brian's album, *That Lucky Old Sun*. *Every Child Deserves a Lifetime*, a benefit album for the Elizabeth Glaser Pediatric AIDS Foundation featured "Country Feelin." Brian coauthored a song with Burt Bacharach and Steve Krikorian, "What Love Can Do" for the Phil Ramone-produced compilation album, *New Music for an Old Friend*.

Taylor Mills, a backing singer in Brian's band since the 1999 show in Ann Arbor, released *Lullagoodbye*, on which Brian sang backing vocals on "Raven." Brian also sang on a cover of "In My Room" for Bill Medley's album, *Damn Near Righteous*. Medley's distinctive voice has become a little rough on the edges, but the two icons delivered a moving performance of Brian's early classic.

Under the Capitol Dome

Brian released *That Lucky Old Sun* in September 2008. It is a strong album and one of the more elaborate works in his catalog. The suite is a celebration of Southern California, and was commissioned by the Southbank Centre and composed in collaboration with Scott Bennett and Van Dyke Parks. The concert premiere took place in the autumn of 2007, with the album recorded in spring of 2008. Early pressings included a DVD documentary about the making of the album. The title track, originally made popular by Frankie Laine, was composed by Haven and Gillespie, the authors of "Old Master Painter" that had appeared on *SMiLE*. His band delivers tight performances and, as with the 2005 holiday album, Brian sounds as if he is having fun with the work. "Forever She'll Be My Surfer Girl" hearkens back to his earlier work, and Van Dyke Parks's narratives are unusually straightforward for Parks, but serve their function within the suite. The tune he composed for *Arctic Tale*, "Live Let Live" is given an update and combined with a reprise of the album's title track. "Mexican Girl" is the heart beat to Los Angeles while the light-hearted "California Role" has a McCartney/Randy Newman feel. "Oxygen to the Brain" is a fun track though it recalls some of his darker memories with "How could I have got so low . . . I laid around this old place, I hardly ever washed my face." This was a trip back to the first Landy era when the doctor forced Brian out of bed by dousing him with cold water. While the album is lighthearted and fun, it is not without its serious themes. "Oxygen . . ." segues into the 1967-era track, "Can't Wait Too Long," in a beautifully reconstructed performance. After all the optimism and upbeat themes, Brian reminds us that his arrival to this point in time was not without enormous struggles. "Midnight's Another Day" opens with a figure that could have been borrowed from Elton John before he dives into a tale of his personal battles in what is perhaps the album's most beautiful track. The line "All these voices . . ." are an acknowledgment of the aural disturbances with which he has struggled for decades, and with "All these people make me feel so alone," he expresses the difficulties that crippled him for so long. A fourth reprise of the title tune leads us into "Going Home," which contains one of the most painful confessions Brian has committed to record since "Til I Die," with "At twenty-five I turned out the light, cause I couldn't handle the glare in my tired eyes." In spite of its serious tone, he crafted an instrumental track that is part hillbilly-shuffle-rock, similar to his earlier Bob Norberg collaboration, "Back Home." The album concludes with the very moving "Southern California," in which he dreams of "Singing with my brothers in harmony, supporting each other . . ." As the last surviving Wilson, Brian's sadness over Carl's death is palpable. Music had been a refuge for all three Wilson brothers and it was their protection against whatever realities Murry constructed around his family and his own ego. As they grew further apart, the harmony was still there, but with Dennis and Carl now gone, Brian faces a world that adores his music and is aware that two-thirds of his signature sound can only exist within his memories. He concludes with "In Southern California, dreams wake up for you. And when you wake up here, you wake up everywhere." Just as Brian's music has followed his fans around the globe, his songs have allowed us to dream of an imaginary and mythical Southern California. The vocal round that concludes the song is a magical coda to the album. There is a hidden track in the run-off groove that provides a final smile to this remarkable album. While sales for *That Lucky Old Sun* were healthy enough to push the album into the low twenties on Billboard, it has not endured as one of Brian's more recognized works. This album, along with *That's Why God Made the Radio* and *No Pier Pressure*, is a trilogy that explores happiness and calm, while each concludes with a contented sadness that only Brian could capture in the late decades of his extraordinary career.

Brian collaborated with noted children's book author Sandra Boynton for her album *Blue Moo.* Brian provides a fantastic read on "Speed Turtle," a song composed by Boynton and Michael Ford. His lead and backing vocal work is fantastic and shows that in his late 60s, Brian's voice can still deliver his complex vocal parts.

Brian signed with Walt Disney Records in 2010 to record and produce an album of music by George Gershwin, *Brian Wilson Reimagines Gershwin*, and the following year on an album of music from Disney movies, *In the Key of Disney.* While the songs of George Gershwin have been interpreted by a range of artists from various genres, Brian's decision to record a Gershwin album was a brave creative decision. Wilson's earlier out-of-the-box efforts seldom elicited excitement or approval, so both Disney and Brian took a substantial leap of faith to pursue projects that were anything but vanity efforts.

Brian worked with Paul (Von) Mertens and Scott Bennett to select songs that fit comfortably within Brian's vocal range and he delivered strong performances across the album. For "Rhapsody in Blue," Brian sang all the vocal harmonies, though with the remainder of the album, his virtuoso band provided backing vocals and instrumental tracks. The Gershwin Estate gave Wilson a number of unfinished musical fragments with their permissions to complete any of them. "The Like in I Love You" was a fragment intended for *Lady Be Good* under the title "Will You Remember Me?" "Nothing but Love" was originally known as "Say My Say." Brian also sang a medley of songs from *Porgy and Bess*, in addition to six of Gershwin's most famous songs. While the album was produced by Brian, Disney Records brought in legendary engineer Al Schmidt (Jefferson Airplane) to remix the album. Mertens was able to translate Wilson's orchestrations so the band could immediately perform the songs in the studio. The instrumental version of "I Got Plenty O' Nuthin' " is one of Brian's most colorful orchestrations since *BWPS* and bears a similarity to *SMiLE's* "Cabinessence" or "Do You Dig Worms." "They Can't Take That Away from Me" has a rhythmic bed that is not dissimilar to "Help Me, Rhonda." Brian gives "Love is Here to Stay," a classic Henry Mancini-flavored arrangement. "I've Got a Crush on You" could have fit on *15 Big Ones* and "I Got Rhythm" is given a straight-up Beach Boys arrangement, while "Someone to Watch over Me" is Gershwin meets *SMiLE* a' la "Wonderful." "Let's Call the Whole Thing off" was a bonus track on iTunes and while less "arranged" than the rest of the album, the duet with Taylor Mills is charming and provides Brian with room to flex his humorous and light-hearted self.

Brian sang "California Sun" for the soundtrack of *Curious George 2: Follow That Monkey!* Best known in its cover versions by the Rivieras and the Ramones, it is humorous to hear Brian's take on a surf-themed song he did not compose.[1] One of Wilson's finest star turns was on Elton John and Leon

Russell's *The Union*, where he provides a ghostly choral arrangement and backing vocals on "When Love is Dying."

Brian recorded his next album *In the Key of Disney* in early 2011. One might expect Brian to feature more "classic" Disney songs from his own childhood, but the album featured five classic songs with the remaining six from Disney's contemporary hit shows composed by Randy Newman (*Toy Story*), Alan Mencken (*The Little Mermaid* and *Pocahontas*), and Elton John (*The Lion King*). As with the Gershwin album, Brian transforms each of the songs into his own and the album is just as enjoyable as the Gershwin collection. Given the unusual nature of the Gershwin and Disney albums, many fans have overlooked these smaller gems. Six days after the release of this album, Capitol released *The SMiLE Sessions*. If *BWPS* let the cat out of the bag in 2004, this release was the final word on a work that had been a Gordian knot that, for three decades, had throttled Brian's emotional well-being. Amidst this creative period, Brian contributed "Listen to Me" to the Buddy Holly tribute album, *Listen to Me: Buddy Holly*.

Think About the Days

At the end of 2011 it was announced that Brian, Mike Love, Al Jardine, Bruce Johnston, and David Marks would reunite as the Beach Boys for a new album and tour in celebration of their 50th year as a band. Brian would rejoin the group for the first time since *Stars & Stripes, Vol. 1* and the first album of original music since the Steve Levine-produced album 26 years earlier.[2] The Beach Boys had splintered after Carl's passing in 1998 and after Al was fired from the band by Mike Love. David Marks rejoined as a touring member of the Beach Boys prior to Carl's death and would become a semipermanent member in the years that followed. The band delivered *That's Why God Made the Radio (TWGMTR)* in June 2012, which became their highest charting album since *Summer Days (And Summer Nights!!)*, where it reached the number three spot on Billboard. While Brian was listed as the album's producer, Mike was given top billing as executive producer, and Joe Thomas was given credit for recording the album. Prior to its release, the Beach Boys began a 50th anniversary tour in April 2012 through North America, Europe, the Far East, and Australia. A good deal of back-room negotiation was required before the project could be formally launched. In addition to Brian and Mike, the band included Al Jardine, Bruce Johnston, and David Marks. They would be augmented by musicians from Brian's touring band and a couple from the Beach Boys's regular touring group. By the end of September, days before their final shows at the Royal Albert Hall and Wembley Arena, Mike announced that he and Bruce would continue on with the Beach Boys, but without Brian, Al, and David.

All but one song of the dozen on *TWGMTR* are composed by Brian with Joe Thomas credited as coauthor. Mike Love has one song "Daybreak over the Ocean," a work he composed in the late 1970s. He recorded it in 1978 and again in the 2000s for solo albums that never came to fruition. The later recording was used for *TWGMTR* with additional vocals by Brian, Al, Bruce, and Jeffrey Foskett that provide the illusion that it was a Beach Boys song. It is the one track on which neither Brian nor Thomas has a production credit.[3] Given it was written in the late 1970s, it bears a similarity to "Sumahama" from *L.A. (Light Album)*. A number of reviews took issue with the excessive use of auto-tune across the album, and while it gives the album a contemporary sound, it also masks the ensemble deficiencies of a band who had not sung together in over 20 years. The album is not dissimilar to Brian's earlier solo work with Thomas and is an enjoyable record. What differentiates it from Brian's earlier solo efforts is the unmistakable colors of the Beach Boys's group vocals. The album contained the largest number of Brian Wilson compositions on a Beach Boys album since *Love You* (1977) and *Friends* (1968).[4] Six of the album's 12 songs originated in Brian's late 1990s *Imagination*-era sessions with Joe Thomas and are among the album's best songs. Of the five newly composed songs, "Isn't It Time" and "Shelter" are the strongest in terms of composition, performance, and production.

The album opens with "Think About the Days," a wordless vocal in the style of "Our Prayer." This leads into the title track that, when we consider it was originally written in the late 1990s, bears a similarity to Robbie Williams's "Millennium" (1998), which was built on a sample of John Barry's theme song to the 1967 James Bond film, *You Only Live Twice*. "Isn't It Time" is a simple tune that gives Al one of his few lead vocals. "Spring Vacation" has a clever vocal arrangement and sounds as if it might have come from Brian's time with Jimmy Buffett, while "The Private Life of Bill and Sue" is another in a laid-back groove and is perhaps the album's least memorable work. "Shelter" has a lovely chorus and though it is one of the newer songs composed for the album, it is stylistically similar to the *Imagination*-era songs. "Beaches in Mind" was coauthored with Love and Thomas and feels similar to Love's "Summer in Paradise."

The last four songs on the album are a melancholy coda to an album where the Beach Boys harmonized with a unity and depth they had not achieved in decades. "Strange World" is similar to the wistful and dreamy tales heard on *That Lucky Old Sun*. "From There to Back Again" provides a wonderful turn for Al Jardine on a song filled with classic Wilson tropes. While Al's processed voice is a little sterile, his emotional reading with Brian is effective and moving. The lyrics are some of the album's most touching as they reflect on a past that, like Brian's mythical Southern California, is an imaginary world where the youthful Wilson and Love families lived happily in some far-away memory of family gatherings at Mt. Vernon and Fairway. The unusually brief "Pacific Coast Highway" opens with a "Celestial Choir" before Brian introduces a wonderfully brief, sunshine-filled moment of melancholy. The album's closing track, "Summer's Gone" is one of Wilson's most beautiful songs of the past 15 years. Like so much of the album, the group's vocals are strong, but Brian's lead is his best of the album.

Mike Love made it known to the press before the end of their anniversary tour that he and Bruce would continue on without Brian, Al, or David. The cautious détente was shattered and each of the parties returned to their pre-reunion roles.

From There to Back Again

Brian's creative activities throughout 2013 included extended periods in the recording studio and a number of concerts with unexpected guest artists. Al Jardine occasionally appeared in concert with Brian, and before the end of the year, Blondie Chaplin would also make guest appearances at Brian's shows. From September through October, Brian toured with Jeff Beck, which led to rumors that the two would collaborate on a new record. Brian was in the studio throughout much of the year, though no specific project was forthcoming to the public.

At the end of August, Capitol Records released the richly packaged, six-disc boxed set, *Made in California*. While compilation albums are the backbone of Capitol Records's Beach Boys catalog, this set superseded the comprehensive, two-decade old *Good Vibrations* set. The 2011 release of *The SMiLE Sessions* was the final word on Brian's masterpiece, so for the new boxed set, Capitol included long-ignored rarities and unreleased tracks. *Made in California* featured a wealth of live tracks and radio promotion spots, in addition to a number of outtakes that included previously unreleased compositions by Dennis Wilson. The set concluded with a sixth disc, subtitled *From the Vaults*, which contained long-overlooked works from the Beach Boys's catalog. Included were the instrumental track for "Guess I'm Dumb," the hybrid 1965–1976 mash-up of "Sherry, She Needs Me," "Where Is She?," the instrumental track of the unreleased "Why," the 1970 version of "Back Home," original versions of "California Feelin' " and "Soul Searchin'," and a 1976 outtake of Phil Spector's "You've Lost That Lovin' Feeling."

Brian appeared on Jimmy Webb's album *Still Within the Sound of My Voice* where he provided backing vocals on Webb's "MacArthur Park." His contributions provide an unmistakable timbral presence, and are a ghostly imprint of the California sound he created. He provides a glorious vocal stack that is unmistakably Brian and adds a rich hue to Webb's elegantly delivered classic.

In December 2013, Capitol Records released an online-only collection, *The Big Beat, 1963*, a collection of unreleased tracks and demos by the Beach Boys, the Honeys, Gary Usher, and two duos that included his original roommate, Bob Norberg, Bob & Sheri, and Bob Norberg and Victoria Hale. Unlike *Made in California*, this collection was released with the intention to extend the copyrights for songs that, due to recently revised laws, would pass into public domain.[5] The collection is a fascinating view into Brian's working methods at a period when he was developing his formidable production skills. A number of the tracks are sourced from acetates and are of middling sound quality, but we hear Brian working through songs and arrangements that he would use in later Beach Boys or Honeys songs. While not for the casual fan, the collection is an enjoyable view into Brian's working methods.

As the year came to close, Brian's trusted guitarist and musical director, Jeffrey Foskett, left his band. As the most senior member of Brian's young group, Foskett was an invaluable asset in Brian's reemergence as a performing artist, and with Darian Sahanaja was central to the reconstruction of *SMiLE.* Brian described Foskett as his "right-hand man," but in a September 2014 interview that appeared in *The Desert Sun*, Foskett (who returned to playing with the Beach Boys in May 2014) acknowledged that he needed a break from the dozen-plus years of service with Brian. He was Brian's touring partner and the surrogate upon whom Brian relied to insure everything ran on time. Following the Jeff Beck-Brian Wilson tour and the indefinite postponement of the rumored Wilson-Beck album, it seemed that Foskett needed to move on.[6]

Brian continued to record throughout 2014, and in July he gave his first shows without Foskett in Ireland and England. Al Jardine's son, Matt, joined Brian's band and would contribute additional instrumental textures and the important falsetto parts that Brian, at age 72, could no longer reach.[7] Al Jardine had been invited back into the Beach Boys that summer but elected instead to tour with Brian.[8] In December, Capitol released two digital-only collections of material from 1964 in an effort to extend copyrights, *Keep an Eye on Summer—The Beach Boys Sessions 1964* and *The Beach Boys Live in Sacramento.* The former features a number of "Vocals-Only" tracks alongside "Sessions" takes, alternate mixes of familiar hits from 1964, and previously unreleased BBC sessions. The live album is of interest because it offers two complete shows recorded on August 1, 1964, which capture the enthusiasm and near mayhem the band could elicit from their audiences. The 1964 release, *Beach Boys Concert*, was recorded in Sacramento over two shows in December 1963 and August 1964, where *Live in Sacramento* offers a complete document of two shows performed on August 1, 1964.[9]

Brian was a guest vocalist (with Al Jardine) on the concert *George Fest: A Night to Celebrate the Music of George Harrison* held on September 28, 2014. A recording of the show would be released over a year-and-a-half later. Brian and Al sang "My Sweet Lord," and while it is a little rough on the edges, they deliver an emotional performance.

The Beach Boys and Brian had, beginning in 1990, been the subject of various made-for-television movies. Whether fabricated (*Summer Dreams: The Story of the Beach Boys*) or grossly subjective (*The Beach Boys: An American Family*), the films were largely forgettable, and each portrayed Brian as a mentally and emotionally incapacitated wreck of a man. Melinda Wilson had worked since 1999 to get a Brian-centric biographical film into production, and through much of the early 2000s, various rumors floated as to the existence of/greenlighting of a film about Brian's life. In the summer of 2014, Bill Pohlad's *Love and Mercy* premiered to strong reviews at the Toronto Film Festival. While Brian had limited involvement in the development of the film, Melinda was a prominent contributor to the production. The movie is constructed on two parallel narratives, Brian of 1962–1967 and Brian of the second Landy period from the mid-1980s. Brian was portrayed by Paul Dano in the early years while John Cusack played the Landy-era Wilson. Melinda Wilson was played by Elizabeth Banks, and Paul Giamatti portrayed Eugene Landy. While some facts were simplified to streamline the narrative, Pohlad's attention to detail in representing both narrative and visual accuracy was superior to any previous effort. The roles that Stan Love and Carl Wilson served in extracting Brian from Landy were largely omitted in favor of Melinda's role in Brian's life, but aside from the slightly rewritten involvement of Mike Love and Van Dyke Parks, the film is considered to be a fairly accurate representation of both periods in Wilson's life. It received a general release in June 2015, two months following the release of Brian's album, *No Pier Pressure.*

In early 2015, Brian appeared as a backing vocalist on "Any Emotions" by Indi-psychedelic-glam popsters, Mini Mansions and on the opening track of hip-hop/alternative-rock producer, Emile Haynie's album, *We Fall.* Brian's ghostly vocal colors the track "Falling Apart," which is built on a descending stepwise progression of the variety Wilson has used in many of his works. Haynie is best known as a producer, and had won a Grammy Award for his work on Eminem's *Recovery*, but *We Fall* is a splendid 30-something breakup album that features guest appearances by Randy Newman, Lana Del Rey, Colin Blunstone, and Charlotte Gainsbourg. Brian's collaborations with a new generation of pop stars set into motion a natural transition for a number of partnerships on Brian's next album.

The Last Song

No Pier Pressure is Brian's 11th studio album and the first solo collection of original material since *That Lucky Old Sun*. It performed admirably on Billboard, where it inched into the top 30. As with so much of Brian's work, it received mixed reviews in regard to the adult contemporary arrangements and the extensive use of auto-tune. The album was coproduced by Joe Thomas, and he is largely responsible for particular timbral choices in the arrangements (his penchant for pairs of woodwinds to "tag" phrases), but aside from these occasional enhancements, the record is Brian's production. The material on this album began life as a follow-up to the Beach Boys's *TWGMTR*, but once Mike Love made it known that Brian, Al, and David would not continue with the band, the materials were reorganized for Brian's solo outing. The tour with Jeff Beck and rumors of a Wilson-Beck album were replaced with rumors of multiple albums. Ultimately, it was announced that *No Pier Pressure* would be a single release from Brian.

The album featured numerous guest artists, the majority of whom enhance the quality of the work. Since Brian had intended that many of these songs would form a second Beach Boys reunion album, it appeared that while this was a solo record, he wanted to have additional ensemble and vocal colors to augment his own contributions. As for the music? It feels and sounds like a continuation of *TWGMTR*, and may be the stronger collection of the two. Al Jardine, David Marks, and Blondie Chaplin make guest appearances on the record and their contributions give the work a Beach Boys "feel."

The opening and closing tracks serve as thematic and emotional bookends, so when Brian opens with "This Beautiful Day," he sets a sweet and wistful tone for the listener to settle into the record. The next track, "Runaway Dancer" is perhaps the most controversial work on the album, not least for his decision to partner with Sebu Simonian from the Indi-pop duo, Capital Cities. Given Brian's recent work with Emile Haynie and Mini Mansions, it is not unexpected that he would choose to work with another contemporary Indi-artist.[10] "Runaway Dancer" is the most unexpected work, since *Sweet Insanity's* abysmal rap-lite exercise, "Smart Girls," but unlike that work, "Runaway Dancer" is a solid pop dance song. The collaboration with Sebu brought a radically different texture and structure to Brian's work and while the song is disliked for its dance-lite character, the work is a fun, radio-friendly song. Al Jardine and David Marks are featured on "Whatever Happened." While the opening is not outstanding, the song builds into a wonderful ballad with an effective chorus. Al and David provide an authentic "Beach Boys" feel and successive verses carry the song into a reassuring groove. The multitalented Zooey Deschanel, one-half of Indi-duo, She & Him, join Brian for "On the Island," which perhaps is the least engaging song on the album. While Deschanel is a wonderful retro-style singer, the duet with Brian feels somewhat artificial, and is an example where the parts are greater than the sum.

The instrumental, "Half Moon Bay" features Mark Isham, the Windham Hill-New Age trumpet stylist. While Isham's playing is fine, the brief work is more of a pastiche than the album opener, "Runaway Dancer." Peter Hollens, a young singer who has built a reputation on his formidable a cappella artistry, is the guest on "Our Special Love." The opening of the song has a classic Wilson choral figure and the duet with Hollens is spectacular. While Brian is a little too auto-tuned, the duet between one of the new generation of vocal artists and one of the greatest composers of popular vocal music resulted in one of the most moving songs on the album. Brian's iconic rise-and-fall melodic contour, similar to a theme he used in "One for the Boys" from *Brian Wilson*, is used to maximum effect. Another Jardine-Marks guest turn is featured on "The Right Time," a good middle-of-the-lane pop song with a beautiful chorus and strong contributions from Jardine and Marks. So much had changed in the lives of all three since they first worked together in Hawthorne 54 years ago, but their ability to blend and find a solid groove has never abandoned them. "Guess You Had to Be There" features country-hipster Kacey Musgraves, who also earned a coauthorship credit on the song. She provides a rich, velvety color in a style reminiscent of Alison Krauss or Allison Moorer, and similar to his duet with Peter Hollens, Brian fits nicely into the lead Musgraves sets and displays a wonderful contour and shape to his vocal line. This song would have been a sure hit had it been included on *Stars and Stripes, Vol. 1*, because it is an honest mix where Brian Wilson meets alt-country.

No Pier Pressure was released in multiple configurations. There was a standard release, a deluxe edition, a Target-exclusive deluxe edition, and a two-disc LP set. The deluxe edition adds three songs into the middle of the album, and the first, "Don't Worry," is one of a handful of the album's up-tempo songs. Brian's lead vocal is not as strong here as it was on the three previous tracks, but it is a good work that serves as an entrée into the next song, "Somewhere Quiet." Scott Bennett was Brian's partner on this song, and they delivered a beautiful rewrite of Brian's 1965 instrumental from *Summer Days (and Summer Nights!!)*, "Summer Means New Love." Al provides a wonderful backing vocal to the rewrite of Brian's original instrumental gem that even preserves the swirling and dreamy string coda. "I'm Feeling Sad" is the last of the "Deluxe" tracks and is another "look-back" into Brian's earlier tool chest. As with the lyrics in so many of Brian's songs from 1968 to 1971 that relied upon "a-day-in-the-life-of" themes, "Feeling Sad" is an unexpected return to this narrative. The song has a cheery accompaniment while Brian delivers a matter-of-fact narration of his daily activities. As with so many of the songs on the album, the lyrics convey a conversational tenor that describes his feelings towards a loved one. Many of Brian's songs on *Beach Boys Today!* and *Pet Sounds* were expressions of love, doubt, fear, and hope directed towards Marilyn Wilson, and he mines similar, albeit in a more mature framework, themes in his lyrics to Melinda on *No Pier Pressure*.

After the "Deluxe" tracks, Brian returned to the core of the album with "Tell Me Why," another song to feature Al Jardine on a shared lead vocal. The vocal arrangement is moving and heartfelt and Al's presence on this song (and throughout the album) brings a richness to the entire work. Blondie Chaplin, whose brief time with the Brian-less Beach Boys from 1972–1974, provided a harder edge to a band that had struggled to find its voice after Brian had withdrawn from the band during sessions for *Surf's Up!* Over three decades later he appears on Brian's album in an unexpected but welcomed return. He provided the lead vocal on "Sail Away," a pleasant tune that echoes "Sloop John B" and the Beach Boys song for which Blondie is best remembered, "Sail On, Sailor." Like Al, Blondie began to make occasional concert appearance with Brian in 2014, and his playing and singing brought a greater level of authenticity to songs such as "Sail On, Sailor" and "Darlin'." Another Wilson-Bennett tune, "One Kind of Love" would be used in the film, *Love and Mercy*, but also appeared on this album. Brian expresses his feeling towards Melinda throughout the album, but on "One Kind of Love" he speaks of his love for her in simple but extraordinarily honest terms.

Brian chose to place "Saturday Night" as the penultimate track and the song, which features Indi-rocker Nate Ruess (he was the connection who introduced Brian to Emile Haynie) on vocals, is an upbeat, fun, country pop-tinged rocker. The production and arrangement are simpler than many on the album, but it is an effective and sincere song. The bridge features Brian's penchant for unexpected key shifts and is a wonderful break from Ruess's expressive lead vocal.

The album's closing track, "The Last Song," is a beautiful and melancholic farewell to an unexpectedly satisfying album. As with "Summer's Gone," the final track on *TWGMTR*, "The Last Song" is an emotional and moving song, for what if this is in fact Brian's last song on his last album?[11] Is he speaking about Dennis and Carl when he sings "There's never enough time for the ones that you love." The choral work is beautifully arranged and provides a glorious conclusion to the album. Brian has given us, his fans, and admirers so much of himself for over five decades, so what if this is his "Last Song?" We have been fortunate to hear the imaginary world of Southern California and his dreams of a perpetually sunny unreality.

Postlude

Beginning in late March 2016, Wilson toured the globe with the *Pet Sounds 50th Anniversary Tour*. A review of Brian's show in Burlington, VT, "Brian Wilson Curates Night of his Beach Boys Songs," was a sympathetic and honest assessment of Wilson's engagement and participation in the concert. While his voice is limited in range, he leads at the piano, introduces the songs, and is the focus of all activity on stage. His lack of facade is an honest reflection of the man. He is known to check his wristwatch during shows. Is it a nervous habit or is he truly anxious to leave the stage? Regardless, it matters to no one in the audience because it is his presence that provides agency to his work with a band that performs his complex and difficult works with relative ease. While he can sing the songs that lay within his current range, it is the vocal prowess of Matt Jardine and his multi-instrumentalist band members who provide an unassailable level of authenticity and legitimacy to the show. If you, as an audience member, accept this, you can derive a great deal of enjoyment and pleasure from his concerts. If you are looking for an exuberant performance from the man who created this work, you may be disappointed. Given all that Brian has survived and endured, his engaged presence is reason enough for celebration.

Since his return to the concert stage in 1999, his band has featured an extraordinary collection of musicians, the majority of whom have remained to the present day. Three musicians who served in various capacities as "right-hand man," "musical secretary," and "musical director"—Jeffrey Foskett, Darian Sahanaja, and Scott Bennett, respectively—are absent from this tour. Foskett left Brian's group at the end of 2013 and returned to his previous job with the Beach Boys. Scott Bennett is no longer in Brian's band, and Darian Sahanaja, who along with Foskett, was responsible for the reconstruction of *SMiLE* and who began the *Pet Sounds* tour in 2016, left at mid-year to pursue other commitments. All three brought both vocal and instrumental leadership to the group, and without Darian there to "conduct" the band, as he so capably managed over the past 17 years, the group has a different energy and "feel" than on previous tours.

What Anderle, Marks, and others used to describe as Brian's innocence and honesty is as present and real now as it was 50 years ago and shows in his performance of *Pet Sounds.* At the end of "Caroline, No," Brian hands the vocal to Matt Jardine after the bridge, and quietly and without fanfare exits the stage before the band is finished. As they play the instrumental closing verse, a sample from the original recording, the sound of a passing train with Brian's dogs barking in the distance, accompanies the band as they exit into the wings. The sight of a septuagenarian Brian walking off-stage is an emotional and crushing reminder of the song's themes on the loss of youth and innocence. The intimate and personal stories that he, at the age of 23, wove into *Pet Sounds* are all the more significant when we acknowledge what he has experienced in the very public and unforgiving light of celebrity. Brian Wilson has survived and lived to see his masterpiece reach its 50th anniversary, and we are fortunate to share these moments and thank him for everything he has given us. The roar of the Santa Fe Scout as it traveled from Hutchinson, KS, to Southern California would have been an indelible memory for the young Murry Wilson when he, his siblings, and his mother came to California in 1921. Nearly a century later, the sound of a locomotive accompanies Brian as he exits the stage and leaves *Pet Sounds* across the globe as a part of all of our pasts.

Notes

Prelude

1. The premiere of "Good Vibrations" occurred on this date in Hill Auditorium on the University of Michigan's Ann Arbor campus. An announcement in the Ann Arbor News on October 20 states that the two shows in the 3,500-seat hall (7:00 and 9:00 pm) were sold out and the Standells were the opening act. Photographs of Brian coaching the Beach Boys on the Hill Auditorium stage confirm his presence at these shows, of which both were recorded. The band played at Michigan State University in East Lansing on October 21, but this show was neither recorded nor did Brian attend this show.
2. Brian appeared on *Inside Pop: The Rock Revolution* (narrated by Leonard Bernstein) that aired on April 25, 1967, where he performed "Surf's Up." This was one of the first news shows to present rock music as both a musical and cultural force that deserved serious consideration.
3. Peter Ames Carlin, *Catch a Wave: The Rise, Fall, and Redemption of the Beach Boys' Brian Wilson* (New York, NY: Rodale, 2006), 277.
4. The legendary Rolling Stone article, *The Healing of Brother Brian* (RS 225, November 4, 1976) opened with the heading "The Abominable Beach Boy."
5. James B. Murphy's *Becoming the Beach Boys* is an excellent study that traces Brian and the band's path from unpolished amateurs to skilled artists.
6. Murry's family came from Hutchinson, KS, while Audree's family was from Minneapolis, MN.
7. James B. Murphy, *Becoming the Beach Boys* (Jefferson, NC: McFarland & Company, Inc., 2015), 42.
8. Her brother Jimmy would later help Brian with the laundry list of surfing spots mentioned in "Surfin' U.S.A."

9. Mike was held up at gunpoint while working the gas station located at La Brea and West Washington St. in the less affluent Crenshaw neighborhood.
10. White, 24.
11. White, 58.
12. David Leaf, *The Beach Boys* (Philadelphia, PA: Courage Books, 1985), 191.
13. Leaf, 10.
14. The family business involved live performances and the management of various Beach Boys business ventures and over the course of 50 years has included Brian's father, his two brothers, and cousins on both sides of his family. Brother Records Inc. (BRI) serves as the formal name of the "family" concern.
15. Kirk Curnutt, *Brian Wilson* (Bristol, CT: Equinox, 2012), 5.
16. Mike Love's contentious lawsuits with Brian in the early 1990s where he sought coauthorship credits for over 70 songs, and the financial gains related to those songs, have their origins in Murry's habit of leaving Mike's name off of the many publishing and contract agreements he managed for Sea of Tunes. Murry also left Al Jardine outside of the business partnership and diverted David Marks's financial share of record sales after he left the band.
17. *The Pet Sounds Sessions*, 111.
18. Ibid.
19. Paul Williams, *Brian Wilson & the Beach Boys: How Deep Is the Ocean?* (London, England: Omnibus Press, 1997), 198.
20. Williams, 206.
21. Williams, 199.
22. Tony Asher has been credited as having overheard this comment from Mike to Brian during February 1966 sessions for *Pet Sounds*.
23. Leaf, 110.
24. Brian Wilson, *Wouldn't It Be Nice* (New York, NY: HarperCollins, 1991), 112.
25. "Do It Again" uses Brian's classic tropes with relative ease and constructs a song in 1969 that sounded like it could have been written in 1964–1965.
26. This was the penultimate track on *Surf's Up*, the Beach Boys's 1971 album that resuscitated and reconstructed the very song the Beach Boys had rejected in 1967 and over which Brian's role as the visionary leader of America's greatest band came to an end.
27. Brian's grandparents on both sides of his family had immigrated from Kansas and Minnesota to California in the first quarter of the twentieth century.
28. Murry Wilson converted their garage into a dedicated den and music room with a piano and an organ that also served as Brian's first musical laboratory.
29. Provincial is not used pejoratively but describes the insular and conservative nature of the new, suburban middle-class.
30. Sports broadcasting of the 1950s tended to include boxing, wrestling, roller derby, and various regional sporting entertainments. Big money major-league sports had not yet arrived on television, and aside from the Los Angeles Rams, major-league sports did not arrive in Southern California until 1958 when the Dodgers relocated from Brooklyn and the Lakers from Minneapolis in 1960.
31. Curnutt, 2.
32. Philip Lambert, *Inside the Music of Brian Wilson* (New York, NY: The Continuum International Publishing Group, Inc., 2007), 43.
33. Williams, 198.

Chapter 1

1. The long-accepted dates of September 15 and October 3 cannot be verified as the correct dates, though many narratives list these as the demo and recording sessions, respectively.
2. Jon Stebbins, *The Beach Boys FAQ: All That's Left to Know about America's Band* (Milwaukee, WI: Backbeat Books, 2011), 37.
3. Stephen J. McParland, *In the Studio with Brian Wilson and the Beach Boys* (Editions Berlot, 2014), 40.
4. *Surfin'* and other tracks recorded by Hite Morgan before the band signed to Capitol records have been licensed and released on multiple occasions and are not part of Capitol's reissue series.
5. McParland, 36.
6. McParland, 36.
7. McParland, 55.
8. Doe, Rusten, Stebbins, and Murphy discuss these items in length in their respective books.
9. Murphy, 157.
10. Murphy, 145.
11. Reported in detail in McParland's *The Wilson Project.*
12. Many sources list these dates as April 16 and 19.
13. McParland, 102.
14. Recorded in some sources as Betty Everett. Murphy believes a case could be made that it was neither person.
15. White, 175.
16. The April sessions are the first when Brian worked with Chuck Britz, who became his preferred engineer until 1967.
17. Keith Badman, *The Beach Boys: The Definitive Diary of America's Greatest Band on Stage and in the Studio* (San Francisco, CA: Backbeat Books, 2004), 25.
18. White, 165.
19. Andrew Hickey, *The Beach Boys on CD: Vol. 1—The 1960s* (lulu.com, 2011).
20. Murphy, 230.
21. Lambert, 44.
22. Gaines, 84.
23. *Brian Wilson Reimagines Gershwin* is the culmination of Brian's skill at mixing disparate styles.
24. Though the name "Wrecking Crew" would not come into use until decades later, I will, for ease of reference, use this descriptor throughout the book. Drummer Hal Blaine used this as the title of his 1990 autobiography. *The First Call Gang* and *The Phil Spector Wall of Sound Orchestra* were also used to describe this collection of musicians.
25. The source for this song was an acetate and not the master tape, so the audio quality has degraded over time.
26. McParland, 127.
27. In Tom Nolan's 1971 article on the Beach Boys that appeared in *Rolling Stone*, Venet is quoted as saying, "I didn't really help Brian that much. I didn't hinder him but I didn't help him because I never really got that close."

28. It has been covered by various artists, including Fleetwood Mac, but is not the Deep Purple song of the same title that appeared on their 1971 album *Fireball.*
29. McParland, 114.
30. A 1931 building located at 1619 Broadway at 49th St. in New York City was ground zero for popular music in post-World War II America (along with a building at 1650 Broadway at 51st St. and one at 1697 Broadway) and was home to songwriters and numerous music publishing concerns. From the mid-1950s into the 1960s, the "Brill Building" sound dominated much of American popular music.
31. There is a lack of consensus about the dates of the Beach Boys shows at Pandora's Box and the number of nights on which they performed there. James B. Murphy's *Becoming the Beach Boys* offers the most plausible argument.
32. He worked with the Honeys throughout the decade and in the 1970s worked with Marilyn and Diane Rovell's project, *Spring* (*American Spring*).
33. McParland, 137.
34. Badman, 85.
35. Philip Lambert refers to this gesture as the "Celestial Choir."
36. The B-side of "Little Saint Nick" featured Brian's a cappella arrangement of Albert Hay Malotte's "The Lord's Prayer." The record did not find favor at Capitol, but showed Brian's vocal arranging skills at their best.
37. ESQ—The Russian River, El Nido, CA.
38. McParland, 143.
39. Both recordings from November 4 are on *The Big Beat 1963.*
40. Doe lists this day as November 6 and gives no mention to any session on November 4.
41. Castells lead singer, Chuck Girard, would go on to work with Gary Usher in the Hondells.
42. McParland, 144.
43. Badman, 44.
44. Lambert, 127–128.
45. Lambert, 139.
46. Lambert, 134.
47. He also returned to "Sherry..." in a retitled song, "She Says That She Needs Me."
48. James B. Murphy has identified this film as Don Brown's *Surf's Up*. This was David Marks's first appearance with the band.
49. Dick Dale & the Del-Tones, Donna Loren, the Hondells, Leslie Gore, and the Supremes were some of the performers who appeared in these films.
50. Elliot, 177.
51. Jon Stebbens, *The Beach Boys FAQ* (Milwaukee, WI: Backbeat Books, 2011).
52. Ian Rusten and Jon Stebbins, *The Beach Boys in Concert: The Ultimate History America's Band on Tour and Onstage* (Milwaukee, WI: Backbeat Books, 2013), 37.
53. Murry's firing initiated a merry-go-round of managers, from solid and competent to misguided and abusive to generally awful. This ended in the 1980s with the arrival of Jerry Schilling and later with Tom Hulett.
54. As with the previous album's cover tune *Why Do Fools Fall in Love*, Brian pays homage to classic songs of early rock and roll era.

55. In 1964, Honda did not sell automobiles but were known for the motorcycles and dirt bikes they marketed to a younger demographic.
56. Brian listed the Rovell home address as his place of residence on the AFM sheets at this period.
57. After 1961, this show would be known as *The Wonderful World of Color*. After 1968, *Disney* replaced the word *Color*.
58. Hickey, Kindle edition, location 886.
59. Author interview with Brad Elliott, November 11, 2015.
60. Brad Elliott, *Surf's Up!—The Beach Boys on Record, 1961–1981* (Ann Arbor, MI: Popular Culture, Ink., 1991), 267.
61. The only original work composed for the album was the Greenwich, Barry, Spector tune *Christmas (Baby Please Come Home)*.
62. A concert film of the same name was filmed at Santa Monica Civic Auditorium on October 28–29, 1964.
63. Campbell added his vocals in March 1965 and the single was released in June of that year.
64. They would adopt Glen Campbell and then Bruce Johnston as a permanent replacement for Brian, who retired from the road in 1965.

Chapter 2

1. Leaf, 64.
2. If we consider David Marks, the band had already listed eight members by the time Bruce Johnston joined the group.
3. While Bruce filled many roles with the band and helped them out well into the 1980s; the Beach Boys have not always been as gracious to Bruce.
4. MOJO and Rolling Stone have each listed this album in their respective list of "must-hear" albums.
5. Wechter was a prominent contributor to many of Herb Alpert's Tijuana Brass albums in addition to his own productions with the Baja Marimba Band.
6. Hickey, Kindle edition, location 1035.
7. Hickey, Kindle edition, location 1012.
8. McParland, 190.
9. Referenced in Chapter 1.
10. McParland, 178.
11. This music program was broadcast on ABC from September 1964 to January 1966.
12. Doe and Tobler have this song written in a brothel in Amsterdam.
13. ESQ gives this date as January 9.
14. Wilson, 111.
15. It was one year earlier when Brian struggled to complete "I Can See Right Through You" for the Honeys, which also dealt with issues of desire and expectations.
16. Lambert, 198.
17. Her last single, produced and authored by Brian, *Thinkin' Bout You, Baby* was released in June 1964.
18. McParland, 175.

19. Its first release was on the 1993 boxed set of *Good Vibrations: Thirty Years of the Beach Boys.*
20. He also returned to work with Brian on his 1988 solo album, *Brian Wilson.*
21. Titelman got Brian to return to the work in sessions for his 1988 solo debut, with a revised title, "Terri, She Needs Me." It was dropped on Eugene Landy's orders.
22. Lambert, 200.
23. Lambert, McParland, Doe & Tobler, Hickey, and others.
24. John Cale has been influenced by Wilson and has recorded no less than two songs that directly quote Brian's work.
25. Lambert, 204.
26. Brian led the band on an incomplete version of "Walk On By" that was included on the 1990 two-fer of *Friends/20/20.*
27. Curnutt, 71.
28. Heard on 1968s Stack-O-Tracks.
29. The Beatles *Let It Be*, the Rolling Stones *Love You Live*, and the cable series MTV Unplugged can be connected to Brian's original *Party!* concept.
30. Sessions included "oldies," songs from the 1950s as well as songs by their peers such as the Beatles and Bob Dylan. On selected songs "loose" also implies that songs were sloppily played.
31. The eight-count silence at the end of each verse is often pointed to as the reason behind its anemic chart performance.
32. The details for this session are outlined in McParland and confirmed on Andrew Doe's *Bellagio* Web site.
33. This is not the familiar children's tune of the same name.
34. The 14-track UK version of *A Hard Day's Night* featured all Lennon/McCartney songs.
35. The 14-track UK version of *Rubber Soul* featured two songs composed by George Harrison and one composed by Lennon/McCartney/Starr.
36. *The Pet Sounds Sessions* liner notes. Wilson shares this narrative in various video documentaries, his autobiography, and in the liner notes to the various editions of *Pet Sounds*, so there is no reason to not accept this as fact.
37. This was the first non-soundtrack Beatles album to retain the same title and cover art as its UK counterpart, though the track listings would differ between the two versions.
38. *The Pet Sounds Sessions* liner notes.
39. Philip Lambert's "Inside the Music of Brian Wilson" provides theoretical analyses for each song on the album.
40. It is believed this was Capitol's response to the ongoing lawsuit between the Beach Boys and Capitol and the impending loss of the group to another label. In doing this, Capitol removed an otherwise consistent revenue stream from both Brian and the band.
41. Author interview with Brad Elliot, November 2015.
42. Warners changed their plan and in 1974 they released 2-for-the-price-of-1 packages with *Wild Honey/20/20* and *Friends/Smiley Smile.* The 2-for-1 package was a popular marketing tool for record labels that enabled them to make available an artists' back catalog at a low cost of production. MCA made the Who's 1960s Decca catalog available through a series of 2-for-1 releases in the early 1970s.

43. As with all of Brian's albums in the 1960s, the album was mixed in monophonic, but released in both mono and duophonic, Capitol's proprietary method and trademark for fake stereo.
44. "Hang on to Your Ego," "Trombone Dixie," and a collection titled "Unreleased Backgrounds." Capitol Records (Japan) released a CD of the album in 1988 without "Trombone Dixie."
45. This was supposed to be released in 1996, for the 30th anniversary, but internal issues within BRI postponed a green light for Capitol to release the set.
46. The videos included original promotional film from 1966 and a newly filmed segment of Brian speaking with Beatles producer, Sir George Martin.
47. In the Summer 2016 Edition of *Endless Summer Quarterly*, Lee Dempsey provided reviews and comparisons of various reel-to-reel and monophonic vinyl issues of the album.
48. In a late 1970s interview with David Leaf, Steve Douglas, a winds player on the sessions as well as an executive at Capitol, said the release of "Caroline, No" as a solo single, "caused problems, man, I just can't tell you."
49. *The Pet Sound Sessions*, Liner Notes, 18.
50. In the 1960s, retail sales of one million dollars or 250,000 units sold constituted a gold record. In the 1970s the ratings were redefined and a gold record indicated 500,000 units sold. Over the course of its lifetime, *Pet Sounds* has achieved 5× Platinum status.
51. It was certified Gold on February 11, 2000, and Platinum on April 6, 2000 (www.riaa.com).
52. Contrary to every other source at the time of the album's release, Mike claims to have supported Brian and this record. It is reported through various sources that at the time of its release, he found Brian's new direction was too avant-garde and felt it lacked commercial appeal.
53. The 2016 release of Mike Love's autobiography, *Good Vibrations: My Life as a Beach Boy*, continues to promote his "alternative" history of the band and its members.
54. Brian held many of the vocal sessions at Columbia studio where they had a new eight-track console.
55. Members of the Wrecking Crew provided instrumental tracks for this album.
56. Excluding Russ Titelman's contribution to the Glen Campbell single and the unreleased "Sherry, She Needs Me," Mike had reasserted himself as Brian's musical partner after Christian's departure, so Asher's entrance into Brian's creative sphere surely reopened earlier conflicts as he was once again passed over.
57. *The Pet Sounds Sessions*, 106.
58. Stebbins, 73.
59. Sellars, ed., 37.
60. In Leaf, Asher recalls that one of the few compromises to which Brian acquiesced was the inclusion of "Sloop John B.," recorded nine months before he began proper sessions for the album.
61. Brad Elliott has documented that "Good Vibrations" was, as of February 23, 1966, slated for inclusion on *Pet Sounds*, but on a revised track listing submitted to Capitol dated March 3 this song is missing. Brian used "Run James, Run" retitled as "Pet Sounds" in its place.

62. David Leaf, *The Making of Pet Sounds* (Los Angeles, CA: Capitol Records, 1996), 44.
63. The original version of the song was first released on the 1990 CD issue of *Pet Sounds*.
64. Leaf, 77.
65. *The Pet Sounds Sessions,* 7.
66. Ibid.
67. Leaf, 79.
68. Kent, 25.
69. Mike Love has taken credit for the title, *Pet Sounds*, in response to the countless takes Brian demanded for each song. He also called Brian "dog ears" because he could seem to hear things that no one else could.
70. *The Pet Sounds Sessions,* 8.
71. Jeff Sellars, *God Only Knows: Faith, Hope, Love, and The Beach Boys* (Eugene, OR: Cascade Books, 2015), 3. The Beach Boys's induction is best remembered for Mike Love's left-field rant, criticizing the Beatles and the Rolling Stones.
72. *The Pet Sounds Sessions,* 109.
73. Brian would continue to produce Marilyn's projects with the Honeys and American Spring into the late 1970s.
74. Ibid., 106.
75. Leaf, 87.
76. Kent, 17.
77. Leaf, 108.
78. Ibid., 110.
79. Ibid., 111.
80. Leaf, 84.
81. To demonstrate that Brian was not the only talent in the family, Capitol, in October 1967, released *The Many Moods of Murry Wilson*, a collection of easy listening instrumentals. It is believed Murry charged this record against the Beach Boys accounts.
82. Badman claims the master at the original speed was delivered to Capitol and only during mastering was the decision made to speed the tape and give Brian a younger sounding voice. If this is true, there is no indication as to who directed this.
83. If anyone in the band expressed reservations with the lyrics, it is generally accepted that the band found Brian's new music to be very beautiful.
84. Mike Love understandably paints a very different relationship between Engemann and Brian in the *Sessions* liner notes.
85. In the Summer 2016 Edition of *Endless Summer Quarterly*, Al Jardine holds Engemann responsible for the album's poor coverage in the United States.
86. Ibid., 109.
87. When discussing *Pet Sounds* a few years later, Venet said he felt "Brian was screwing up . . . he was no longer looking to make records, he was looking for attention from the business."
88. Kingsley Abbott, *The Beach Boys Pet Sounds—The Greatest Album of the Twentieth Century* (London, England: Helter Skelter Publishing, 2001), 93.
89. Gaines, 149.
90. Ibid., 150.

91. Capitol's publicity and sales teams were reading the wrong tea leaves in 1966 because they did not understand their best-selling artists. In June 1966 they released the Beatles's *Yesterday and Today*, one of the great marketing disasters in their history.
92. The Capitol compilation, *Endless Summer*, 1974.
93. Johnston is seldom credited for his business savvy, and as the "other" Beach Boy, he was only noticed after everyone else in the band had been given due attention. His skills as businessman and producer would help out the Beach Boys on many occasions in the upcoming decades.
94. In Abbott, Lou Adler claims to have brought an acetate of *Pet Sounds* to England prior to Bruce's arrival, and played the album for Stones manager Andrew 'Loog' Oldham and Paul McCartney. This implies McCartney had already heard the album and brought Lennon along to Bruce's suite to hear it for himself.
95. In *Wouldn't It Be Nice*, Brian relates a story when he met the Rolling Stones in 1965 at Hollywood's RCA Studio while they recorded tracks for *Aftermath* (1966).
96. Leaf, 86.
97. Capitol never released a Beatles greatest hits album in the band's lifetime, though their UK label Parlophone did release a hits compilation at the end of 1966.
98. Capitol passed on a number of the British Invasion artists and with progressive artists later in the decade who, in England, were on the Harvest label. While they had Pink Floyd, they managed to lose them to Columbia.
99. Leaf, 89.
100. Ibid., 80.
101. The original Asher lyrics were featured on *Brian Wilson Presents SMiLE* (2004).
102. While the Beach Boys's song hit number one in both the United States and England, the Beatles single peaked at number two in England.
103. While "Good Vibrations" had sections called "Untitled" and "Inspiration," Pink Floyd used similarly amorphous working titles such as "Return of the Son of Nothing" or "Nothing Parts One to Twenty-Four" when constructing "Echoes." On *Meddle*, Pink Floyd offered their own pet sounds with the filler track "Seamus," but released *Animals* six years later as a less friendly and more Orwellian take on four-legged creatures.

Chapter 3

1. Luis Sanchez, *SMILE* (New York City, NY: Bloomsbury, 2014), 6.
2. Leaf, 97.
3. Timothy White, David Leaf, Peter Ames Carlin, and others have provided a thorough overview of events involved in the making of the album.
4. Sellars, 5.
5. Members of the Beach Boys have at various times claimed there were between six and seven versions of "Heroes and Villains."
6. *The SMiLE Sessions*, Liner Notes.
7. Van Dyke called the album an "American Gothic Trip."
8. As Wilson had *SMiLE* rejected, Gaye's magnum opus from 1971 was also rejected. Motown boss Barry Gordy left Detroit in 1968 to decamp to

Hollywood and wanted to reject the album. He thought it was the worst thing he had ever heard. Both albums address the importance of the spirit and of hope, and share a great deal more in common than one might expect.

9. Leaf, 95.
10. Marilyn has often described Brian as a "gentle soul" and her displeasure with the less appealing members of Brian's circle was in response to the negative influences they piled upon Brian's open, honest, and curious nature.
11. Taylor's talents were more adept at promoting "Brian Wilson Is a Genius" than in bringing the band into to the modern era. It would remain for Jack Rieley to make this a reality in 1971.
12. Brian's recording of "Teeter Totter Love," a quirky, humorous song sung by photographer Jasper Dailey may be an example of the sort of work with which he wanted to experiment for Brother Records. The AFM paperwork for the sessions lists Brother Records under "Employers Name."
13. Brian insisted that everyone in the family and group was included because he still believed in the unity of family and would not consider himself as distinct or separate from the Beach Boys.
14. Leaf, 101.
15. Leaf, 102.
16. *The SMiLE Sessions*, Liner Notes.
17. Abbott, 114.
18. When Van Dyke Parks left *SMiLE*, he recorded his first Warner Brothers album, *Song Cycle* (released December 1967).
19. Priore revised this collection in 1995.
20. Bob Dylan's *Blonde on Blonde* and Frank Zappa and the Mothers of Invention's *Freak Out* released in May and June 1966 were the first double album releases in rock music. Within three years we would have double albums by the Beatles, the Jimi Hendrix Experience, the Who, and the Pink Floyd.
21. "The Elements" were to represent earth, air, fire, and water. With the exception of "Fire," also known as "Mrs. O'Leary's Cow," the other elements have never been definitively connected to other works on *SMiLE*. It is generally accepted that "Earth" is "Vegetables," "Air" is "Wind Chimes," "Fire" is "Mrs. O' Leary's Cow," and "Water" is "Cool, Cool Water/In Blue Hawaii."
22. It was assumed for many years that the *20/20* version of this track was reconstructed from fragments of the original 1966 recordings. McParland confirms the *20/20* track is the original recording that Brian finished in 1966 while recording engineer Stephen Desper maintains that Carl added a lead vocal part for the "Home on the Range" section in 1968.
23. Brian did not make too great an effort to deflect discussion of this song, and spoke of it in some depth for an interview in Rolling Stone and in an interview with Jack Rieley on KPFK radio. Rieley would go on to manage the Beach Boys and direct them to include more socially relevant themes in their music.
24. A practice not dissimilar to users who share their personal playlists on streaming music services.
25. The German "leitmotif" (guiding motive) can also be used to describe this.
26. One month before the CBS taping on November 4, 1966, Brian and Van Dyke provided an in-studio performance at KHJ-AM Radio for "Humble Harve" Miller. They presented a version of "Heroes and Villains" that incorporated

"I'm in Great Shape" and "Barnyard," but the CBS performance of "Surf's Up" was the first public airing of a complete work from *SMiLE.*

27. Kent, 35.
28. Lyric books were uncommon for pop albums at this time. The Beatles's *Sgt. Pepper's Lonely Hearts Club Band* (released June 1967) was the first rock album to include all of the album's lyrics on the record jacket.
29. *The SMiLE Sessions* liner notes.
30. Dailey was a middle-age photographer who documented most of the in-studio shots from *SMiLE.* Brian wanted to record him and "Teeter Totter Love," now available on the boxed set for *The SMiLE Sessions*; this demonstrates Brian's love for the absurd. Two other demos were recorded with Dailey, "Crack the Whip" and "When I Get Mad I Just Play My Drums."
31. Picture sleeves for a single that featured parts 1 and 2 of "Heroes and Villains" (Capitol 5826) were printed but scrapped when Brian pulled the single. A reproduction of the sleeve and single was included in the boxed set of *The SMiLE Sessions.*
32. Siegel and others have blamed Brian's ongoing use of amphetamines in conjunction with the bands resistance to the new songs and mounting business and legal stresses for his repetitive and obsessive methods at this juncture of his work on *SMiLE.*
33. Mark Linett's essay in the *Sessions* boxed set talks about the limitations of predigital recording technology in the creation of mixes in 1966, as each segment on tape had to be physically cut and spliced to the next segment. This time-consuming and labor-intensive process would have to be redone each time Brian wanted to move or shuffle any individual modules. He credits current digital technology for making it possible to reconstruct Brian's work from the dozens of fragments and modules.
34. Mike has always maintained that he felt the instrumental parts of *SMiLE* were amazing recordings, but he did not like the lyrics, and described them as "acid alliteration." He had issues with drug use, both perceived and real, among members of Brian's circle, and saw Brian and Van Dyke as speed freaks who were more interested in being creative than they were in making songs that people could relate to. Even Carl, speaking in 1994, recalls Mike did not like the lyrics because they were "not relatable and too abstract."
35. Leaf, 112.
36. With an obsessive drive that was not dissimilar to what he had expressed in the "Heroes . . . " sessions just weeks prior.
37. Leaf, 105.
38. Leaf, 99.
39. It would be 17 years before Angel Records would release an album by a rock music artist. *Boulez Conducts Zappa: The Perfect Stranger* was released in 1984.
40. Considered to be one of the first rock and roll records, "Gee" was produced by one of the less savory characters in the early history of rock music, George Goldner. Another colorful, dubious character and colleague of Goldner's, Morris Levy, added his name to the list of authors for this song.
41. Authorship for this song is often attributed to Jimmie Davis, whose recording of the work helped to make it a standard. But it is widely known that Davis bought the song from Rice and listed himself as the author.

42. Ironic because this work held such negative memories for Brian.
43. This also presented as complete a version of *SMiLE* as could be had from the original sessions from 1966 to 1967.
44. An earlier release of *SMiLE* was largely impossible because of the fragmentary nature of Brian's original studio tapes. The *BWPS* reconstruction provided Boyd and Linnet with the template by which they could reconstruct Brian's original recordings.
45. In Brian and Van Dyke's studio performance at KHJ-AM Radio on November 11, 1966, they incorporated sections of "I'm in Great Shape" and "Barnyard" into their performance of "Heroes and Villains," which provides a valid argument for the adjusted track order on the 2011 set. Further investigation of tape sources also supports its placement in the opening movement.

Chapter 4

1. Leaf, 98.
2. Rusten and Stebbins, 90.
3. Carlin, 121.
4. The Beatles had abandoned live concert appearances just nine months earlier in August 1966.
5. Leaf, 110.
6. Lambert, 294.
7. Byron Preiss, *The Beach Boys: The Authorized Biography of America's Greatest Rock and Roll Band* (New York, NY: Ballantine Books, 1979), 87.
8. Which supports Anderle's description of a period composed of "different, interchangeable projects floating around."
9. These would finally surface on the 1990 two-fer of *Smiley Smile/Wild Honey*, the *Good Vibrations* boxed set, and on *The SMiLE Sessions.*
10. It was not uncommon for Beach Boys singles to feature a B-side that appeared on an earlier album, but this was an instance where the B-side was never released elsewhere.
11. In initial pressings of the album, Van Dyke's name was not credited for the songs on side two.
12. Preiss, 86.
13. I refer to this song as having the rhythm of a three-legged march.
14. These appeared with catalog numbers 1001 and 1002. The second single was credited to Brian and Mike not to the Beach Boys.
15. Brother 9002 is a number that has been spoken of in connection to an unreleased, 10-track *SMiLE*, as well as the frequently referenced, but never released live album, *Lei'd in Hawaii.*
16. Priore, 196.
17. In this label's brief (1964–1970) existence, they mostly served artists whom they felt would have a low profile with smaller audience appeal. They released the first three Pink Floyd albums in the United States until they adopted the Harvest imprint for *Ummagumma* through *Dark Side of the Moon* and the compilation, *A Nice Pair.*
18. It is generally believed this excuse was for the benefit of the press and Syd's fans. The band's management would drop them once Syd was out of the group as they chose to represent Syd as a solo artist instead of a Barrett-less Floyd.

19. While the five Beach Boys served as equal shareholders in the new company, other artists were signed to the label, but the only non-Beach Boys record released on Brother was the Carl-produced the *Flame,* which featured Blondie Chaplin and Ricky Fataar.
20. The Brothers Records imprint would not reappear until the band moved to Warners/Reprise in 1969.
21. The rest of the Beach Boys declined the opportunity to sign Redwood. They changed their name to Three Dog Night and achieved enormous success in the 1970s on the Dunhill label.
22. Chuck Negron, *Three Dog Nightmare* (Los Angeles, CA: Renaissance Books, 1999), 76–78.
23. According to online reviews and various Beach Boys blogs.
24. An UK review described it as "... a qualified disaster ... ."
25. Wilson, 176.
26. This two-week sojourn resulted in Mike missing two weeks of sessions for the album.
27. This first appeared as a bonus track on the two-fer CD of *Friends/20/20.*
28. *Landlocked* is a disputed album, as engineer Stephen Desper claims it was never a proposed album, only a proposed working title. Then-manager Jack Rieley claims it did exist and he had cover art to prove it. David Leaf states it either is "an elaborate hoax ... or ... an entire Beach Boys LP that is hidden ... (in) other than the tape library of Brother Studio." If it exists, it was a wonderful, 13-track collection from which three songs survived the cut for the second Warners album, *Surf's Up*, three ended up on, *15 Big Ones*, *Love You*, and *Keepin' the Summer Alive*, and five have been released on various post-1993 compilations. Two tracks have yet to be commercially released, Brian's "Carnival," and Mike's beautiful, duple-meter version of "Big Sur."
29. This album was rejected by Warners, and many of these tunes were given new, non-holiday lyrics, and resubmitted for the *M.I.U. Album.*
30. Diane and Marilyn Rovell, without cousin and fellow Honey, Ginger Blake, comprised *Spring*. Brian produced a pair of singles and coproduced an album for them on United Artists in 1972. They were renamed *American Spring* when a British group named *Spring* threatened legal action.
31. It has been posited that Murry charged the costs for this album against the Beach Boys's accounts.
32. Curnutt, 27.
33. Where it was matched with a fragment of Stephen Foster's "Old Folks at Home." A stand-alone version of "Old Man River" was released on *Made in California.*
34. It is believed Deutsche Grammaphon lost interest in the band after Brian's admission in the press that the band was nearly broke.
35. An ardent Beach Boys fan, Cale would go on to compose "Mr. Wilson" for his 1975, Island Records solo album, *Slow Dazzle*, and in 2013, released "All Summer Long," an homage in reference to Wilson and Cale's own memories of life in Southern California in the early 1970s.
36. The non-delivery of *SMiLE* by May 1, 1973, required the band to return $50,000 of their signing advance to Warner Bros.
37. Capitol chose to not release the submitted studio album for the band's final commitment, but instead chose to release a live album for the UK market.

38. McParland, 320–321.
39. This song has appeared on various *Landlocked* bootlegs and has been rudely critiqued on liner notes for those albums. As quoted in McParland, one critique read " ... over-produced, over-orchestrated, over-blown in general, and just plain dumb."
40. The 1970 recording was included on *Made in California*.
41. It is also known by its English title, "When You Are in Love (It Is the Loveliest Night of the Year)."
42. There exists a narrative that a second Warners album titled *Landlocked* was rejected by the label. Though the name appears on a Stephen Desper track sheet, all parties maintain it was never submitted as an album but simply was a preliminary title for a second album.
43. With *Pet Sounds* and *Sunflower*, the Capitol and Warners sales teams bore a significant responsibility for the poor sales of these records in 1966 and 1970.
44. There is much contradictory information about the name and the number of configurations the Beach Boys submitted to Warners. All that can be definitely stated is that more than one album configuration was submitted before what we know as *Sunflower* was accepted. It is known that at least one configuration was titled *Add Some Music*, but there is no clear agreement as to whether this was the first or second offering to Warners.
45. Brian still believed in, and carried into his own work, the feelings expressed on the Kalinich production into his songs on *Sunflower*.
46. Intended for the follow-up album to *Sunflower*, this song remained unreleased until the 1993 boxed set. It had the lighthearted humor similar to other of Brian's works of this period.
47. Brad Elliott's research has provided the most thorough information about this period in the band's history. See Doe's Web site for further information.
48. Nolan stated that Wilson first met Rieley at the Radiant Radish, which led to the interview in July 1970.
49. "A Day in the Life of a Tree" from *Surf's Up* and "Mount Vernon and Fairway (A Fairy Tale)" from *Holland*.
50. Doe confirms that the Flame served as their opening act. The Carl Wilson-produced, South African group would soon provide the Beach Boys with two new members, Blondie Chaplin and Ricky Fataar.
51. *Wild Honey* reached number 24 on Billboard and *Surf's Up* reached number 29.
52. Dragon was a keyboard player in the Beach Boys live band and would later go to great successes in the mid-1970s as one-half of the Captain and Tennille.
53. Brian Wilson was listed as the executive producer.
54. The Beach Boys would use the same backing track for their recording of "Good Time."
55. The choice to record in Iowa is unusual though but had no connection to the Beach Boys's later decision to record at the Maharishi International University in Fairfield, IA.
56. "Fallin' in Love" was one side of Dennis's solo single released under the name, Dennis Wilson and Rumbo. The single, with "Sound of Free," was only issued in the United Kingdom and Europe, making the Spring recording the first time domestic audiences would hear the song. "Had to Phone Ya" would be recorded in 1977 for *Love You*.

57. Bruce claims he left under friendly but mutual agreement. Jack Rieley said he fired Bruce. In an interview soon after Bruce's departure, Mike Love stated that the band decided Bruce should be let go. The truth is somewhere in the middle. Bruce's straight-arrow lifestyle and uncomplicated personality likely was out of sync with both sides (the hard-living or hard-meditating) of the group.
58. Though Brian and Blondie never performed with the Beach Boys at the same time, Blondie has toured with Brian in 2015–2016 to enthusiastic acclaim from audiences as he sings "Sail On, Sailor," "Darlin," and other songs, in addition to providing classic guitar work of a bygone era.
59. Their catalog pre-*Pet Sounds* was still unavailable as Capitol licensed various albums and tracks to other labels or continued to release their own compilation albums comprised of their early hits.
60. Carlin, 179.

Chapter 5

1. The film was made on a three-quarter-of-a-million-dollar budget and went on to gross over $140 million.
2. As of 2016, it has achieved triple-platinum status.
3. Rusten and Stebbins, 177.
4. This song also served as a working title for the album that became *M.I.U. Album*.
5. Leaf, 172.
6. They were mistaken as they owed a further album that they had to deliver after having signed to CBS 1977.
7. The year 1976 was also the year of the Montreal Summer Olympics.
8. This was not helped by the fact that Capitol had reissued a single of the Beatles 1964 recording of the song, as it was the title track of a Beatles compilation released that summer.
9. This followed Roy Wood's break from Jeff Lynne and the original Electric Light Orchestra.
10. Leaf, 178.
11. The show aired on NBC on August 5, 1976.
12. Leaf, 179.
13. Lorne Michaels was only interested in Brian. He could have had the Beach Boys on the show as they played Madison Square Garden on the three nights preceding Brian's guest appearance.
14. Leaf, 179.
15. Eugene Landy would, upon his second term in treating Brian, make himself the beneficiary to Brian's estate after he had secured a percentage of Brian's income.
16. Carlin, 215.
17. Carlin repeated Stan Love's recollection at hearing his brother Mike ask Brian "What the fuck are you doing?"
18. A point of irony because the band would soon start to perform at casinos.
19. Costello was picked up by Columbia, who would release *My Aim Is True* in December of 1977.
20. Whether it was the final decision of Warners or the Beach Boys, this was the most utilitarian title ever given to a Beach Boys record.

21. Carlin refers to this as "the most unsettling moment in the entire recorded history of the Beach Boys." I believe few would disagree.
22. Brian is not credited on "Bells of Christmas" but is given compositional credit for "Belles of Paris."
23. The "Match Point" of this unusual title is borrowed from the world of tennis.
24. When the Brother Records era albums were first issued on compact disc, they were released through Caribou Records/Epic Associated, a subsidiary of CBS. Though the band no longer was represented by CBS Records, Caribou distributed their Warners era catalog outside of North America.
25. Leaf, 193.
26. "Good TImin" from *L.A. (Light Album)*, "Goin' On," and in 1985, "Getcha Back" from their eponymous, Steve Levine-produced album. Each of these songs has a strong group feel, a positive, upbeat tone, and sound like "Beach Boys" songs.
27. They would of course find greater success when they took "Kokomo" to the top of the charts with its tourist calypso-lite rhythmic bed.
28. Dennis rejoined the band for this tour.
29. Whenever Brian took a lead, one of the members of the group would call out his name to the audience as if some miracle had occurred.

Chapter 6

1. The connection between Padgham, Gabriel, and Collins was first posited in Albin Zak's *The Poetics of Rock*. Coincidentally, Padgham mixed five songs on *Brian Wilson*.
2. Stephen McParland provides a detailed account of the highs and lows of their collaboration in *The Wilson Project*.
3. It was used under the final credits of the redoubtable *Police Academy 4: Citizen on Patrol*, a film released by Warner Brothers, the parent company of Sire Records.
4. *Ultimate Music Guide, the Beach Boys*, 96.
5. Matt Dillon, *Fifty Sides of the Beach Boys—The Songs That Tell Their Story* (Toronto, ON: ECW Press, 2012), 256.
6. One such example is "I'm So Lonely" from the Beach Boys 1985 album.
7. Carlin, 261.
8. Alexandra Morgan was Eugene Landy's significant other, and was credited for having provided lyrics to many of Brian's songs.
9. This album managed to earn a gold record with sales approaching 700,000, and was their first gold record since *15 Big Ones* (1976).
10. Conversely, Brian was gratuitously added to two other songs to further the image that the Beach Boys were a unified band. The album also featured "Kokomo" and older Beach Boys songs that were licensed for use in recent films.
11. Brian performed "God Only Knows," "Love and Mercy," and "I Sleep Alone."
12. Shaffer is music director for late-night television host David Letterman.
13. Though *Sweet Insanity* was not an official release, it was the subject of stories in various publications and received positive reviews.
14. John Sebastian attempted to work with Brian on *Brian Wilson*, but was blocked by Landy and Morgan.

15. With a few exceptions, a majority of the album could have a stood a post-Landy redo.
16. *Brains and Genius* was a partnership set up to represent the Wilson and Landy.
17. This resulted in lawsuits filed against Brian by Carl and Audree Wilson, Mike Love, and members of the Beach Boys (Brother Records, Inc.).
18. This agreement did not extend to Landy's many assistants who continued their daily watch over Brian.
19. *Los Angeles Times,* Irv Letofsky, September 19, 1989.
20. *Los Angeles Times,* September 18, 1990.
21. Love originally claimed authorship on 79 songs.
22. In interviews from this period, Brian might display trembling in the hands or facial tics, and his habit of speaking from the left side of his mouth became more pronounced. It was rumored that he had suffered a stroke, but the enormous number of medications Landy prescribed Brian likely had resulted in Tardive Dyskinesia, where embodied gestures can mimic stroke-like symptoms.
23. A significantly slimmer, though still hirsute, Brian appeared with the Beach Boys on the June 29, 1984, episode of The Tonight Show. He appears to be nervous singing a work from their earliest years, "Graduation Day." Bruce appears with the group, to complete the quintet, as Dennis had passed away seven months earlier.
24. Their eponymous 1985 album was an early album to be fully recorded and mastered on the digital platform.
25. This was the final piece of Wasserman's trilogy that comprised *Solo* (1983), *Duets* (1988), and *Trios* (1994).
26. In the film, Brian, Carl, and Audree gather around the piano to sing "In My Room" and "God Only Knows" in a final, moving performance from all three Wilsons.
27. The Quentin Tarantino film *Pulp Fiction* was released the previous year, and the cover of *Pulp Surfin* was modeled after the cover of the *Pulp Fiction* soundtrack.
28. Three songs had lyrics by Michael Hazelwood and the final track on the album is a wistful reading of George Gershwin's "Lullaby."
29. In the liner notes to the soundtrack for *I Just Wasn't Made for These Times,* Was admits that his first hearing of these works was in 1989, a half-decade before he made the documentary.
30. Carlin, 283.
31. Brian is simply a prop in this show.
32. Carlin, 284.
33. Dillon, 102.
34. Another project in which Brian was not involved.
35. Vol. 1 implied a Vol. 2 would follow, but this never came to pass.
36. www.esquarterly.com
37. Carlin, 291.
38. A vocals-only track of "Your Imagination" proves this quite handily.
39. Leaf confirmed that Brian still had his falsetto in the 1970s, contrary to many observations after the *Love You* album, and could sound like "anyone he wants to sound like, including Brian Wilson." No one seemed to notice that his falsetto had seemingly "returned" on the next Beach Boys record, the *M.I.U. Album.*
40. Curnutt, 71.

41. The track remained unreleased until its inclusion on *Made in California* in 2011.
42. A few of Thomas's musicians would end up joining the Wondermints in Brian's post-1999 touring band.

Interlude

1. Carlin, 294.
2. This was released on Brian and Melinda's personal label, BriMel Records, and was originally offered through the QVC home shopping channel and on Brian's Web site. It would be reissued the following year on Oglio Records.
3. Carlin, 300.
4. Steven Gaines understandably distanced himself from the production.
5. Love had, by this time, already removed Al Jardine from the band.

Chapter 7

1. Morris Levy coauthored this song that was first recorded by Joe Jones in 1961, though the Rivieras version is the most widely recognized.
2. While the 1992 *Summer in Paradise* album was the last original album credited to the Beach Boys, Carl and Al had minimal involvement and Brian was absent from the entire project, though one of Brian's song, "Surfin" was rerecorded for the album.
3. Beach Boys collaborator Paul Fausero is credited as producer.
4. While the majority of songs on *Stars and Stripes, Vol. 1* (1995), were composed by Brian, they were remakes of his earlier songs.
5. *The Beatles Bootleg Recordings 1963* was released in response to the revised laws.
6. Jeffrey Foskett first joined the Beach Boys touring band in 1981.
7. Matt Jardine had been part of the Beach Boys live band in late 1980s and provided similar instrumental and vocal parts for the band.
8. David Marks took the spot Al had been offered in the Beach Boys, when he replaced Al in 1962.
9. In December 2015, Capitol released *Live in Chicago, 1965*, which provides a similar experience to the Sacramento album, offering two shows recorded on consecutive evenings. Though he retired from the road at the end of 1964, Brian performed in these shows.
10. The core of Brian's current band was the Wondermints, Indi-pop artists from the 1990s, so his choice to continue work with Indi artists is not at all unexpected.
11. Possible, but unlikely, for as of late 2016 he has hinted in the press his intention to record a new album.

Selected Bibliography

Abbott, Kingsley, ed. *Back to the Beach: A Brian Wilson and the Beach Boys Reader.* London: Helter Skelter Publishing, 1997.

Abbott, Kingsley. *The Beach Boys Pet Sounds: The Greatest Album of the Twentieth Century.* London: Helter Skelter Publishing, 2001.

Anthony, Dean. *The Beach Boys.* London: Crescent Books, 1985.

Badman, Keith. *The Beach Boys: The Definitive Diary of America's Greatest Band: On Stage and in the Studio.* San Francisco, CA: Backbeat Books, 2004.

Blaine, Hal, and David Goggin. *Hal Blaine and the Wrecking Crew.* Alma, MI: Rebeats Publications, 2003.

Carlin, Peter Ames. *Catch a Wave: The Rise, Fall, and Redemption of the Beach Boys' Brian Wilson.* Emmaus, PA: Rodale, 2006.

Covach, John, and Graeme M. Boone, eds. *Understanding Rock: Essays in Musical Analysis.* New York, NY: Oxford University Press, 1997.

Curnutt, Kirk. *Brian Wilson.* London: Equinox Publishing Ltd, 2012.

Denisoff, R. Serge. *Solid Gold: The Popular Record Industry.* New Brunswick, NJ: Transaction Books, 1975.

Denisoff, R. Serge. *Tarnished Gold: The Record Industry Revisited.* New Brunswick, NJ: Transaction Books, 1986.

Dillon, Mark, ed. *Fifty Sides of the Beach Boys.* Toronto, ON: ECW Press, 2012.

Doe, Andrew G., and John Tobler. *Brian Wilson and the Beach Boys: The Complete Guide to Their Music.* London: Omnibus Press, 2004.

Elliott, Brad. *Surf's Up! The Beach Boys on Record, 1961–1981.* Ann Arbor, MI: Popular Culture, Ink., 1991.

Everett, Walter. *The Beatles as Musicians: Revolver through the Anthology.* New York, NY: Oxford University Press, 1999.

Everett, Walter. *The Beatles as Musicians: The Quarry Men through Rubber Soul*. New York, NY: Oxford University Press, 2001.
Fusilli, Jim. *Pet Sounds (33 1/3)*. New York, NY: Continuum, 2005.
Gaines, Steven. *Heroes and Villains: The True Story of the Beach Boys*. New York, NY: Dutton/Signet, 1986.
Hickey, Andrew. *The Beach Boys on CD: Vol 1—1961–1969*. Seattle, WA: Kindle Edition, 2011.
Hickey, Andrew. *The Beach Boys on CD: Vol 2—1970–1984*. Seattle, WA: Kindle Edition, 2011.
Kent, Nick. *The Dark Stuff: Selected Writings on Rock Music*. Cambridge, MA: Da Capo Press, 2002.
Lambert, Philip. *Inside the Music of Brian Wilson: The Songs, Sounds, and Influences of the Beach Boys' Founding Genius*. New York, NY: The Continuum International Publishing Group Ltd, 2007.
Lambert, Philip, ed. *Good Vibrations: Brian Wilson and the Beach Boys in Critical Perspective*. Ann Arbor, MI: University of Michigan Press, 2016.
Leaf, David. *The Beach Boys*. Philadelphia, PA: Courage Books, 1985.
Lewisohn, Mark. *Tune In: The Beatles: All These Years, Vol. 1*. New York, NY: Crown Archetype, 2013.
Love, Mike. *Good Vibrations: My Life as a Beach Boy*. New York, NY: Blue Rider Press, 2016.
McParland, Stephen J. *It's Party Time: A Musical Appreciation of the Beach Party Film Genre*. New South Wales, Australia: PTB Productions, 1992.
McParland, Stephen J. *The California Sounds: An Insider's Story: The Musical Biography of Gary Lee Usher*. 5 volumes. New South Wales, Australia: CMusic Publishing, 2000.
McParland, Stephen J. *The Wilson Project*. France: Editions Berlot, 2012.
McParland, Stephen J. *In the Studio with Brian Wilson and the Beach Boys: Our Favorite Recording Sessions: A Look at Various Recording Sessions of the Beach Boys, 1961–1970*. France: Editions Berlot, 2014.
Morgan, Johnny. *The Beach Boys: America's Band*. New York, NY: Sterling, 2015.
Murphy, James B. *Becoming the Beach Boys, 1961–1963*. Jefferson, NC: McFarland & Company, Inc., 2015.
Negron, Chuck. *Three Dog Nightmare: The Chuck Negron Story*. Los Angeles, CA: Renaissance Books, 1999.
Passmore, Mark Thomas. *Dead Man's Curve and Back: The Jan and Dean Story*. Bloomington, IN: 1stBooks Library, 2003.
Preiss, Byron. *The Beach Boys: The Authorized Biography of America's Greatest Rock and Roll Band*. New York, NY: Ballantine, 1979.
Priore, Domenic, ed. *Look! Listen! Vibrate! SMILE!* San Francisco, CA: Last Gasp, 1995.
Priore, Domenic. *Smile: The Story of Brian Wilson's Lost Masterpiece*. London: Sanctuary Press, 2005.
Ribowsky, Mark. *He's a Rebel: Phil Spector, Rock and Roll's Legendary Producer*. New York, NY: Cooper Square Press, 2000.
Rusten, Ian, and Jon Stebbins. *The Beach Boys in Concert: The Ultimate History of America's Band on Tour and Onstage*. Milwaukee, WI: Backbeat Books, 2013.
Sanchez, Luis A. *Smile (33 1/3)*. New York, NY: Bloomsbury Academic, 2014.

Sellars, Jeff, ed. *God Only Knows: Faith, Hope, Love, and the Beach Boys*. Eugene, OR: Cascade Books, 2015.

Siegel, Jules. *Goodbye Surfing, Hello God!* The Atavist. Seattle, WA: Kindle Edition, 2011.

Stebbins, Jon, and David Marks. *The Lost Beach Boy*. London: Virgin, 2007.

Stebbins, Jon. *The Beach Boys FAQ: All That's Left to Know about America's Band*. Milwaukee, WI: Backbeat Books, 2011.

Tobler, John. *The Beach Boys*. London: Hamlyn, 1977.

White, Timothy. *The Nearest Faraway Place: Brian Wilson, the Beach Boys, and the Southern California Experience*. New York, NY: Henry Holt and Company, Inc., 1994.

Williams, Paul. *Brian Wilson & the Beach Boys: How Deep Is the Ocean?* London: Omnibus Press, 1997.

Williams, Richard. *Phil Spector: Out of His Head*. Revised ed. London: Omnibus Press, 2003.

Wilson, Brian, and Todd Gold. *Wouldn't It Be Nice: My Own Story*. New York, NY: Harper-Collins, 1991.

Wilson, Brian. *I Am Brian Wilson: A Memoir*. Boston, MA: Da Capo Press, 2016.

Selected Web sites

www.beachboys.com
www.thebeachboys.com
www.brianwilson.com
www.esquarterly.com
www.smileysmile.net
www.surfermoon.com

Selected Interviews

Cooper, Chet, and Gillian Friedman. "Brian Wilson Interview." *Ability Magazine* (2006).

Crisafulli, Chuck. "Why Can't Brian Wilson Get a Record Deal." *Request* (June 1997).

Holdship, Bill. "Lost in Music." *MOJO: The Music Magazine* (August 1995).

Selected Articles

Aquila, Richard. "Images of the American West in Rock Music." *Western Historical Quarterly* 11, no. 4 (October, 1980): 415–432.

Beneker, Jeffrey. "And Now for Something Completely Different: Addressing Assumptions about Myth." *The Classical Journal* 109, no. 1 (October/November, 2013): 114–122.

Carter, Dale. "Beyond the Stars and Stripes: Charting Van Dyke Parks' New World Musical Voyage." *Popular Music* 28, no. 2 (May, 2009): 197–216.

Chidester, Brian. "Brian Wilson's Secret Bedroom Tapes." *LA Weekly* (January 30, 2014).

Chidester, Brian. "Brian Wilson's Secret Bedroom Tapes: A Track-by-Track Description." *LA Weekly* (March 5, 2014).

Cooper, Leonie. "The Beach Boys' Brian Wilson Lends Vocals to New Mini Mansions Song—Listen." *NME* (January 13, 2015).

Cucos, Mihal. "A Few Points about Burt Bacharach." *Perspectives of New Music* 43, no. 1 (Winter 2005): 198–211.

DeWitt, Jack. "The Cars of American Graffiti." *The American Poetry Review* 39, no. 2 (September/October, 2010): 47–50.

Felton, David. "The Healing of Brother Bri." *Rolling Stone Magazine* (November 4, 1976).

Hedegaard, Erik. "The Ballad of Mike Love." *Rolling Stone Magazine* (February 17, 2016).

Kerstetter, Todd M. "Rock Music and the New West, 1980–2010." *Western Historical Quarterly* 43, no. 1 (Spring 2012): 53–71.

Nolan, Tom. "The Beach Boys: A California Saga, Part One: Mr. Everything." *Rolling Stone Magazine* (October 28, 1971).

Nolan, Tom. "The Beach Boys: Tales of Hawthorne." *Rolling Stone Magazine* (November 11, 1971).

Payne, Chris. "Brian Wilson Has Never Heard of Punk Rock." *Billboard Magazine* (April 10, 2015).

Reum, Peter. "Adult Child—An Album Lost." *peternreum.blogspot.com* (January 9, 2016).

Reum, Peter. "Freeing Brian Wilson." *peternreum.blogspot.com* (January 8, 2016).

Wilonsky, Robert. "The Forever Frown." *Phoenix New Times* (December 23, 1999).

Index

About the Author

CHRISTIAN MATIJAS-MECCA is an associate professor of dance and music at the University of Michigan where he teaches courses on accompanying movement, research methods, and the history of music in dance. He is a leading practitioner in the area of dance/music studies and has collaborated with artists from many of the world's leading dance companies. Christian has presented papers at academic conferences in North America, Europe, and Asia, and has produced albums of original compositions (*Standing Alone; Suites for Dance;* and *Na Razie, bez Ciebie*) and music for dance technique class (*Etoile Solo Ballet Variations* and *Music for Modern Dance*). A native of Los Angeles, he earned degrees in harpsichord and early music from the University of Southern California and spent much of his youth in the same neighborhoods and schools as Brian Wilson and has related to his music for over 40 years.